TOWARD A HARMONY OF FAITH AND LEARNING

TOWARD A HARMONY OF FAITH AND LEARNING:

Essays on Bible College Curriculum

Kenneth O. Gangel, Editor

William Tyndale College Press
Farmington Hills, Michigan 48018

Toward a Harmony of Faith and Learning: Essays on Bible College Curriculum
Copyright © 1983 by William Tyndale College Press
35700 West Twelve Mile Road
Farmington Hills, Michigan 48018

Library of Congress Cataloging in Publication Data

Toward a harmony of faith and learning.

    Bibliography: p.
    1. Bible colleges—Curricula—Addresses, essays,
lectures. I. Gangel, Kenneth O.
BV4022.T68 1983   207'.11   83-4799
ISBN 0-912407-00-X (pbk.)

Copy edited by Diane L. Zimmerman and Maureen W. LeLacheur
Designed by Heather L. Richter
Cover design by Richard Lambert

Printed in the United States of America

CONTENTS

The Editor

Kenneth O. Gangel has served in Christian higher education for almost a quarter of a century. He has earned the B.A. degree from Taylor University; the M.Div. from Grace Theological Seminary; M.A. from Fuller Summer Seminary; S.T.M. from Concordia Theological Seminary; and Ph.D. from the University of Missouri. After completing his formal schooling, he spent ten years at Calvary Bible College in the roles of instructor, registrar, academic dean and vice president for academic affairs. In 1970 he joined the faculty of Trinity Evangelical Divinity School as founder and director of the School of Christian Education. Four years later he was called to the presidency of Miami Christian College, a post which he held for five years before returning to the classroom of that institution in 1979. Currently he is professor and chairman of the Department of Christian Education at Dallas Theological Seminary.

Gangel is the author of over one thousand magazine and journal articles and fifteen books. In addition to teaching and writing, Dr. Gangel is active on the lecture and preaching circuit, speaking almost two hundred times a year. He brings to this effort a firsthand knowledge of Christian higher education, coupled with an understanding and love of the Bible college movement.

PREFACE

Kenneth O. Gangel

For the past two decades educators in the rapidly growing Christian elementary and secondary school movement have placed great emphasis on what has come to be called "the integration of faith and learning." Hundreds of workshops have been designed, articles and books prepared, and faculty training seminars conducted to produce in the movement a holistic approach to Christian education. From the work of Mark Fakkema in the old National Union of Christian Schools to the new materials presently being released by the NUCS successor, Christian Schools International, and by the Association of Christian Schools, International, a concern for effective integration has sharpened as we face the last two decades of the twentieth century.

Meanwhile, Christian thinkers in liberal arts colleges have made significant contributions. Faculty seminars held at Wheaton, Calvin, Covenant, and other evangelical institutions have produced a host of monographs supplemented by effective handbooks on integration such as *The Idea of a Christian College* and *All Truth Is God's Truth*, both by philosopher Arthur Holmes of Wheaton College.

A significant contribution dealing with the role of the Christian student in the secular college or university has been available since 1972. I refer of course to *Christ & the Modern Mind*, edited by Robert W. Smith. Of more recent vintage is the Zondervan Probe Series initiated in 1977 under the general heading "The Christian Free University Curriculum." Ultimately it will include a collection of fifteen handbooks in various study fields providing a "perspective on the integration of the academic disciplines and historic Christianity."

To this point virtually nothing has been done to assist the faculty of the more than two hundred Bible colleges in North America to implement such a harmony of truth in learning and life. Yet the Bible college is a unique institution with unique characteristics. It is different from a Christian liberal arts college, for example, in its *objectives* which center primarily on vocational Christian service. It is different also in *curriculum*, mandating a Bible-theology major core for every student, a requirement very rare in the Christian liberal arts college movement. It is different in *student ministry orientation*, requiring each student to be active in some form of "Christian service" during his college years, a practice once maintained by almost all Christian colleges but long since abandoned by most.

These differences make necessary this present volume. It is to be hoped that great value lies herein for colleagues who serve our Lord in other fields of Christian education, whether liberal arts college, elementary school, or secondary school. The very design is geared to the threefold Bible college curriculum structure—biblical education, professional education, and general education. And it is to the member schools of the American Association of Bible Colleges and those who will join its ranks in the future that this effort is dedicated.

Terminology and Definitions

One hesitates to use the word *integration* while at the same time recognizing that it cannot be avoided. The hesitation stems from two difficulties. First of all, in common vocabulary the term generally refers to the social incorporation of equals in a culture. But even when understood in its pedagogical sense, it has been so frequently used of late that one wonders about the extent of its present impact. Nevertheless we must use it and as we do we shall mean *the forming or blending into a whole of everything that is a part of a Christian student's life and learning*. The emphasis is upon the teaching of all subjects as a part of the total truth of God, thereby enabling the student to see the unity of natural and special revelation. As Bruce Lockerbie puts it,

> It calls for a correlation between what we believe and how we respond to the world we live in. But *integration* must never become an evangelical cliché reserved to professional scholars. Instead, there must be an integration of faith with every vocation—the selling of used cars, the making of political decisions. We need an integration of faith and *living*.[1]

Nevertheless, while yielding to the necessity of using the term *integration* we reserve the right to emphasize the concept of *harmony* and have preferred that term for the title of our work. The emphasis and the meaning remain the same—to merge, blend, correlate; to connect, associate, and apply. The process is both principial and practical, both philosophical and pedagogical.

Assumptions

As the research began it was necessary to identify some premises on which the various authors would work. At all points these assumptions were open to challenge and amenable to change or even deletion. Most, however, have stood the test of study and continue to form the bedrock foundation for this volume. The knowledgeable readers of such a book as this will be immediately aware that any one of the following could be expanded into a major monograph, even a book manuscript. It is merely our purpose here to state them briefly without extensive justification for their selection.

A comprehensive view of Scripture serves as a base for all aspects of the integration of faith and learning in higher education. It is not technically correct to say that "Bible courses" are more important in the Bible college curriculum than any other courses. On the other hand, there must be an integrative core for the curriculum, and in the Bible college that core is special revelation. Indeed, the Bible college curriculum pattern is often drawn in the form of the following diagram (Figure 1) to show how an understanding of Scripture interrelates with an understanding of professional skills and general education to find impact in real life.[2]

The unity of learning built around the centrality of the Bible is described most clearly by Frank Gaebelein.

> Now Christian education, if it is faithful to its deepest commitment, must renounce once and for all the false separation between secular and sacred truth. It must see that truth in science, and history, in mathematics, art, literature, and music belongs just as much to God as truth in religion. While it recognizes the primacy of the spiritual truth revealed in the Bible and incarnate in Christ, it acknowledges that all truth, wherever it is found, is of God. For Christian education there can be no discontinuity in truth, but every aspect of truth must find its unity in the god of all truth.[3]

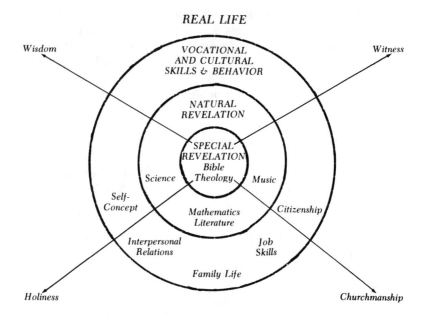

Figure 1. Biblical, Professional, and General Studies

Traditional Bible college curriculum does not satisfactorily provide for the teaching of a comprehensive view of the Bible. Though we have come a long way from the one-hour book synopses which characterized Bible institute curricula half a century ago, the smorgasbord effect still prevails. To be sure exegesis and exposition of certain books and passages are most valuable and that value dare not be minimized. But specialization of exegesis and hermeneutics may very well be inappropriate until the student has internalized a comprehensive view of the Bible and its message, including a clear perception of the unity of Old and New Testaments. Fragmentation has sent our students through commencement lines with high concentration in, let us say, the eschatology of the Pauline epistles while at the same time holding scarcely a clue to the flow of history from Enoch to the exile.

An undergraduate grasp of theology should center more on what can properly be identified as "biblical theology" than the traditional approach of "systematic theology." I am fully aware that there is no assumption in this volume on which we will be more frequently and more vigorously challenged than this. Let it be said most clearly that the value of systematics is not questioned for one moment nor is it implied that a study of systematic theology is less important than a study of biblical theology. The point is that undergraduate theological education (i.e., Bible college curriculum) more appropriately achieves its objectives by aiming at a flow of theology as found in the normal handling of the Bible as the student finds it rather than in the superimposition of historic categories. In short, we are recommending an inductive rather than a deductive approach to theological studies while at the same time assuming a strong dose of both systematic and historical theology during graduate theological education in seminary.

Bible college students should not be encouraged in any manner to study general education courses in a secular environment. Many Bible colleges currently recommend this practice, sometimes out of convenience or economics, sometimes out of a genuine concern for more broadening educational experiences. Surely a commitment to the unity of God's truth forces a philosophical denial of the validity of such a practice. The bifurcation of curriculum which results when a student is encouraged to attend two institutions—a Bible college for Bible and theology and a secular university or community college for general education—is precisely the counterproductive curriculum plan which a proper understanding of integration repudiates. If, indeed, it is only necessary for a student to learn Bible and theology, from which learnings he makes his own integrative applications in other disciplines, then the pure institute with no commitment to general education coupled with the best secular university is the only sensible model. Such a conclusion denies the common commitment of both Bible colleges and Christian liberal arts colleges.

In the process of integration, it is essential not only that the teacher be able to integrate his subject matter with special revelation, but also that he teach students how to do it. Our movement faces numerous problems on this front. Too many faculty have inadequate theological credentials, or perhaps inadequate academic credentials, thereby lacking one or both dimensions of preparation for the harmony of faith and learning. By the same token, faculty who do have the background and ability to integrate in the classroom too often come off as "performers" rather than people who have the ability to lead others to the well, teach them how to drink, and ultimately teach them the craft of well digging. The words of David Kornfield sting a bit.

> The Christian cliché of "integrating faith and learning" seeks to overcome this dichotomy (between education and life, education and ministry), but it needs both some further definition and some clearer operationalization. As they are thrown around, the terms "faith" and "learning" both refer to bodies of information, the former being the Bible and doctrine, and the latter being in academic discipline. This is debasing the original terms "faith" and "learning" which are both meant to be more in the sense of verb forms (faith equals believing equals faith) than nouns that are passive, bound items that can be put into a book. Both faith and learning are intended to be active ongoing processes that are of necessity integrated in the individual and when properly understood as such cannot be only external documents and field study as some seem to think.[4]

Authorship and Structure

In the earliest weeks of this research project certain qualifications were set down for participants although not every author possesses every qualification. Three characteristics were paramount: an earned doctorate; at least five years teaching experience in a Bible college; and evidence of ability to integrate and teach others to do so. Obviously the first two items are very measurable and the third quite subjective. The reader will be the ultimate judge of the value of each author's contribution to the collective work.

The overall structure of the book follows the threefold Bible college curriculum pattern of biblical, professional, and general education described earlier. Fifteen chapters represent fifteen fields of study commonly found in Bible colleges. The terminology may differ and certain schools may offer programs not mentioned in these pages but, in general, the patterns are fairly standard. Within each essay, the authors were asked to follow a format roughly approximating the following outline:

INTRODUCTION
BIBLICAL FOUNDATION
PHILOSOPHICAL FORMULATION
PRACTICAL APPLICATION
CONCLUSION

However, each author was free to develop a model within his/her own field that was felt to be appropriate. Thus, the format of the essays varies somewhat. The editor's introduction to each essay attempts to explain the uniqueness each contains. As a part of his conclusion, each author was asked to speak to the question of "passing the torch" to students, enabling them to carry out the process of integration well beyond the confines of the Bible college classroom.

Objectives and Utilization

As Wendell G. Johnston points out in the Introduction, this volume is a beginning contribution which we hope will stimulate additional work. Our concern is to demonstrate that a complete approach to the harmony of faith and learning, if it is really to be a practical paradigm for an educational institution must have impact on every area of the college—mission, curriculum, faculty recruitment, faculty training, board orientation, and communication with the institution's many publics. As academic deans utilize these chapters in faculty training sessions we hope for a new emphasis on interdisciplinary studies and interdepartmental cooperation. We want to see a united effort on the part of all faculty to adopt and adapt the "harmony" to curriculum structure and teaching process. As we say many times throughout the book, the integrative approach is not an end in itself but rather a means toward involving the student in the faith-learning synthesis. Robert W. Smith reminds us,

Because our present state of knowledge is incomplete, we cannot comprehend the unity of truth possible perhaps a century from now nor the unity that some scholars alleged in the Renaissance. We do know, however, that solid faith in God as He is revealed in Jesus Christ provides a perspective on one's education unattainable by human insight alone. Christianity and scholarship comprise two sides of the same coin of God's truth: a Christian commitment reminds the scholar that all truth ultimately comes from God while scholarship cautions the believer not to descend to superstition and fanaticism. These commitments do not preclude, but rather supplement, each other.[5]

If that can be said of the Christian student in a totally secular environment, how much more must it be true of the student in the Bible college where Christ is the key to the Scriptures and the Scriptures are the key to learning.

Notes

1. D. Bruce Lockerbie, *The Cosmic Center* (Grand Rapids: Eerdmans, 1977), p. 122.
2. Diagram appears as a part of my article entitled "Integrating Faith and Learning: Principles and Process," *Bibliotheca Sacra* 135 (1978): 102.
3. Frank E. Gaebelein, "Towards A Christian Philosophy of Education," *Grace Journal*, 3 (Fall 1962): 13.
4. David Kornfield, "A Working Proposal for An Alternative Model of Christian Higher Education" (unpublished monograph, 1976), p. 12.
5. Robert W. Smith, *Christ & The Modern Mind* (Downers Grove, Ill.: Inter-Varsity, 1972), p. vi.

The Author

Wendell G. Johnston has served the Bible college movement for many years as a pastor, professor, academic dean (Washington Bible College) and now president of William Tyndale Colege, a post he assumed in 1968 when William Tyndale College was known as Detroit Bible College. He holds the B.A. degree from Bob Jones University and the Th.M. and Th.D. from Dallas Theological Seminary. He has provided impetus and guidance for this entire project since its inception, and appropriately writes the introduction to our study.

The Subject

Dr. Johnston's task in this brief introduction is to alert us to the unique nature of Bible college education in the rapidly changing, indeed kaleidoscopic, world of higher education at the end of the twentieth century. He addresses himself to basic questions and pinpoints the central thesis of the book when he writes, "Christian education is . . . the integration of the Scriptures into every academic pursuit thereby developing a truly biblical world and life view."

INTRODUCTION

Wendell G. Johnston

Christian higher education is faced with a tremendous challenge. The future of our Christian colleges and universities is at stake. One of the threats—to the entire educational system in the United States as well as to Christian schools—is limited financial support. *The Chronicle of Higher Education* reports that 32 percent of public colleges are losing ground financially. Also there is growing concern over the signs of hidden deterioration in the form of deferred maintenance of assets, both physical and human, an incipient enemy which does not show up in the normal accounting statements of institutions.

The statistics for the seventies reveal that 141 private colleges failed to survive during that decade. Almost all were small (under 500 students), church-related, and coeducational. This indicates that our Christian colleges are just as vulnerable to financial problems as secular colleges and universities. The National Center for Educational Studies is predicting that as many as 200 small colleges could close during the eighties.

Limited financial resources is not the only problem to be faced in Christian higher education. A vital issue involves the philosophy and conceptualization of Christian education. There is an urgent need to articulate clearly the distinctives of Christian education, to express the value and the significance of what we have to offer. Specific questions must be addressed and evaluated: Are Christian colleges offering an education that is significantly different from secular schools? How are these differences defined and communicated? Are evangelical colleges maintaining a high academic quality and yet retaining their Christian emphasis and mission?

Higher education that is Christian involves more than having a doctrinal commitment—more than maintaining good relations with churches. It is more than requiring students to be Christians or hiring a Christian faculty. It is more than having a Bible department in the curriculum, more than requiring students to be engaged in Christian service. Christian education is all these plus another very important ingredient—*the integration of the Scriptures into every academic pursuit thereby developing a truly biblical world and life view.* It is this single concept that really distinguishes Christian education from other approaches to education. Christian educators have repeatedly affirmed this position. Edward Hayes writes:

> The Scriptures, rightly divided and directly studied in proper sequence, are essential to Christian education. The centrality of the Bible, however, is not conditioned by pragmatic concerns or even by communicative necessity although we admit that the Scriptures do possess animation and the communication of God's truth is a major concern of the Christian disciple. The Bible is central to Christian education primarily because it is central to Christian epistemology. Divine revelation, while it incorporates the dimensions of human motivation, cognition, and learning, goes far beyond these concerns in its application of truth. Jesus Christ is revealed to be more than a historic, superteacher, as the earlier religious educators would have us believe. He introduced a new supernatural dimension to knowledge. We recall how He said: "Ye shall know the truth, and the truth shall make you free." [1]

The point is that a Christian educator does not ignore the scholarship of the day, nor is he intimidated by research and discovery. On the contrary, a Christian scholar is genuinely committed to study the facts of history, science, and other disciplines. Christian education recognizes the contributions of men and women who have labored in various academic fields. In reality, Christian education leads to a depth of understanding beyond mere knowledge of academic content. It requires the Christian to analyze and evaluate all the facts and theories and opinions from any and every source available, and then submit these to the inerrant Word of God. The Christian educator must develop a philosophy of education in which he is able to integrate the Bible with all that can be known in the world today.

Not only must the Bible be taught, but it must be related, applied, and integrated into every aspect of life and learning.

An educational philosophy that involves the integration of the Bible into all of life and learning is both exciting and challenging for faculty and students alike. Faculty members must be chosen who are qualified in their own disciplines, have a working knowledge of the Bible, and are able to integrate the Scriptures into their fields of expertise. Faculty are not automatically equipped to teach in an integrated manner because they have graduated from a Christian college or seminary. Unfortunately, there are very few Christian graduate schools that teach the concept of integration and, thus, most faculty members are left on their own to develop this all-important concept as they teach their students.

Students also must be taught how to evaluate and integrate, a goal which cannot be accomplished by a superficial understanding of the Bible. Every student will need a basic comprehensive view of the Word of God and doctrine so that he can assimilate, correlate, adapt, and apply what he has been taught. It is conceivable that it might take longer than four years for students to receive a degree in some areas of study. Students cannot be short-changed in their pursuit of an academic degree.

For several decades Christian educators have, in articles and books, explained the philosophy of integrating the Bible into academic subjects. However, the practical aspects of methodology have often been neglected. How can godly faculty members integrate the Bible in their classes? Certainly integration is more than quoting verses of the Bible at appropriate times throughout the lecture. The integration process is not, nor should it become, just a mechanical exercise. This manual can only be an aid to the harmony we seek. Since there is no simple formula for teacher or student that will suffice, it will be necessary to develop a biblical framework, a significant challenge in itself.

This volume is simply the first step in an effort to provide some literature on both principal and practical levels to assist administrators, professors, and students in this whole concept of integration. The point of departure is the Bible college, its uniquenesses having been already explained. It is hoped that others will improve and expand it so that all of us involved in Christian education can increase effectiveness in this important dimension.

This is not a golden era for secular education. This philosophy of the world is inadequate for the complex days in which we live. The

years ahead can be the most significant for Christian higher education if we really believe the truth of God can be integrated into all of
life and learning. Let John Howard's legacy once again pervade the
Christian college movement:

> Let every student be plainly instructed and earnestly pressed to con-
> sider well the main ends of his life and studies; to know God and Jesus
> Christ which is eternal life and therefore to lay Christ in the bottom as
> the only foundation of all knowledge and learning and see the Lord
> only giveth wisdom.[2]

Notes

1. Edward L. Hayes, "The Centrality of the Bible In Christian Education," *Bibliotheca Sacra*, 126 (July 1969): 230.
2. *The Dan Smoot Report*, Dec. 6 1965.

Part One

DIVISION OF
BIBLICAL EDUCATION

The Author

A veteran Bible college teacher with many years of pastoral experience as well, Robert Hilgenberg holds degrees from the University of Illinois (B.S.) and Dallas Theological Seminary (Th.M.; Th.D.). During thirteen years of pastoral ministry he was a member of the faculty at Moody Bible Institute before joining the faculty of Calvary Bible College in 1972 where he served as chairman of the Bible department. After that he served as chairman of the biblical studies division at William Tyndale College. Currently he is engaged in Ph.D. studies in education at Michigan State University.

The Subject

The centrality of the Bible in Bible college education is so basic as to be a *sine qua non*. Dr. Hilgenberg assumes an orthodox view of inspiration and inerrancy, then goes on to show how one's educational philosophy depends upon his view of the Bible and its role in the college curriculum. Philosophically, the Bible provides the foundation for a Christian approach to metaphysics, epistemology, anthropology, and axiology. Its rubrics establish the boundaries of our study in all disciplines. Dr. Hilgenberg urges his colleagues to demonstrate godly lives by modeling their subject matter before their students to the end that both teacher and student realize "that what we are studying together is truth and not just a set of notes."

1

ENGLISH BIBLE

Robert J. Hilgenberg

Introduction

The uniqueness of the Bible college is the central emphasis given to the direct study of the English Bible. An examination of the curriculum of Bible college catalogs, both past and present, reveals the standard requirement of a core of biblical and theological studies (usually thirty to forty hours). This emphasis on the English Bible is the heart of the Bible college movement. Frank Gaebelein, in summarizing the movement, observed in 1951 that "The foremost characteristic . . . is the central place given to the direct study of the English Bible."[1] Today, member schools of the American Association of Bible Colleges must require a minimum of thirty hours in biblical and theological studies of all graduates. Consequently, each student graduates with a double major, one in biblical studies and one in his chosen field of specialization.

To maintain this emphasis Bible colleges normally have a Bible department which, in addition to teaching the required core studies in Bible, offers many other courses in biblical and theological studies. Students who adopt preseminary or pastoral ministries programs have additional required and elective courses in Bible-related subjects, such as biblical languages, analysis of selected Bible books, and further studies in systematic or biblical theology. Students whose majors are in such other areas as psychology, music, history, or philosophy must take the required core of biblical studies.

There are three basic reasons why the discipline of English Bible provides the foundation of a Bible college education. The first reason becomes apparent when the educational purposes and objectives of the Bible college are understood. The primary aim is to prepare its students for Christian ministries and church-related vocations. *Since Christian ministries necessitate a good foundation in knowledge of the Scriptures, a major in Bible meets that need.* In addition, the Bible major becomes a stimulus to the student to become involved in Christian work.

The second reason is that a major in Bible *is the most effective way to emphasize the centrality of the Bible in all educational pursuits.* If those who are involved in Christian education really believe the authority of the Bible as the focus of all truth, then our practice should demonstrate that fact. Our curriculum arrangement should demonstrate that the Bible has authority in permeating every other discipline in the college's program.

With this in mind, we might take issue with Gaebelein's point that a separate Bible department is unnecessary in a school which is serious about making Christ and the Bible integral to all areas of studies.[2] In the ideal Gaebelein may have a point, for then every teacher becomes a Bible teacher along with his or her other discipline(s). But history denies us examples of such an ideal.

Since we are serious about making the Bible the center of an educational program, then we should make it obvious by employing teachers who devote their abilities specifically to the exposition and explanation of the Scriptures. Some levels of biblical study, in an academic setting, require specialists who can keep the level of Bible instruction in the curriculum on a par with that of other disciplines.

The nature of the student who enters a Bible college provides the third reason for requiring an English Bible major. Bible college education is established for the student who knows Jesus Christ as Lord and Savior, and who senses to a greater or lesser degree that Christ has claims on his or her life. For the Christian student, then, the words of Solomon are appropriate, "The fear of the Lord is the beginning of wisdom, and the knowledge of the Holy One is understanding" (Prov. 9:10, NASB). The area of knowledge *most* appropriate for Christians is the Bible, so the Bible must have that central emphasis in their education. Being related to Jesus Christ affects all aspects of life and only a thorough knowledge of Scripture will equip the Christian for every facet of his life—family, economic, social, and spiritual dimensions.

Another characteristic of the Christian student points to the weakness of contemporary Bible education in North American churches. Too many college and seminary students are woefully ignorant of the English Bible. It is presumptuous to expect that eighteen or twenty year olds will enter college with the capacity to integrate biblical information with other disciplines when their only biblical instruction came from a Sunday school setting or from the pulpit. They need a biblical exposure which demands as much from them academically as any other discipline. This serious Bible study will best prepare them to integrate biblical truth with other sources of information in their educational process.

The Bible major, then, is necessary if one is to realistically recognize the deficiency of the student in terms of his or her lack of biblical knowledge while at the same time meeting the need of the student as one who is a Christian and specially related to the Scripture.

The rationale supporting the Bible major in a Bible college is not superfluous. The major in Bible and theology supports the very purposes for which the college exists and it is the most effective way to emphasize the centrality of the Bible in all of education. Finally, it meets the needs of the type of student who attends a Bible college.

Biblical Foundation

The theological and biblical foundation for the educational approach of the Bible college rests upon the understanding of the nature of the Bible. Put simply our basic conviction affirms that the Bible is the authoritative Word of God and is the focus and measure of all truth. The belief that the Bible is the written, accurate, Word of God is the only valid reason for keeping it at the center of our educational philosophy and practice. Without this perspective, we have no basis for affirming biblical truth as the hub into which every spoke of relative truth must converge.

Our doctrine of inspiration, then, determines our educational philosophy and this doctrine rests upon what the Bible says about itself. Several key Scripture passages deductively establish the nature and authority of Scripture. The purpose here is not to go into minute exegetical detail but simply to stress some salient features which support our high regard for the authority of the Bible.

Inspiration

The first passage is Paul's statement in 2 Timothy 3:16: "All Scripture is inspired by God and profitable for teaching, for reproof, for correction, for training in righteousness" (NASB). Here Paul states the origin of that which is called Scripture (*graphē*). It is God-breathed (*theopneustos*) and hence, it originates from the heart of God Himself. The Bible owes its existence to the very creative activity of God, who is, therefore, the first cause of that content called "Scripture."

Even though the expression *graphē* in this passage has primary reference to the Old Testament, the term is used also to point to a New Testament book. Paul in 1 Timothy 5:18, uses *graphē* in designating both an Old Testament passage, Deuteronomy 25:4, and a New Testament passage, Matthew 10:10, thereby equating these two Scriptures. In addition, Peter, in 2 Peter 3:16, referrred to Paul's letters as *graphē*. By deduction, therefore, we can conclude that the New Testament writers accepted the Old Testament books and the New Testament books, the Gospels and Epistles, as *graphē*, and therefore that these necessarily have their origin solely in God. We accept, then that both the Old Testament and the New Testament are *graphē* and inspired of God.

This concept of the origin of Scripture is extended somewhat in the second key passage, 2 Peter 1:20–21. Peter's point in these two verses is that no human being by his own initiative, his own thinking, or his own investigation into the nature of things, brought prophecy (i.e., Scripture) into being. This appears to be Peter's meaning in using the word *epiluseōs* (unloosing) which is translated as "interpretation" in several English versions. He carries the Pauline thought even further by indicating that men were used as instruments in speaking from God as they were "borne along" by the Holy Spirit. These men were speaking God's word by the Holy Spirit and consequently what they spoke was His, not theirs.

Jesus and the Bible

Two additional passages stress the authority of Scripture. In Matthew 5:17–18 Jesus indicates that the smallest aspect of the Law (represented by the jot and tittle of the Hebrew alphabet) must have its fulfillment as long as the cosmos remains. Every ethical commandment, every statement concerning God's intentions, every statement of His character and His works must find its fulfillment with the same sureness as the stability of the cosmos.

This same confidence in the Word of God was expressed by Jesus in John 10:35. The main point of this verse rests on Christ's statement that the Scriptures cannot be broken. By this expression Jesus is saying that it is impossible for Scripture to be annulled or denied. Furthermore, the very manner or form of expression stands with irrefragable authority. *The words stand as equivalent to what God thinks, and what one reads is what God meant.* Jesus upholds the indefectible authority of the written word in all of its particulars and, in doing so, emphasizes the verbal authority of God's revelation.

One of the most interesting aspects of Jesus' recognition of the Old Testament was His complete acceptance of the historicity of many people and events. He accepted creation by God and the existence of Adam and Eve along with Cain and Abel (Matt. 19:4; Luke 11:51). He recognized the existence of Noah, the Ark, the reality of the flood, the destruction of Sodom, and the death of Lot's wife (Matt. 24:37–39; Luke 17:28–32). He based the reality of His own resurrection on the historicity of Jonah's experience (Matt. 12:40).

Perhaps the key impression of Jesus' attitude toward the Old Testament is seen in His response to Satan's temptations in the wilderness. Repeatedly Jesus said, "It is written," not for the purpose of teaching Scripture memorization, but rather to indicate His obedience to the written word. He could not do what Satan suggested because He was committed to the Old Testament which was equivalent to His Father's will.

Jesus Christ's attitude toward the Old Testament was one of total trust. In no way did He ever distinguish between that which was true in faith and practice from that which was true in historical matters. The New Testament authors reflected this same perspective in their writings. In several places (for example, Matt. 19:5; Acts 13:35), they represent God as the speaker of an Old Testament text when, in fact, He is not mentioned in the text itself. New Testament writers often stated, "Scripture says" when quoting an Old Testament statement that God is said to have made (Rom. 9:17). There seems to have been such habitual identification of the text of Scripture with what God said that it became natural to use the phrase "Scripture says." The disciples did not question, argue, or repudiate the authority of Scripture.

The Holy Spirit and the Bible

One other point needs to be made here concerning the authority and truthfulness of the New Testament. Jesus, who claimed he was truth (John 14:6), also spoke of the Holy Spirit as truth (John 14:17; 15:26; 16:13). As the Spirit of truth guided the New Testament writers and enabled them to remember all that Jesus did and taught, and as He instucted them about things to come, He did so without error. Therefore, He who held the Old Testament in such high regard also insured the same high standard for the New Testament writings.

In light of the preceding discussion, we can affirm that the Bible, God's word to man, is the final word regarding the nature and identification of truth from any other source. Jesus not only obeyed the written word as the pattern for His earthly ministry but also accepted it implicitly as that which reveals the nature and truth about God, the invisible world, history, culture, and man. ´

Jesus' attitude toward the Old Testament also established the pattern for our hermeneutics. Our approach to Scripture must be to accept it as written, in its normal, cultural, historical setting just as He did. We should interpret the text with as much implicit trust in its words as Jesus had. The Scriptures stand as the source book for truth and we must contend that *whatever is declared as true outside of the Bible must bear positive correlation to the written truth*. This is *not* to say that all truth is found in the Bible; but it is to say that any aspect of existence which is declared true will be in harmony with what God has revealed in the Scriptures concerning that area.

The nature of the Bible, then, is the very reason for placing the study of it in the center of the Bible college curriculum. A faculty member or student without a thorough grasp of special revelation cannot and will not develop a distinctly Christian world and life view and will be unable to harmonize faith and learning in the sense that it is being discussed in this volume.

Philosophical Foundation

The basic premise from which the Bible teacher must instruct his student for the ultimate purpose of integration is this: *the Bible is the foundational sourcebook for man's investigation into all areas of learning.* By this is meant that regardless of what area of inquiry is pursued, the Bible has something to say about that area. This is based on the assumption that when God focused truth in the Scriptures, He touched *in some way* all truth in the universe. Not every particular of truth is mentioned, but certainly every particular of truth has a broader framework given in the Bible. To illustrate this principle, the section below relates Scripture to four areas of philosophical inquiry: metaphysics, epistemology, anthropology, and axiology.

Metaphysics

The Bible has much to contribute in the area of metaphysics. Beginning with the aspect of ontology, certainly the opening statement of Genesis, "In the beginning God," sets the parameters of being. Ultimate reality resides in the God of the Bible who throughout Scripture revealed Himself as Jehovah, the I Am, the Eternally Existent One. Paul's statement on Mars Hill relates to ontology when he said of this God, "In Him we live and move and exist" (Acts 17:28, NASB). From Paul's message, ultimate being and reality relate to the God of Genesis for the same God in whom we live is also the One who Paul said created the world (Acts 17:24). Throughout the Bible all things—stars, snow, water, animals, trees, man—ultimately relate to the God of the Scriptures. This same God, by His own words, precludes the existence of any other: "I am the Lord, and there is no other; Besides Me there is no God" (Isa. 45:5, NASB). In his Bible courses the student soon realizes that all questions of ultimate meaning and reality must be studied within the parameter of the God of the Bible. The attitude of biblical writers was one of faith. They naturally assumed the existence of God, an attitude commanded in Hebrews 11:6—anyone who comes to God must believe that He is.

The Bible also circumscribes cosmology, the branch of metaphysics dealing with the universe as a whole. According to Genesis, God brought into being the entire natural universe. This God is identified further as Jesus the Christ who not only created everything, but also sustains everything (John 1:1-3; Col. 1:16-17; Heb. 1:1-3). The writer of Psalm 104 establishes for us how one is to view the creation account in Genesis. He believed in the literal, normal understanding of what was written, and his belief led him to worship the God spoken of there. In the psalmist's approach the Bible provides the rubric for one's view of creation. A biblical view of the cosmos entails both an acceptance of the statements of Genesis 1, and an acceptance of the psalmist's perspective of that passage. In other words, the Bible not only gives us the facts but also provides examples of how one is to respond to those facts. The Bible teacher must guide the student in understanding creation in the same manner as the psalmist did. In addition, he must help the student perceive that increasing knowledge of the natural world should be understood within the context of biblical information. The student of astronomy, for example, in his perspective of the ever expanding knowledge of the universe, must be guided by the Scripture's statement concerning the sun, the moon, and the stars.

Epistemology

In addition to these areas of metaphysics, the Bible provides foundational parameters of epistemology dealing with *how* we know *what* we know. From the Christian's perspective the Bible is the source of knowledge concerning God, man, sin, angels, and nature, so we *know* in these areas because we read of them in this book. However, there are other sources of information recognized and debated by philosophers: experience, reason, and nature. These also are evident within Scripture.

Experience, for example, became a source of knowledge for Solomon. In Ecclesiastes he experimented and tried a number of life's involvements and learned that "all is vanity." Job's experience of suffering became an avenue of knowledge for him to understand the sovereignty of God. Even Christ Himself *learned* through His sufferings (Heb. 5:8) the discipline of obedience. The apostle Paul stated that he "learned to be content in whatever circumstances" he found himself. He learned by experience that Jesus could and would supply all his needs (Phil. 4:12,19). The Bible records experience as a valid source of knowledge.

The same could be said for reason. Man's ability to think, to reason, to approach problems and issues rationally and logically is clearly evidenced in Scripture. A thorough reading of Romans points up the fact that Paul thought through issues logically and arrived at knowledge by this mental exercise.

Finally, Jesus indicated that the only way we can "know" in some areas is by direct opening of the mind by God. He told Peter that Peter's recognition of Jesus as the Messiah came only by the Father's having opened his understanding to perceive this (Matt. 16:17). Jesus also indicated to His apostles that their ability to remember events and teachings of Jesus's life, as well as knowing future events, would come through the special work of the Holy Spirit (John 14:26; 16:13).

Anthropology

The third area of philosophy for which the Bible provides a perspective is anthropology. All information one can assimilate from Scripture on this subject will provide the framework for any study of man. Several Scripture passages establish that man, the highest of God's creation, is accountable to Him. The origin of man coming directly from the hand of God and being made in His image (Gen. 1:26–27) plus the commandments given to man (Exod. 20:1–17) establish the accountability of man to Someone outside himself. David, in accepting the literality of the creation account, stressed in Psalm 8 the high value of man in view of God's having entrusted His creation to him. This information from Scripture, therefore, must govern the ultimate perspective of a student in his study of any discipline regarding man. Consequently, any conclusion which places man on the same level as an animal must be rejected as error.

Furthermore, any estimation of man as being inherently good must be rejected in light of the fall of man in Genesis 3, and Jesus' statement in Mark 7:21–22 that out of the heart of man proceeds "evil thoughts, fornications, theft, murders, adulteries, deeds of coveting and wickedness, as well as deceit, sensuality, envy, slander, pride and foolishness" (NASB). Certainly this information from Scripture regarding man's thoughts has a bearing on studies of psychology, and other social sciences. In fact, interpretation of research data in these areas is governed by the biblical concept of redemption which tells us that behavior modification can be experienced through forgiveness of sin and the indwelling Holy Spirit.

Any research and continuing study of man must operate within the limitations established by the Bible. As long as the interpretation of new information harmonizes with the scriptural data and relates comfortably to the Bible's framework, then we can say it is truth about man.

Axiology

The fourth area of philosophy for which the Bible provides a framework is that of axiology. Here we want to consider ethics (what is right), and aesthetics (what is beautiful).

It is not difficult to pinpoint for the student that ethics is a chief concern of the Scriptures. The basic concepts given in the Ten Commandments set the stage for all types of ethical behavior given in the casuistic laws of the Mosaic legislation. Especially in Exodus and Deuteronomy there are laws dealing with ethical issues regarding master-slave relationships, business and economic dealings, the treatment of elderly people and children, and the regulations governing war and jurisprudence.

Because of its inclusion of many art forms, the Bible also speaks to the issues of aesthetics. The accounts concerning the tabernacle and temple deal with many facets of artwork such as color combinations, embroidery, metal sculpturing, woodworking, and tapestry (Exod. 25–40). God even went so far as to supply His Spirit to Bezalel and others to give them abilities in craftsmanship (Exod. 31:1–6). From God, then, comes provision and enablement to take the materials of His creation and use them artistically.

Another art form was Hebrew poetry, used not only in the Psalms and other poetical books but also in many of the prophetic books.

Music certainly was a key aspect in the worship of Israel for both the community as well as the individual. The sweet psalmist of Israel, David, not only was a musician himself, but directed others when he "spoke to the chiefs of the Levites to appoint their relatives the singers, with instruments of music, harps, lyres, loud-sounding cymbals, to raise sounds of joy" (1 Chron. 15:16, NASB). In the New Testament, Paul indicates in Ephesians 5:18–19 that music is a necessary aspect of the Christian's spiritual life. Even a cursory reading of Alfred Sendrey's *Music in Ancient Israel* should convince anyone that music was an important art form in the worship of the God of Israel.

To conclude, the Bible has its contribution in whatever area of philosophy one studies. This contribution, moreover, represents the position of authority. Those of us who teach in the area of Bible must guide the student into conscious recognition of the biblical boundaries governing man's acquisition of truth outside of the Bible. *Biblical revelation and natural revelation are both reflections of God's truth but the appropriate educational scheme requires the latter to be understood in the light of the former.* Some ways this can be accomplished are dealt with in the next section.

Practical Application

What is it that we want to achieve when we discuss integration and the issues of faith and learning? After we have spent hours with our students in Bible courses, what do we really want them to do? James Michael Lee, a Roman Catholic educator, has succinctly identified the key issue regarding integration:

> For the integralist the aim of religious instruction is to empower the learner to act in the interest of God: God as he is in himself; God as he is in the Church; God as he is in the community of men; and God as he is in the learner. To the intellectualist the integralist responds that the real Christians are not necessarily the people who know or even notionally believe the right things, but rather the people who live the kind of life which Christ lived. To the moralist, the integralist answers that a Christian lifestyle devoid of or deficient in a pervasive intellectuality is neither human life nor human style, and hence can scarcely be considered Christian.[3]

What Lee has given as the aim of religious instruction is that which the apostle John stated, "I was very glad to find some of your children walking in truth" (2 John 4, NASB). Ultimately, those of us who teach Bible desire that our students would walk in truth, to "act in the interest of God" in every aspect of their lives. This objective demands consideration of three areas: (1) the teacher, (2) the subject matter, and (3) the student.

The Teacher

First and foremost, the Bible teacher must know the English Bible. Perhaps this sounds unnecessary to seminary graduates who not only have Bible courses but also Greek and Hebrew to their credit. Effective Bible teaching is more than just repeating Bible notes from seminary or from books. The best Bible teacher is the one who is saturated with the English Bible so that at his or her disposal is God's revelation at a moment's reflection. The Bible teacher must be a master of the Book if he expects his students to be the same.

In addition to a thorough saturation from firsthand study of the English Bible, the teacher who would foster integration of faith and learning must be aware of world events. Issues of politics, economics, medicine, entertainment, and social concerns, when placed within the context of Bible teaching, will effectively remind students that the Bible is relevant and applicable to every situation.

The teacher's awareness must also include issues and subject matter being taught in the other departments of the college. The teacher of Bible fosters integration when he relates to his own Bible teaching the concepts, methodologies, and historical background learned from interaction with his colleagues. If the teacher can, in the process of teaching Romans, discuss the syllogism from logic; in teaching from Isaiah, the need for understanding Assyrian history; in teaching the Gospels, point out the historical development of Pharisaism; and in teaching Ephesians, the importance of music; he will be leading the student into integrative thinking.

There is, however, another dimension concerning the teacher that goes beyond content. There is also the crucial dimension of *communication*. Bible teachers need to think through not only what they are going to teach, but also how they can best communicate that content to the types of student in their particular teaching environments. Gaebelein emphasizes that teachers should have some grounding in the basic theory of their profession.[4] An understanding of both teaching and learning theory would help Bible teachers more effectively lead their students into an in-depth understanding of God's Word and its relationship to other areas of truth. With this understanding can come Christ-like behavior which does not necessarily result from simply dispensing theological and biblical information.

The Content

James M. Gray, over three-quarters of a century ago, emphasized how to handle our subject, the English Bible. In setting forth his case he said, "How to master the English Bible! High sounding title that, but does it mean what it says? It is not how to study it, but how to master it; for there is a sense in which the Bible must be mastered before it can be studied." He goes on to say, "And it is the Bible itself we are to master, not books about the Bible, nor yet 'charts.'"[5] Gray's words need to be reemphasized. On the Bible college level, it is the Bible we want our students to know, not so many other books.

We must remember Paul's words that it is the Scriptures which are "profitable for teaching, for reproof, for correction, for training in righteousness" and because of the Scripture's profitability, the man of God is adequately equipped for every good work.

The most effective way a student can master the English Bible is by reading it firsthand. Gaebelein's statements here are also significant, "Granted that the Bible is the Word of God, the most rewarding study must be the Bible itself in its books of history, poetry, prophecy, and doctrine. . . . Granted the experiential value of Bible study, it follows that each generation should have an immediate, direct, and original experience of divine reality."[6]

Speaking from personal experience, when I taught the Old Testament exposition course at William Tyndale College, I simply required the reading of the Bible rather than using another textbook. Every week the student was required to master fifty pages of biblical content to the point that he was able to take an objective quiz on the details of that text. The students did not always enjoy the quiz, but they did testify how much they learned when they had to read the Bible carefully. The student who really knows what is in the Bible through firsthand study of its pages is best prepared to integrate its material with information learned from other disciplines.

The Student

The student's development of integrative thought processes begins with how well he perceives the Bible's relevance to his world as he views it.

Teachers will do well to know culture, family, and academic backgrounds of their students. In addition, teachers must become more sensitive to the students' understanding of the Bible and spiritual matters. Even Jesus limited what He taught because his followers were not able to bear the material at that point (John 16:12).

Recently, in order to give consideration to the background of its students, William Tyndale College modified its Bible curriculum. The entering student receives a Bible overview which exposes him to the entire Bible from Genesis through Revelation in three semester hours. During the second through fifth semesters, the student studies all of the books of the Bible in exposition courses. In the sixth semester, after he has had Old Testament exposition, the student takes Old Testament theology. In the seventh and eighth semesters, the student is offered New Testament theology along with an overview of systematic theology. This curriculum structure moves students gradually from an overview of the Bible to a basic study of all the books; then from direct Bible study, to biblical theology, and finally to systematic theology. The student moves through various levels of biblical studies in line with his ability to perceive truth.

Ultimately, the task of the Bible teacher is to lead his students along a path whereby they gradually develop an awareness of the Bible's relevancy to their life situations. One of the ways this can be done is to relate illustrations from students' own life milieu to the concepts given in the Scriptures. For example, in the process of expounding on ethics from passages in the Bible a teacher could point out to students that payment of their school bills is an ethical issue. By so doing we will help students realize that studying Bible and theology in a college curriculum is ultimately meant to make their behavior more Christ-like. Another way this can be done is for the teacher to relate illustrations from his own personal experiences of how the Word of God has met particular needs. This will help the student relate biblical truth to all aspects of his own life. As Bible teachers we must teach students in such a way that they perceive that what we are studying together is truth and not just a set of notes.

Conclusion

The centrality of English Bible in the curriculum is one distinctive which makes the Bible college unique among educational institutions. Keeping the Bible central in our educational endeavors is going to be a significant issue in the years to come. This is precisely why a high view of inspiration needs to be maintained. An infallible and inerrant Bible is essential for a Bible college education. Anything less will eventually erode the uniqueness of our institutions. Anything less will contribute to a loss of identity. As Elton Trueblood pointed out in an interview, "If the Christian college ceases to be consciously committed to the Christian revelation, it has nothing to give."[7] If the Bible college ceases to consciously emphasize the centrality of the Bible in its educational approach, it too has nothing to give.

Our high view of Scripture is the basic reason why all other subject matter must be related to the Bible and why biblical subject matter is to permeate every other discipline taught in the Bible college. Gordon Clark's comment that, "Christianity, far from being a Bible-department religion, has a right to control the instruction in all departments,"[8] is to some degree legitimate if we understand "control" as meaning that every teacher and his subject matter are to be guided by the principles given in God's Word.

Bible teachers would do well to take additional studies in the art of teaching their subject matter. The Bible college movement needs to devote more effort toward fostering educational expertise among its teachers, especially in the area of Bible. I would think that those of us who teach the greatest subject in all the world would work at doing it with as much expertise as possible. Bible colleges should make provision for their teachers to specifically study the art of teaching through required reading, education workshops, and special seminars; and they should also give grants for further education.

Finally, the goal of our Bible teaching must continually be kept before us. What we are always aiming for is that our students will live the remainder of their lives intellectually, emotionally, morally, psychologically, and spiritually *under* the full teaching of the Word of God. For them to do this means they must see the wholeness of life as related to the Scriptures; consequently, they must think "integratively" and we must lead them to do so. Gaebelein's words are still appropriate: "Much work in Christian education has yet to be done in the integration of methodology to Biblical truth. . . . It will take pioneer work coupled with original thinking."[9]

Notes

1. Frank E. Gaebelein, *Christian Education in a Democracy* (New York: Oxford, 1951), p. 161.
2. Frank E. Gaebelein, *The Pattern of God's Truth* (Chicago: Moody, 1968), pp. 48–49.
3. James Michael Lee, *The Flow of Religious Instruction* (Mishawaka: Religious Education Press, 1973), p. 12.
4. Gaebelein, *Christian Education*, p. 204.
5. James M. Gray, *How to Master the English Bible* (Chicago: The Bible Institute Colportage Association, 1904), pp. 13–14.
6. Gaebelein, *Christian Education*, p. 161.
7. Elton Trueblood, "A Life of Broad Strokes and Brilliant Hues," *Christianity Today*, 23 May 1980, p. 22.
8. Gordon H. Clark, *A Christian Philosophy of Education* (Grand Rapids: Eerdmans, 1946), p. 210.
9. Gaebelein, *Christian Education*, p. 198.

The Author

Since 1980 Richard Melick has been at Palm Beach Atlantic College, West Palm Beach, Florida, first as chairman of the religion department and currently as academic vice president. Prior to that he served eight years in two AABC schools, Columbia Bible College and Miami Christian College. Richard Melick holds the B.A. from Columbia Bible College, an M.Div. from Trinity Evangelical Divinity School, and the Ph.D. in New Testament from Southwestern Baptist Theological Seminary, Ft. Worth.

The Subject

In what may be the most difficult chapter of the book, Dr. Melick carefully and logically builds a case for the teaching of biblical rather than systematic theology at the undergraduate level. While affirming the importance of systematics in ministerial training, Dr. Melick warns us against the immaturity, tendency toward "proof-texting," and minimal grasp of progressive revelation frequently characteristic of college students. The chapter aims at the development of a theological pedagogy which utilizes discovery learning and an emphasis on "doing theology," as both teacher and student work at the application of theological principles to the world around.

2

THEOLOGY

Richard R. Melick

In a Sunday school class several years ago a psychology professor was lecturing on the nature of man. Intending to survey the contributions made by differing disciplines, he said: "Psychology says man is good. What does the Bible say? The Bible says man is bad." Then, realizing for the first time the implications of his statement and the context in which he said it (a Sunday school class), he stopped in unresolved frustration and moved quickly to another subject. The professor's approach was too simplistic; not all psychologists say man is good, and certainly the Bible does not say man is "bad" in the sense in which he used it. In addition, the dichotomy itself was an awkward one. His artificial polarization of authorities posed interesting questions regarding the nature of truth and how revelation is to be integrated with the social sciences.

How is the theologian to respond to a situation like this? Obviously that professor should learn Christian theology. Equally important, the traditional "secular" disciplines must accept the primacy of theology as a guideline for understanding all truth. Legitimately, the theologian may fault the secularists for lack of perception in theological areas, particularly since the professor claimed to be Christian. On the other hand, the theologian also has a responsibility in the integration of truth. His task involves more than affirming the standard for all other disciplines and those who teach them. The theologian must seek to integrate from his perspective, to

take initiative in understanding the entire scope of God's revelation
generally and specifically. He must become involved in every
aspect of life, seeking to redeem each area by subjecting it to the
Lordship of Christ.

If this task is to be accomplished, from the beginning the student
must have a holistic approach. In the theology classroom a twofold
foundation is laid. First, a student begins to learn the *basic doctrines*
of Christianity. He embarks on a life-long adventure of discovering,
exploring, and enjoying the truth of God. A proper introduction
results in the development of deep-rooted convictions held with the
confidence born of personal involvement. Secondly, the student
learns a *perspective*. He develops attitudes toward theological study
and involvement in life. He should also learn how to approach the
issues of the day with strong confidence in the biblical materials as
the guide. These two basic areas are not only the foundation, but
they are also the goal of theological study. All of life becomes a
laboratory for learning God's truth and applying it to man. The
theologian or theological student must have an accurate, solid base
of conviction, and he must always endeavor to communicate these
convictions accurately and lovingly to his world. It is of utmost
importance, therefore, that introductory theology be approached
properly.

Introduction

The Traditional Approach

The traditional Bible/theology curriculum reflects a proper development. The first year consists of survey courses in which the
student achieves a knowledge of basic information about each book
of the Bible. With proper guidance he also gains insight into the
message of each book and its distinctive contribution to the whole of
Scripture. After the survey courses, a student undertakes studies of
individual books and topics (e.g., biographical studies such as "The
Life of Christ"). At this point he should begin to see the significance
of each book in depth. Finally, usually in the upper levels of a four
year program, the student begins systematic theology.

This outline is consistent with the logical development of theology
in general. Beginning with an awareness of contextual matters, the
theologian works with exegesis and hermeneutics, then biblical
theology, and finally systematic theology. Maturity and preparation
are indispensable for profitable study of systematics.

Although the traditional curriculum outline is proper, it must be challenged with two basic questions. Can undergraduate students really assimilate the broad range of materials included in these areas of theological studies? Is there a better way to lay a proper foundation for understanding theology and current applications? These questions guide the following discussion.

Problems in the Traditional Approach

A number of difficulties arise from the traditional approach to theology. These problem areas arise not because the logical progression of theological discipline is violated (although frequently students register for courses out of sequence), but because of the difficulty of dealing with every area adequately on the undergraduate level. For example, by the third year of Bible college study the student normally begins studying systematic theology. Prior to that, he has had a survey of the Bible, but probably not many studies of individual books or introduction to theological method. Naturally there is a strong desire to expose the student to Christian theology early. A premature exposure, however, perpetuates the difficulties outlined here.

Identifying these problem areas does not imply absolute failure of the traditional approach. Neither does it suggest that all students will graduate with these characteristics. This section simply points out areas of difficulty which do characterize many Bible college graduates, and it serves as a preliminary to suggestions for improvement.

Insufficient Background. One of the greatest difficulties in the study of theology is that undergraduate students usually do not possess the background necessary to grasp the truths of systematics. This is reflected in two diverse but related areas: (1) biblical background, and (2) intellectual maturity and interests.

Systematic theology builds on an extensive knowledge of the Bible. One cannot begin to collate teachings, or reason theologically, without understanding the historical context, perspective, style and vocabulary of the author, and personal factors which influence the writing. There must be some awareness of the original languages and the thought patterns they reflect. In addition, an appreciation of hermeneutics is absolutely necessary. While it is true that many theology professors have developed these skills, it is also true that virtually no undergraduate student has, nor could be expected to have, such expertise. Often, therefore, the students grasp theological conclusions without understanding the process. Undergraduate students should focus on acquisition of the facts and contexts of revealed truth, with elementary aspects of systematic arrangement of these truths.

The second aspect of this problem is the lack of intellectual maturity. In any college setting there is a broad range of student development and interests. Recent demographic studies reveal that the average age of Americans is getting higher, and therefore, there will be fewer young students available to colleges. Survival in the educational world will be in part dependent upon programs suitable to the older students. Most Bible colleges have already shown a high percentage of mature individuals, many with families, enrolled in their programs. Nevertheless, intellectual preparation must be considered.

Recently, I tested a sample of theology students to determine their "natural ability" to do theology, based on a test of their learning capabilities. The learning style inventory used plotted the students in terms of "abstract conceptualization" and " concrete experience" preferences. A basic presupposition was that systematic theology generally requires a more developed ability in "abstract conceptualization." Barely 10 percent scored significantly in the abstract areas of the spectrum, while a strong majority were very high on the concrete experience end. Almost the same figures (though not as polarized) separated "active experimenters" from the "reflective observers," the other two categories of the inventory.

There were no significant differences between the scores of the various ages and sexes, although some had suggested that males and older students would generally score higher in the abstract and experimentation ends of the spectrum. The interpretive materials supplied with the inventory stated that adults would show movement from concrete to abstract as they matured.[1] As a whole, these students preferred interaction and experience rather than lecture, and tended to postpone using what they learned rather than actively integrating it with other academic subjects or with life in general.

Although the control group in the test was not scientifically selected, an important question arises: Do undergraduates have the capacity for and interest in the kind of theological study demanded by systematics? Should systematic theology be taught to the undergraduate? Some would opt for omitting theology from the curriculum, but that is the wrong answer. Rather, one must approach it on the level of the undergraduate student. The teacher must teach in such a manner that the truth is "encountered" in a living context and is, therefore, more immediately and obviously relevant.

"Proof-Texting" Methodology. A second problem raised by an early dose of systematics without adequate preparation is that of a tendency toward "proof-texting" mentality. "Proof-texting" refers to the practice of quoting a verse or verses to prove a point without regard to context (textual, literary, historical/cultural). At times the quoting of verses on a given subject is quite in order and sometimes even possible methodology. Many categories of theology many be legitimately "proof-texted" because the text quoted means exactly what a cursory reading suggests. Although the result may at times be acceptable, the practice is suspect and should be avoided.

The difficulty here is not so much the use of biblical texts to support basic statements of theology as it is the mentality that often results. Many students develop the idea that simply quoting a Bible verse proves the issue. In one Bible college situation every senior was asked to write a doctrinal exam as a prerequisite to graduation. Each exam was graded and returned to the student, followed by a discussion between the student and grader (always a faculty member). In multiple cases, almost at certain predictable places in every paper, students resorted to quoting a verse without comment, as though the presence of a supporting verse—even without interpretation—proved the point. This practice occurred in spite of a fine faculty who warned verbally and in practice against such an approach.

"Proof-texting" may reveal an underlying superficiality and inflexibility. A "proof-texter" assumes that the Scriptures are always self-evident and that there is no need to understand the very subject matter he may be studying in other courses. Matters of historical background, context, language, and culture are diminished in an almost simplistic fashion. A student may assume early in his theological training that this method is the sum total of theology and may demand it of all who contribute to the discipline. Further, this mentality has far-reaching implications into areas of ministry in general (*understanding* his culture), and of personal witness in particular (*listening* to the person he encounters). Since the theology classroom often sets the direction in these areas, care must be exercised here.

Static Concept of Revelation. A third difficulty with the traditional teaching of systematics as the primary exposure to theology on the undergraduate level is that it often restricts one's awareness of progressive revelation. Many systematic textbooks quote freely, and correctly, from both Old and New Testament passages, assuming the reader will understand the differing stages in God's revelation. The student, however, often assumes that the Old Testament saint understood as much as the men who walked with Jesus, or, on a different level, that Adam understood as much as Daniel. Gross mistakes have been made in this area, particularly in relation to salvation, the meaning of the blood, the understanding of the sacrificial system, and other concepts fully revealed in the New Testament.

Related to the concept of progressive revelation is that of "movement" in theology. Although the evangelical firmly holds to one basic, ultimate theology, he also recognizes that theology is revealed in real-life situations. The nature of the Bible reveals that clearly. History is primary. God spoke on specific occasions, through men whose words related to a given context. Even the common statement that the Word of the Lord *came* to the spokesmen reveals a dynamic quality. Theological discussion was never divorced from life. Truth came in a life-setting, and many of the modern charges of irrelevancy would be silenced if that dynamic force were more appreciated.

A further aspect of this category is that often a young theology student fails to appreciate the contributions made by the individual personalities of the biblical authors. This problem is of major concern, extending beyond mere lexicography and culture, since inspiration focuses on this point. All of the writer's personality serves as a vehicle to communicate God's revelation. The student who recognizes that God used various types of personalities who expressed truth differently because of their situations will have a better grasp of the way God works today. As a classification of biblical theology, it is a logical prerequisite to systematics and must be emphasized before the systematic courses. In the traditional curriculum, time does not permit adequate coverage.

Lack of Commitment to Continuing Theological Study. The final matter of concern may be the most alarming from a practical viewpoint. Often a student views theology as *peripheral to his purpose* in college and in life. Several factors contribute to this. First, there is a natural intimidation in the term *theology*. Like philosophy, theology bears a reputation of being somewhat esoteric, a discipline for the erudite few who can make sense of it. Secondly, *theology often confuses students*. Theologians naturally differ and although many differences help preserve a necessary balance and protect the universal church, the average Bible college student may assume that differences in theological conviction prove that the particular subject is unimportant. Furthermore systematicians argue laboriously over what students often consider minor points. The resulting confusion encourages students to concentrate on what they know positively (i.e., what the church agrees on).

The focus on a consensus of truth, however, may cause a disregarding of other important truths about which there is no general agreement. The fallacy that "if it is not clear it is not necessary" persists. Third, students often feel *theology is irrelevant*. Though few would verbalize that conviction, many approach theological study with that presupposition. Christian living and ministry occupy their thoughts and theology simply does not fit. They may reason that God will explain Himself in eternity, and theology can wait until then.

These factors, among others, lead some to ask: why continue to study theology? Many students realize that graduate seminary training demands further theological study. But frequently theology texts sit on the shelf collecting dust while the "practical" books wear out.

This situation must be reversed. Students must see the value of theological study and commit themselves to life-long habits of work in this crucial discipline. In many cases the theology classroom diminishes this desire rather than encouraging it.

Each of these problem areas leaves much room for discussion. Some areas apply more to certain schools, teachers, and students, than to others. Some will question whether or not they represent *bona fide* problems. Yet a holistic approach to life demands that students overcome these potential misemphases. Early exposure to theology sets the direction one way or another. Perhaps Bible colleges should reexamine their approach in order to achieve a better, more productive, and incisive product. Indeed, theology should improve one's life and thinking, so that he has a basis for Christian growth and ministry.

Biblical Foundation

Presenting biblical foundations for the study of theology may seem tautological. Evangelicals affirm not only the importance of the study, but also its centrality. Nevertheless, some brief description of the biblical foundations serves two good purposes: first, to remind one of the biblical evidence supporting the teaching of theology and second, to discover how that teaching was done. In this presentation it is necessary to consider briefly both explicit statements and implicit suggestions as to the importance of theology.

Explicit Statements

Many passages state the importance of transmitting truth by teaching and no competent evangelical is ignorant of these. Since such familiarity can be assumed, this section is representative and in no sense exhaustive.

Deuteronomy 6:4–9. This passage, including the well-known proposition that "Jehovah our God is one Jehovah," was foundational in Israel. Of particular importance is verse 7: "and thou shalt talk of them when thou sittest in thy house, and when thou walkest by the way, and when thou liest down, and when thou risest up." Moses commands both formal and informal instruction in the words of God. Because of the Hebrew meshing of theology with the ethical and practical, this command must relate to both areas of life. Ethical and moral practices in Israel were commended because of a God who had revealed Himself (theology) to the fathers. From the earliest days of the nation to the later scribes and Pharisees, this teaching function, more than any other aspect of life, preserved the nation. Clearly the Jews were "theologically oriented."[2]

2 Timothy 2:2. Paul writing to his younger companion Timothy penned words now almost foundational to any aspect of Christian living: "And the things which thou hast heard from me among many witnesses, the same commit thou to faithful men, who shall be able to teach others also." Although this applies to personal growth, any program of discipleship, and practical truths in general, it seems most likely that Paul had theological content in mind here. The practical concerns which come to the fore in Paul's letters grow out of more foundational, philosophical/theological concepts. Timothy not only traveled with Paul, spending hours learning from him, but also represented Paul to many of the churches, carrying out the apostle's words of instruction. Theological controversy often sharpened both minds and their conclusions were to be preserved.

Both Israel and the early church attempted to objectify and transmit the truth given them by God. Several examples reveal that, including the rabbinic preoccupation with understanding tradition and Scripture, the separation of *kerygma* and *didache* in the New

Testament writings, and the content of the early "hymns" now preserved in the biblical materials.[3] There was a determined effort to preserve the "words of the Lord" so as not to confuse them with the words of an interpreter, however inspired he may be. Clearly teaching was the primary means of conveying truth, and that truth was theological.

Implicit Passages

In addition to these explicit statements, the careful reader observes many examples of the importance of theology to the early church. A brief and simple classification of these passages reveals those things for which theology is valuable.

Developing Christian Character and Attitudes. A clear example of this is found in Philippians 2:5–11. Here, commending unity and service to each other, Paul illustrates the point with his famous *kenosis* passage. The illustration reveals that theology promotes Christian character, since the Christian is to have the same attitudes as Christ. Similarly, Peter explains that suffering produces character, therefore demonstrating purifying value, even as Christ's sufferings were redemptive (1 Peter 2:21–25). Although used as illustrations, these theological truths provide the proper basis and focus for Christian growth.

Providing Comfort and Strength to the Distressed Believer. Both Old and New Testament examples abound. As for the former, one might examine the number of passages in which God, addressing Israel, introduces Himself as the God of the Exodus, the mighty one (Isa. 43:14–17 is a clear example). The theological content expressed by God (omnipotence, eternality) gives comfort in discouraging times. A New Testament example is 1 Thessalonians 4:14. There, in comforting the hearts of bereaved Christians, Paul appeals to a well-known theological tenet ("If we believe that Jesus died and rose again"—note the first class condition in Greek) to postulate another one equally important ("them also that are fallen asleep in Jesus will God bring with him"). Theology provides strength and comfort.

Detecting Error Within the Church. Warning about those who destroy the church from within, John suggests a theological test of orthodoxy, "Jesus Christ is come in the flesh" (1 John 4:1-6).

Confronting Error from Outside the Church. Of the many examples which may be cited, Colossians 1 is typical. Paul's discussion there, including many specific terms he uses, has particular reference to the tenets held by those seeking to infiltrate the church with their philosophy. Paul counters them from a strong theological base as foundational to apologetic content.

Averting Potential Apostasy. Hebrews 5:12–6:12 teaches that theological maturity involves growth beyond the knowledge necessary for conversion. For the author, these truths involve comparisons between Christ and Melchisedek, and the earthly and heavenly tabernacles. This section of Scripture graphically portrays a broken-hearted pastor sensing the tensions of the congregation as they are faced with apostasy in the church. This return to Judaism could be countered by theological progress.

The brief treatment given here does not imply that biblical foundations are insignificant. Every area of life, including Christian college life, should rest on clear biblical principles. Since, however, evangelicals accept the centrality of theology in the curriculum, these points are representative. Two important principles are seen in this section: first, it is necessary to transmit theology from one Christian generation to the next, and second, theology is suited to the "give and take" of life. Without good teaching of theology, Christian truth will be lost both intellectually and practically.

Philosophical Formulation

In the introduction to this study the question is asked: "Is there a better way to teach theology on the undergraduate level?" Having surveyed some of the problems often resulting from theology classes, and having examined some aspects of the biblical foundation, we may now consider that question more directly. A philosophy of teaching theology involves both the manner and the content of teaching.

In a significant doctoral dissertation (1978), Dr. Al Hiebert surveyed theology teachers and their students in selected schools of the American Association of Bible Colleges. Particularly, Dr. Hiebert attempted to determine whether theology professors and their students preferred *expository* or *discovery* methodology in theology classes. He discovered that both teachers and students preferred the *discovery* method, although most teachers used lecture (expository) because of class size and limited time to cover the specified material.[4] In fact, over half of the teachers and students reported *never* having questions or discussions in class.[5] Since many students learn best by discovery methods, the classroom expository experience did not produce the desired results. "Discovery students" showed less commitment to the doctrines studied when they were under "expository" teachers.[6] All students preferred Bible exposition (not to be confused with "expository" methodology) as a means of approaching theology.[7] Dr. Hiebert concluded that theology teachers must reexamine their teaching with an eye to a better methodology. Far more is at stake than simple pedagogical preference. In beginning classes student attitudes are shaped, forming a perspective toward theology and truth. Ultimately this attitude, negative or positive, expresses itself in the Christian leader's view of life and ministry.

Theology in Relation to Other Disciplines

All evangelicals agree on the importance of theology. In acquiring knowledge, natural revelation provides truth from the so-called "secular sources" and special revelation guides the quest for ultimate truth. In both cases, theology becomes the canon for determining truth. The more a subject area approaches the realm of knowledge found in the Bible, the more directly the conclusions of theological study apply.

The particular relationship between theology and other disciplines may be viewed from two perspectives as the stance of the teacher influences his teaching philosophy. Model 1, in its three stages, attempts to picture the centrality of theology from one perspective. Model 1-A shows theology in relation to biblical studies; Model 1-B indicates how theology is central to other disciplines in the college curriculum; and Model 1-C extends this viewpoint beyond the college setting to life in general.

The graphics assume that an attitude learned in the beginning will probably persist to the end. In each phase, theology is viewed as an isolated "body of truths" somewhat segmented from other disciplines. The relationship pictured is unilateral. Theology determines what is truth from any source. Its authority is, thus, "pontifical." Some would modify the graph to resemble 1-D, where there is some limited interaction between theology and other areas. The philosophy, however, is basically the same.

One of the many difficulties with this perspective is that of seg-

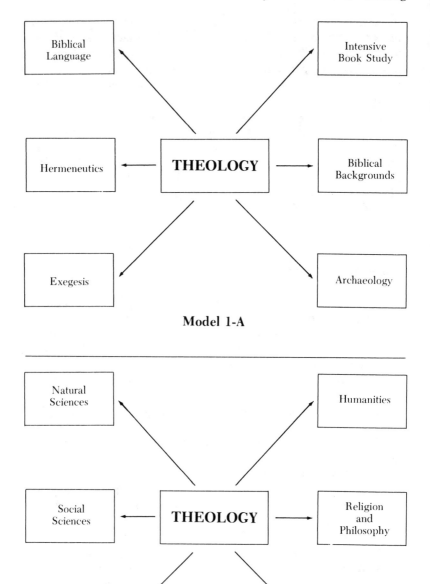

Model 1-A

Model 1-B

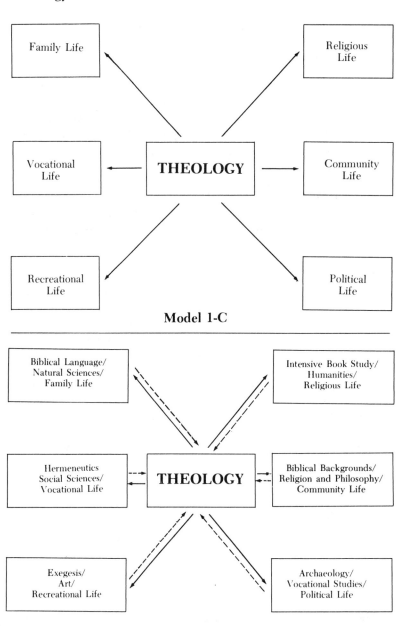

Model 1-C

Model 1-D

Note:
The outside rectangles are intended to recall Models 1-A, B, and C. Thus various categories are included in each rectangle. There is no correlation between subject matter listed within each rectangle. "A" appears first, "B" second, and "C" third.

mentation. Students begin to see theology as a set of truths which must be "internalized." Once learned, they give one absolute authority over every area of life. While it is true that theology does consist of propositions to be learned, and theological study does increase evaluative skills, a question remains as to the long-range value of such an approach. The isolationist attitude often leads to arrogance.

The Model 2 series pictures another perspective. Here, theology interacts with related biblical studies (Model 2-A); other disciplines in the curriculum (Model 2-B); and life in general (Model 2-C). This perspective, considering carefully the context, becomes a "theology in context." The historical, cultural, and linguistic context serves as a guide, a protection, and a motivator.

As a *guide*, the context points the student toward more deeply held convictions by enabling him to see theology as interrelated with biblical studies, other disciplines, and life situations. By exposing the roots of theology in context, the teacher helps the student grasp a principle which contributes to a lasting perspective. The context also *protects* conclusions. Since biblical truth is always clothed in historical garb, a necessary reciprocity develops: theology interacts with a life situation, and the life situation shapes theology. The tension between these two keeps both in balance. Finally, the context becomes a *motivator*. The more the student understands the issues of a particular era, the quicker and more perceptive is his response to God's Word. Sometimes unknowingly, a framework develops enabling the transfer of a theological principle to similar contemporary contexts. Thus the entire theological cycle provides immediate incentive for further study.

Successful theological study enables a student to apply revealed truth to the problems of contemporary life. Biblical authors did not anticipate the complexity of modern issues such as social and medical ethics, genetic engineering, and nuclear arms discussions. Thus, little is said directly about them. The modern theologian, however, must address these issues and his students cannot be passive. When a discovery is made in one context it easily leads to an application in another. The theology classroom should prepare for that task.

Theology in Relation to Itself

The models presented suggest some tensions which must be addressed. First, what is central and what is peripheral? The question pertains to the philosophy of theology on the undergraduate level as well as to the teaching of theology. Naturally, the teacher must focus

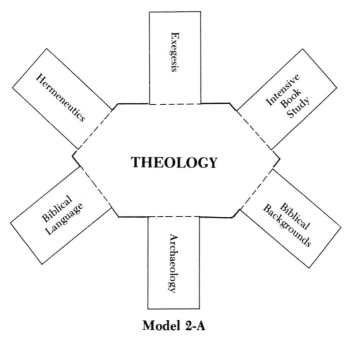

Model 2-A

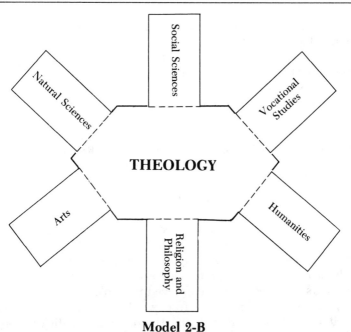

Model 2-B

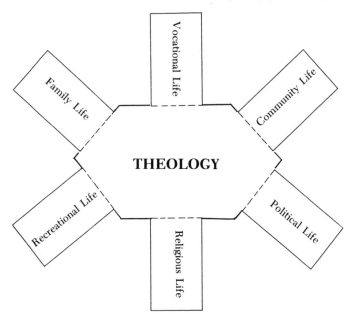

Model 2-C

on the primary. Secondly, what tension exists between "stating" and "doing" theology?

Three basic areas of tension may obscure the central-peripheral distinction: (1) the role of tradition, (2) the necessity of a philosophical framework for viewing theology, and (3) the developing or progressive understanding of theological truth. Each of these demands brief consideration.

The Role of Tradition. Tradition influences theology. The spectrum of influence moves from the Eastern Orthodox and Roman Catholic churches on one hand to modern Fundamentalism on the other. The former are characterized by a purposeful and stated acceptance of tradition as necessary to interpretation. The latter, characterized by strong individualism, prefers to go "strictly by the Bible," although tradition still guides its interpretation. Total objectivity cannot be achieved, and the insights of the past significantly help modern interpreters. A realtively harmless example of this occurs in the categories employed in theology. Early Christian Greek thought produced the framework for understanding and describing truth even though the Hebrew outlook differed from

Greek.[8] Overreaction, however, may lead to the trap of assuming that quoting a verse proves the point.

With such a legacy from the past, it is necessary to state a principle regarding the philosophy of teaching theology. The biblical data must be primary, interpretations secondary. The undergraduate course should focus on the primary—the raw material—and only secondarily include historical interpretations. The teacher bears the responsibility of clarifying his perspective for the class, and consistently subordinating his understanding to the biblical materials. In modern theology, theological systems form a major concern in Dispensational, Reformed, and Lutheran circles. A healthy tension must be maintained: the system provides understanding, but the system must always grow from the biblical raw materials. Thus, while traditions of various sorts are helpful, they must remain subordinate and not become determinative. Elementary theological study must impart that perspective.

A Philosophical Framework. Each generation of Christian scholars has faced the problem of integrating theology with some particular philosophical perspective. Beginning with the New Testament itself (where the Book of Hebrews in particular seems to reflect a "platonic dualism") history records this phenomenon. The early church was impressed with Augustine's Neoplatonistic framework. That was later met by Anselm and Aquinas with their Aristotelian orientation. Hegel and Marx influence some parts of the church even today, although Bultmann's antisupernaturalism and modern existentialism have posed more recent threats. On the contemporary scene an increasing number are trying to wed biblical truth with process philosophy.[9] No doubt man will persist in that quest.

However, any such philosophical approach to the Scriptures faces subtle dangers. First, it may diminish the significance of divine inspiration and the Bible's own claim to uniqueness. Secondly it may suggest that we, because of our more refined understanding, may be able to express reality better than the apostles. After all, they were men of their day speaking God's truth to their world; we must speak it to ours. The conclusions of radical form critics with their philosophical/theological assumptions reveal a multitude of inherent dangers.

Theological educators must balance perspective. A clearly defined line separates the depositor of divine truth from reflection on that truth. In other words, the Bible, which is truth, must be categorically different from attempts to understand and apply divine truth. Since a definite philosophical perspective was part of the writers' world view and thus partially shaped that truth, there will always be the tendency to "improve theology" as our knowledge of reality improves. This, of course, cannot be done and leads to theological impotence. On the other hand, theology should be taught in such a fashion that the student comfortably relates God's truth to contemporary culture and a distinctly Christian philosophical world view. The biblical materials, including the world view adopted by the writers, are central; philosophical interpretation is at best peripheral.

Progressive Understanding of Theological Truth. The assumption that man progressively understands theological truth must be discussed because it lies close to the heart of the previous two sections. "Progressive understanding" must not be mistaken for "progressive revelation" which culminated in the pages of the New Testament. "Progressive understanding" refers to the possibility that successive generations of Christian scholars may build upon each other so that Christian truth is refined and sharpened. Few would deny that such is the case (e.g., lexicography, archaeology). Scientifically we accept it, and most interpreters readily appreciate historical theology for the insights it affords. The tension is not between the Bible and history, but between *understanding* theological propositions as revealed in the Bible and *changing* these propositions.

An example of this tension exists in the realm of modern science. No doubt scientific discovery helps our understanding. On the other hand, the Darwinian theory of evolution and Einstein's theory of relativity have produced revolutionary changes in all thought. The theologian must beware. Just as philosophy and tradition may alter truth, the evolution of ideas and insights presents a definite threat.

Each of these areas has dealt with the central and the peripheral. As always, the biblical materials must stand above the insight afforded by other disciplines, yet the thinking Christian must listen to truth from any source, particularly from Christian sources. The teacher must impart (1) what the Bible actually says, and (2) his understanding of what it means—in that order! The interpreter may be wrong, but the Scriptures remain true.

"Doing" Versus "Stating" Theology

Many theologians today speak of "doing" theology rather than merely stating principles to be believed. By "doing theology" one means that the student and teacher are both actively involved in the process of deriving theology and applying it to the world around. Doing theology involves interaction with the context (then and now) and formulation of theological principles, incorporating insight gained from the history of thought. The student must be exposed to theology in such a way that he is not afraid to "be a theologian," both in discovering theology for himself and in applying it to his contemporary context. This involves a healthy understanding of what we have called "theology in context," with a purposeful interaction between theology and other disciplines. Finally, the teacher must see himself as much a *guide* to discovering truth as an *imparter* of truth. Although this may cause a reduction in the amount of material covered in class, it will encourage better cognitive results because of the relevancy of the theology to life.

Practical Application

Curriculum Design

The curriculum of any Bible college reflects its philosophy of teaching. In traditional course offerings (e.g., christology, anthropology, bibliology, etc.), the teacher must be sensitive to areas of concern and adjust his methodology accordingly. Perhaps, however, more effective approaches would yield better long-range results in relating theology to life and faith. Here is one suggestion.

The theology curriculum might begin with an Introduction to Theology. Like any other survey course, it should be prerequisite to other theology courses and should be a genuine introduction to the discipline, including such subjects as the foundations for theology, theological methodology, types of theology (exegetical, biblical, systematic, historical, etc.), commonly used classifications of the segments of theology (e.g., christology), and the contributions made by certain systematicians such as Calvin and Luther. Properly taught, the course could prepare the student for advanced theology of any type.

Following the survey, the curriculum consists of biblical theology modules. Taken in sequence, these are the heart of the undergraduate program. Beginning with the Pentateuch, the student is exposed to the historical/ideological backgrounds of each period (patriarchal in this case), along with the significance of these books both theologically and redemptively. With such preparation, each predetermined theological category is discussed in order (e.g., bibliology, christology, etc.), along with the necessary insights from that time period. Prophetic and typical elements can be seen and appreciated in proper perspective.

Not all categories of systematics would be included in every module, since all are not relevant to each segment of the Bible. At the end of each module, a survey summary relates the findings to the current study and the others previously studied. At the same time, the teacher sets the direction for future theology modules as the student watches for developing themes to emerge in clearer focus. The following modules, typical of biblical categories, might be helpful:

Course One   *Course Three*
Intro. to Theology   Theology of Gospels and Acts
Theology of Pentateuch   Theology of Paul
Course Two   *Course Four*
Theology of Historical Books   Theology of General Epistles
Theology of Wisdom Literature   Theology of Revelation
Theology of Prophetic Books   Summary course

Further, each section of biblical theology would have an introduction to the backgrounds and thought of the period. For example, the first theology course may be outlined as follows:

Introduction to Theology
A. Definition of theology
B. Types of theology (biblical, systematic, historical, etc.)
C. Classifications within theology (anthropology, theology proper, christology, bibliology, etc.)
Theology of the Pentateuch
A. Context
   1. Thought patterns of the day (Hebrew)
   2. Historical setting/life situation (Old Testament survey could have cared for this area and only a review would be necessary)
   3. Relation to former and latter historically developed areas (for Pentateuch there would be little need for this and other areas would tie in to what was covered in Pentateuch, etc.).
B. Content
   1. Selected areas of the classifications of theology which are pertinent to the Pentateuch. These would include anthropology, hamartiology, christology, etc.

At the end of the theology sequence, when all modules are completed, a final course would summarize and organize each category into the traditional systematics format. Model 3 graphically explains this curriculum design.

Several values would emerge from such a study. The student would *develop a sense of biblical theology* as prerequisite to systematics. Yet there is not a total separation of the two since an introduction has been given to theology in general and systematics in particular. Additionally, the categories of systematics could still be used, providing a traditional framework (even though all the categories might not be utilized in each module). Then there is a

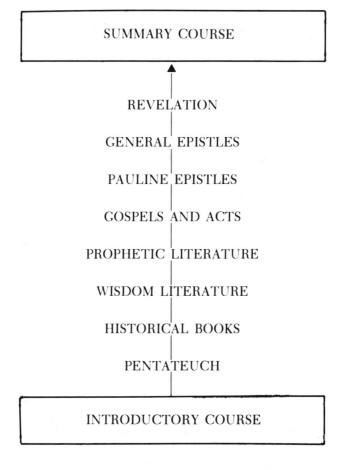

SUMMARY COURSE

REVELATION

GENERAL EPISTLES

PAULINE EPISTLES

GOSPELS AND ACTS

PROPHETIC LITERATURE

WISDOM LITERATURE

HISTORICAL BOOKS

PENTATEUCH

INTRODUCTORY COURSE

Model 3

more direct sense of progress in revelation and movement in theology. Finally, the student, discovering how theology has developed in various contexts, senses *the relevance of theology to life*. As theology is integrated into a student's thinking process, he "does" theology. He sees what God said and how God said it, and he knows immediately how to apply it to himself and his world.

There are, of course, some objections to this proposal. It *may* take longer to present the materials necessary in order to achieve proficiency in theology. Normally, the Bible college curriculum strains to allow an adequate survey of the categories of theology. To repeat them in this fashion, module by module, would require even more time unless some delimiting was done. In addition, the student's *grasp of the whole* awaits the summary course at the end so he *may* lose the "big picture" from his interaction with the parts. However, this problem is countered by the possibility of surveying the entirety of a doctrine at the place it is most fully developed, by the better orientation to theology at the beginning, and by careful selection of a satisfactory textbook.

Although many may not be interested in changing traditional methodology, some thought must be given to avoiding the dangers inherent in most systematics courses. An orientation toward biblical theology provides a promising alternative.

Classroom Procedure

If the classroom experience is to be integrative, the teacher of theology must be an "integrator." He must see life holistically, be able to appraise it carefully, be willing to interact with it honestly, and be able to initiate dialogue with the problems of his world. If theology is central to knowing all truth, and there is legitimate dialogue between disciplines, the teacher must enjoy interaction with other disciplines. Such an interest may be developed to some degree in any field, but the theologian naturally senses its importance and shares this outlook with the class.

The classroom experience must actually relate theology to other areas of life. Whenever appropriate, the teacher must call attention to current related issues in science and the arts. Whether he has answers to contemporary questions or not, the theologian must be willing to initiate dialogue by providing the biblical and theological resources necessary for evaluating the issues. One helpful means is to plan sessions in the class schedule, or as an extracurricular

interdisciplinary seminar, for interaction between and among disciplines. Other faculty resources (along with persons outside the
college community) should be utilized. In such a class a tangible
model displays the integration of God's Word and human
understanding.

A better use of class time, providing a total learning experience,
can be helpful. More direct use of the theology text (by requiring
students to know it as a prerequisite to class) allows freedom in the
classroom for making applications and encouraging holistic learning. If the textbook is not sufficient for outlining theology, the
professor should produce an extended syllabus which explains his
concepts. There is no need for class lecture to reproduce the text.
The teacher should do something for the student that he cannot
receive from reading alone, e.g., *an integration of theology and life.*

Improved teaching methods help. If the teacher has access to a
text which he can use as a basis for content, he is then free to use
various methods to help students grasp the subject. Case studies,
parables, ethical or moral dilemmas, are particularly helpful for
involving students in theological issues.[10] In addition, panels,
forums, and group activities encourage discovery and interaction.
The methods used, however, must be appropriate to the subject and
must not be overused or misused. Certainly a higher purpose than
variety should control.

Class size matters. Some administrators take the stance that if
there are thirty students enrolled in class there might as well be two
hundred, since the teaching method requires lecture. Two factors
point up the fallacy in such thinking. On the one hand, teacher
productivity diminishes since the total teaching load requires
grading of papers and other extra-class involvement. On the other,
theological concepts require reflection and interaction. Theology
differs from Bible survey, for example, which tends to be more
factual. A good teacher-student ratio is a necessity in "doing
theology."

These suggestions point toward effective teaching but they do not
guarantee it. Each Bible college theology department bears the
responsibility for determining its particular approach, and the
individual professor is the effective agent. Far too often courses are
approached the same way year after year. Many are copies in
miniature of the professor's seminary theology classes without any
reflective or creative thought given to methodology. Routine may
become a rut: good theology teaching avoids that pitfall.

Conclusion

Theology still reigns as "queen of the sciences" if by that one means she is the most demanding and most satisfying of the disciplines. However, the pragmatism of modern life, along with philosophical disdain for classic course offerings, have caused the queen's crown to tilt. Bible colleges recognize the central place of biblical and theological studies. To the degree that centrality is retained, to that degree our schools will be successful.

Two assumptions guided this study. First, that biblical theology (rather than systematics) produces better long-range results and is, therefore, the better choice for teaching introductory theology. It is hoped that case is presented sufficiently to gain some hearing. Secondly, that most college students who plan to continue in full-time ministry will apply for graduate training. The benefits of seminary training, coupled with its ready availability, make it the logical choice. No doubt the trend in that direction among Bible college graduates will increase. But even if the student does not opt for further training, he must start correctly in his theological pilgrimage, building on a foundation which will serve him throughout his life of ministry. The issues raised in this chapter must be addressed, for the beginning question still remains: "Is there a better way to approach and teach theology on the undergraduate level?" It is the writer's hope that Bible college administrators and teachers will examine their programs in light of these suggestions.

Notes

1. David A. Kolb, *Learning Style Inventory* (McBer and Company, 1976).
2. One may argue at this point from the practical viewpoint since the majority of the nation did not adhere to the strictness of the law. Yet they were called to be a theologically sensitive people and were blamed pointedly when they failed in that area.
3. The most famous of these passages is Philippians 2:5–11 (cf. also Col. 1:15–20) which displays a lyric, poetic nature. These "hymns" reveal a strong theological affirmation which became a confession in the early church.
4. Albert A. Hiebert, "Expository and Discovery Teaching of Systematic Theology: An Analysis of Instructional Models Preferred by Teachers and Students of Systematic Theology in Accredited Schools of the American Association of Bible Colleges" (Ph.D. diss., New York University, 1978). The references are to a paper read by Dr. Hiebert at the annual conference of the American Association of Bible Colleges, 1978, entitled, "Teach Sound Doctrine," p. 29.
5. Ibid., p. 32.
6. Ibid., pp. 41–42.
7. Ibid., p. 44. This dissertation presents a thorough and carefully analyzed approach to what is being done in the AABC schools. It should be given great consideration in the future.
8. The titles of systematic theology represent this: "omnipotence, omnipresence, omniscience, aseity, and eternality" are examples.
9. A recent example of a growing number of works seeking to view doctrine as "in process" is: David Gasperson, "Transformation of the Cross: A Process Perspective in Light of New Testament Thought" (Ph.D. diss., Southern Baptist Theological Seminary, Louisville, Kentucky, 1980.) Its bibliography suggests others who are working in the area.
10. The case study method has particular promise for theology. An excellent explanation of this method is found in Jack B. Rogers and Forrest Baird, *Introduction to Philosophy: A Case Study Approach* (San Francisco: Harper & Row, 1981). Of particular interest is "An Introduction to the Case Method for Students and Teachers," by Robert A. Evans, pp.xv–xxvi. Although this particular case approach deals with philosophy, one title in this series is *Christian Theology*, by Robert A. Evans and Thomas D. Parker.

The Author

Stephen B. Woodward has served at Winnipeg Bible College and Winnipeg Theological Seminary since 1970. He has been professor of Greek and New Testament Literature at the seminary since 1975. Before that time he was active in pastoral ministry. Dr. Woodward brings to his craft impressive credentials: the B.A. from the University of Tennessee; the B.D. from Columbia Theological Seminary; and the Ph.D. from the University of Aberdeen.

The Subject

It is, of course, impossible to treat both Greek and Hebrew within the confines of one short chapter. Since Dr. Woodward's expertise centers in Greek, he has chosen to use the language of the New Testament to build his case. Perhaps it is appropriate to note that what pertains to Greek also pertains to Hebrew except in the details of classroom methodology. He criticizes the misunderstanding which comes from confusing accidence with syntax and argues strongly for a syntactical approach to biblical language study which points the student to a Christ-in-life grasp of the Scriptures.

3

BIBLICAL LANGUAGES

Stephen B. Woodward

Introduction

Though often forgotten in our day, the historical utility of Greek for Christian doctrine and experience cannot be doubted. Most people recall the tremendous impact of the ministries of John Wesley and George Whitefield but too few are aware that their ministries drew deeply from an intimate knowledge of and commitment to the languages. Wesley produced a revised New Testament version which contained 1200 variations from the Authorized Version and, more germane to our subject, overtly placed special faith in ministers who knew the original languages.[1] Similarly, Luther, through whose writings Wesley grasped the reality of justification by faith, also underscored the value of such preaching and teaching:

> So although the Faith and the Gospel may be proclaimed by preachers without the knowledge of languages, the preaching will be feeble and ineffective. But where the languages are studied, the proclamation will be fresh and powerful, the Scriptures will be searched and the faith will be constantly rediscovered through ever new words and deeds.[2]

This may be hyperbole, or perhaps Luther speaks relatively. Nevertheless, his conviction fairly represents the mind of some of those whom we deem to have done most in a pragmatic sense for the household of God. Historically, the correlation of language and faith did not imply an impractical, uneasy, or unnecessary union.

But historical precedent and practice do not always mean that the same holds for the present. Things change. Based on this general reasoning, several overt objections to learning the original languages have been lodged.

Time and Translations

Some object that the time and energy expended mastering the languages is out of proportion to the advantage gained. Would not the time- and energy-consuming devotion to the memorization of paradigms and conjugations better be redirected to the immediate study of one of the illuminating translations?

Ronald Ward holds that the objection overlooks the obvious— who will be the future translators (and commentators)?—and does not explain the imprecision of present preaching/teaching when compared with the precision of Lightfoot's day.[3] However, Ward's reply is inconclusive and misses the essential flaw in the argument. One could reason that God calls some specialists to free the rest of us to study what they have translated and commented upon. With respect to his second charge, similarly, one could reply that a better choice of commentaries and translations, coupled with a more intensified perusal of the text would tighten up the exegetical laxity.

The essential inconsistency which Ward misses is that the objection confuses the importance of accidence with that of syntax and so with one sweep obscures the unique value of Greek. Accidence—the often tedious study/memorization[4] of the forms of words (their spelling, conjugation, declension)—foists upon the whole discipline a reputation for pedantry, and it interests no one but the specialists.[5] Syntax, however, concentrates on the way the words within the sentence or phrase are logically or emotionally hooked together to reflect the author's thought pattern, and consequently should be of interest to everyone.

Since on the whole word-forms can be *reproduced* into another language, while syntax can only be *reflected*, syntax becomes a unique window to the writer's mind and personality.[6] Because of the limitations of the English language, no translation (ASV, Berkeley, KJV, NIV, Phillips, RSV) of Romans 8:1 captures the force, color, and finality of the emphatic word *no* by which Paul dispatches the last nagging doubt with respect to the staggering doctrine of justification of the ungodly. Hence, though one should be grateful for illuminating translations, one should face the fact that translations cannot reproduce the mind and personality of an inspired writer as they are found in the original. Therefore when one identifies Greek with "translation" and "accidence," rather than with "unique insight" and "syntax," he confuses and obscures the whole matter and enervates serious desire to integrate language and faith, doctrine and experience.

Word-books and Commentaries

Some may think that "word-books" and commentaries make up the difference between translation and syntax. Of course, there is no doubt that our increased knowledge of the meaning of single words has illuminated New Testament interpretation. But James Barr has effectively proven that "theological thought of the type found in the NT has its characteristic expression not in the word individually, but in the word-combination of the sentence";[7] that is, without respect for their syntactical context, the words lose their integrity! No doubt particular commentaries evidence a pragmatic awareness of approacing the text syntactically. However, rising production costs and the desire for economy prohibit even the best commentaries from presenting more than the minimum syntactical comment and thereby truckloads of valuable personal and pastoral insight are lost. Moreover, since one is forced to weigh the material listed in commentaries, a personal knowledge of syntax becomes a necessary theological safeguard. Without it, how can one assess the theories and observations of the commentators, not to mention the translators themselves?

Subjectivism

Others wonder whether or not the study of Greek is a precise science. They may suspect that the study of syntax is an artificial tool which can be manipulated consciously or unconsciously at the whim and prejudice of the exegete.

If by *precise* one means that probabilities must be excluded, then almost any endeavor into any subject is precluded and we have ruled out exegesis in Greek, Hebrew, or English! With respect to the charge that syntax is artificial, one is at a loss to prove to those who have little knowledge of the discipline that it is truly a science, and not a pretext for the unbridled imagination. Unless the one who objects consents to examine the evidence for himself, all that can be done is to cite the conclusions of those who have worked through the documentation. As Nigel Turner concludes,

> This is a science, not a field for unbridled imagination, nor for reading things into an innocent text. All the discipline and patience which men devote to empirical science is demanded and the results are as reliable.[8]

Consequently, though all empirical sciences require the judgment of the observer, and though *at times* the evidence may warrant no more than the conclusion "probable," there is no mandate to dismiss the whole as "imprecise" and "subjective."

Pietism

For the conservative Christian, perhaps the most subtle objection to integrating language and faith is *pietism*, an anglicized term which springs form the Latin title of a book by the Lutheran pastor, Philip Spener (1675), *Pia Desideria (Heartfelt Desire).*[9] As the title implies, the term originally characterized the protest of a living faith against the (German) state's often arid, pseudo-intellectual and impersonal religious caricature. Positively, it called Christians to recultivate and implement the biblical emphases of the priesthood of all believers, personal holiness, evangelism and missions, separation from the world, gentleness in controversy, and Bible study fellowships. From the latter eventually developed several Bible colleges. Its enormous positive influence may be traced to the present through the ministries of George Müller, Jonathan Edwards, D. L. Moody, and many others.[10]

Given the enormity of pietism's positive contributions, it is not suprising that its negative tendency to overemphasize the subjective and to partition religious feeling and zeal from the intellect went almost unnoticed. Thus an understandable reaction against pseudo-intellectualism subtly swung too far and resulted in the valuative imbalance and confusion between the devotional experience and genuine biblical intellectualism.

For education, the effects of pietism are serious. Academics, and especially language study, come to be equated with irrelevance to Christian growth and are consistently confused with that which classical pietism originally protested, "pseudo-academics." Arising from the confusion, the immediate reward of the heart is played off against the seemingly inconsequential long-term benefits of the head, in this instance learning to integrate language with faith.

Subtle axiological redirection has occurred, the subjective for the objective.

The objections to the study of Greek can be met with appropriate responses: although good Bible translations are helpful, they do not communicate the mind and personality of the writers as does the original text. "Word-books" provide inadequate data about the meaning of the words in context, and commentaries are often deficient in the amount of such information as well. The possibility of subjectivism on the part of the exegete can be best overcome through careful study of comparable contexts and constructions.

Although some who emphasize head knowledge lose sight of the significance of the heart and an individual's devotion to the Lord, it need not be so. If we do indeed grow in grace and in knowledge of the Lord Jesus Christ as a result of our interaction with the Word, then the more accurate an understanding of the Word we have, the more growth should take place. With this in mind we shall consider more fully a biblical rationale for the study of Greek.

Biblical and Philosophical Rationale

The rationale for the integration of language and faith is uniquely Christian. One does not study Greek simply for scientific or aesthetic reasons. Since syntax controls the freshness, correctness, and fullness of doctrinal studies and their profound application to experience, its correlation to the other important disciplines within the Christian curriculum is basic and vital. Indeed, since translations cannot reproduce the mind and personality of the author to the degree that a study of the original can, it is no waste of time to study Greek syntax. On the contrary, such a study "gives an aid to . . . the preacher [and teacher] which is unsurpassed for detail and power of insight.[11]

Indispensable Tool Through Which to See Christ

Indeed the contribution of Greek to the Christian faith makes it an indispensable tool through which to uncover the fuller color, range, variety, and force of the personality of Jesus, in whom the inexhaustible fullness of deity resides.[12] Without it, all the other disciplines within the Christian curriculum run the risk of blurring the image of the very Christ they are attempting to uncover and of discarding a theological and christological safeguard.

Putting it concisely, one loves syntax because it uniquely discloses the Christ whom he loves, and because it enables him to minister far more effectively to those for whom Christ died.

Christian View Of Man

The Bible declares that God originally created man in His own image or likeness. This was later marred; and for those in Christ, is presently being renewed (Col. 3:10; cf. Eph. 4:24). Based on the premise that what is presently being renewed in man must have characterized at least part of what was originally marred, Calvin defined essential humanity as the "inner good of the soul." By the latter term he included the reason, affections, and will.[13] This essential correspondence served as the prerequisite to man's unique relationship to God and clothed man with the dignity requisite to serve as God's earthly vicegerent (Gen. 1).

Three *general* implications of this definition of humanity are relevant to the implementation of our rationale that Greek is an indispensable tool through which to see more of the unblurred Christ.

First, since by *nature* those in the class are designed for "correspondence with God," progression towards solidifying this union (ethical, intellectual, emotional, volitional) with the Creator (without loss of individuality, Gal. 2:20) remains the goal. This is what is good in life and determines the direction in which the class ought to move. It also implies that the values of the class are objective and not subservient to the sometimes transient desires or pleasures of the student and/or his social milieu. The content of the course is based upon this goal, whose full attainment remains tempered by a recognition that the student is something of a hybrid, an unfinished product in terms of his renewing.

From this two things follow. (1) Primary motivation rests upon the fact that the renewing process has begun. One does not whip or pamper the student, but basically and continually (as Paul) appeals to this "given." This is affirmation. (2) Because the renewing is incomplete, one realistically faces limitations of character development in the student and himself. Because character fluctuations occur, it is the teacher's art to speak to this appropriately, but always within the context of the renewing reality. The lazy are to be repeatedly admonished, the discouraged are to be continually encouraged, while particular attention and help is to be perpetually devoted to the weak. Since this is an arduous task, it demands continual forbearance and patience. Indeed, welding the two realities together, while retaining the integrity of both, demands a gifted and self-sacrificing sensitivity to the Chief Teacher, the Holy Spirit.

Secondly, the Christian student has a social dimension which must be respected. He learns best in the company of others. Since the restoration of full humanity is progressive, the teacher must attempt to familiarize himself/herself as much as possible with the varying stages of development of each student. This emphasis on the relational, however, implies neither a democratic nor autocratic approach to community, but a theocratic one. The teacher supposedly is a gifted person (Eph. 4) who, for the good of the community, *directs* the class toward a goal. Yet, since he and the students are a family in Christ, the relationship turns relatively on their subservience to the greater direction by and submission to the Holy Spirit. This keeps the relationship flexible and truly reciprocal, but nevertheless does not destroy the integrity of the theocratic nature of the social emphasis.

Thirdly, since the class is by nature creative, it learns best inductively. This feeling of "discovery and contribution" should be fostered through corresponding educational methodology. However, it is the responsibility of the teacher to safeguard the integrity of what is induced by providing synthetic directives from which perspective is maintained (i.e., the relationship of the parts to the whole).

Philosophical Barriers

Unfortunately, because of the differing philosophical views of the nature of man, the educational state of affairs today is extremely confused.[14] To be sure, this implies that experts disagree upon means and goals in education. Indeed, the sheer range of the field, coupled with the rather negative publicity which the experts' disagreements have engendered, has caused many to give up their attempts to understand the total picture (synthesis) and have turned in despair to the provincialism of special studies.[15] But such metaphysical nihilism[16] simply drives the essential problem underground and through tacit neglect heightens the very dilemma which it seeks to avoid: what is human nature and for what is it designed?

Consequently, derivative answers to other questions with respect to values (axiology) and ethics receive no basis for consensus. Yet answers to whether values are objective, i.e., of intrinsic worth apart from personal gain *per se*, or subjective, i.e., dependent upon satisfying personal desire; whether they are constant or relative (and so possibly hierarchical or not) certainly shape what one feels is the "good" for his class and the manner by which the whole discipline ought to be pursued. The real problem, as Plato noted long ago, is that *apart from valid revelation, certainty is unobtainable.*[17] One either swings to the positivist extreme which commits the inductionist error, or to Collingwood's idealism, which turns "objectivity" into mere "coherence."[18]

In the midst of this confusion, the Christian view of man can make a contribution to secular education. Whether this occurs or not, it is imperative that the Christian concept should govern educational practice within the Christian classroom. Otherwise, subtle philosophical barriers vitiate the Christian contribution and thereby distort the goals, method, and content of education that is Christian.

Practical Application

It was necessary in the previous section to discuss something of the teacher's role with respect to the implications of the Christian view of human nature. In this section we wish to focus primarily on his task as model and motivator in the Greek class.

Teacher as Model

With respect to the integration of language with faith, the value of the teacher's function as model cannot be overestimated. While he must not artificially or selfishly perform, he must communicate naturally his genuine thrill of discovering more of his Savior through a unique tool. Yet at the same time, he must candidly identify the limitations of the language (e.g., not all difficult questions are solved by a knowledge of Greek). If he teaches Greek so that others can grasp the Savior and their Christian responsibility more fully, he must demonstrate his own gift at applying the insights, so that the class may see the pragmatism of the tool. This requires a certain homiletical and pastoral skill, which, unfortunately, has not always surfaced in some classrooms.

Most importantly, he must convince the students that he can help *them* to develop their ability to locate, communicate, and apply the rich insights which Greek affords. Otherwise, though he may cause the class to marvel at their teacher's ability, in the long run, since they cannot reproduce, the teacher-model simply discourages. This of course requires the professor of biblical languages to maintain patience with himself and the student (1 Thess. 5:14). Some students are fast starters, others develop more slowly. All must receive affirmation in unmistakable doses.

Textbook Selection

Part of the integration breakdown in the teaching of Greek is traceable to our textbooks. Usually the teacher selects a text because it reflects his major emphasis and so his goal.

It is alarming that an examination of the textbooks used over the last half century reveals that little overt effort has been expended to wed syntax to exegesis, and both to personal application.[19] Such a hiatus violates the cardinal Christian criterion for teaching Greek and indicates that the students during this interim have constantly stood in danger of missing the motivational point of the whole discipline: *syntax (not morphology per se) applied to exegesis provides the unique basis for a fuller and more vivid picture of Christ and an ensuing application to life.* Exegetical insight and consequent motivational power is understandably (but nevertheless, incorrectly), sacrificed to "completeness and breadth" (Turner)[20] and presentation of the "chief features of grammar" (Dana and Mantey).[21] Thus as Turner candidly admits, "interesting discussion" (motivational discovery of insights unique to the use of the language)[22] was forestalled.

To their credit, some teachers did attempt to bridge the gap between syntactical data and their application to exegesis. In 1941 William Chamberlain recognized the "unbridged gulf in the student's mind" and sought to bring the distilled work of the pioneer grammarians to bear on interpretation.[23] In 1944, Max Zerwick avoided the beguiling attraction to the "purely scientific or philological" purpose, and turned "to encourage future ministers of the Word to have recourse to the original Greek."[24] As a result of his pastoral thrust, Zerwick multiplied examples which reflected the importance of the study of the New Testament within the Koine as a whole, and apart from a few remarks given in his conclusion with respect to morphology, devoted his energies exclusively to the cruciality of syntax for interpretation.[25]

Yet sadly, syntactical textbooks of this stripe seem to be the exception rather than the rule. Thus the true motivational rationale for studying Greek continues to be obscured.

Overcoming The Language Barrier

At first sight, the beginning student views Greek with considerable apprehension. The letters are unfamiliar and strange, and the word order unusual. Also, with increasing frequency, students are entering language classes with insufficient knowledge of English syntax and grammar.

How does the teacher explode or at least decrease the size of the language barrier? The following are suggestions, some of which will be further developed in the succeeding section on overcoming methodological barriers.

1. Since some students have not learned English grammar properly, J.W. Wenham (following Nunn) summarizes English grammar in fifteen lucid pages before he tackles the Greek alphabet.[26] This procedure is effective because it recognizes that lack of a working knowledge of English grammar enervates class morale and prohibits learning.
2. Since the student's fears primarily relate to morphology, the teacher should take pains to stem the initial rising sense of pedantry by untangling the popular but confused overidentification of morphology with Greek. If one introduces a few examples of the crucial relevance of syntax to exegesis and life early enough, the student will be encouraged to focus on the marvelous objective which awaits his redoubled efforts.
3. Advanced Greek students can be encouraged to minister to the more inexperienced classes. Their encouragement and excitement is contagious and in effect sells the value of the program. It also builds a sense of Christian concern and combats the pietistic tendency to differentiate "academics" from "true ministry."
4. Instructors must continually remind the student that the competency at which he is aiming is ministerial. He will probably not be speaking Greek, nor will he have inexorable need to have his devotions in Greek, nor will he normally need to exegete great swaths of Scripture in Greek. We picture him at his desk—assorted helps at the ready—ransacking a limited portion of Scripture. This encourages those with less language aptitude and rarely stops those others whose eyes and hearts are opened to the pragmatic value of the language.

Overcoming Methodological Barriers

Method is largely "orderly procedure."[27] It should evidence purpose, order, and consistency or definiteness. The latter implies that
the participant follows a well-marked path which keeps him (in his
lucid moments) on the correct road and thus allows him time to
develop his abilities.

Since purpose depends upon one's philosophy and a resulting
psychology of man the method must be philosophically and psychologically groomed to achieve the Christian goal, i.e., a progressing
union with God and man, and should reflect the hybrid nature of the
renewed and renewing man, including his essential need to create
and discover. The latter implies a major role for inductive learning
which, within the theocratic setting of the classroom, is safeguarded
by the synthetic perspective provided by the teacher. Consequently,
within these parameters, we attempt to provide the student with
procedures by which eventually he may achieve the integration of
language and faith independently.

Syntax Observation. Since translations can reflect but not fully
reproduce syntactical insights, it is crucial that the student quickly
learn an orderly procedure by which the syntactical pointers are not
regularly overlooked. One which has proven its merit falls into five
basic categories or parts. With respect to the sentence, the student
examines consecutively (1) the presence or absence (asyndeton) of
particles (including conjunctions); (2) word order (the tendency is:
particle, verb, subject/object and modifiers, supplementary participle);[28] (3) tense; (4) mood; (5) and the presence or absence of the
article. As the procedure is limited to five steps, it covers the area
comprehensively enough to be of exegetical value, without being so
ponderous that it becomes self-defeating. We find also that once this
basis is mastered, the students begin to add additional steps of their
own.

Though it is impossible to illustrate adequately in this chapter,
perhaps the following description will provide something of the
exegetical value which such a procedure provides. The identification of particles supplies the contextual relationship between sen-
tences and paragraphs; or if absent implies that a new paragraph (cf.
Gal. 3:15), rhetorical or emotional involvement of some kind (cf.
Gal. 3:1–5) and/or closeness of thought (e.g., 1 Thess. 5:19f.) is
present. Word order reveals the author's emphasis and so aids the

exegete to precision. Tense describes and sometimes vivifies the kind of action the author wishes to emphasize (or not emphasize) and illumines and colors many a dreary sermon or lesson; while mood signals whether the writer relates the verbal action or state to reality (actual or possible from the writer's vantage). Finally the article provides rich insight into many areas of contrast, quality, unity, and the like. With such a procedure, the student begins to escape the translation syndrome, whereby he continues to think in English, begins to grasp from "feel" for the author's style and so his thought patterns, and reduces wasted time and effort with respect to reading Greek.

Diagramming the Sermon Outline. In this next step, we wish to strengthen the tendency to pragmatic application which begins to occur in the procedure outlined above. Students are given a simple method for diagramming a passage.[29] From the diagram they then draw lines to a skeleton English outline to indicate that they are using syntactical insights to enrich and sharpen their interpretations and applications. Philosophically, this fits quite well since it feeds the renewed man's desire to grasp and apply the truth, and also stems his unrenewed (natural) penchant for immediate and subjective reward. Psychologically, this fits quite well since it feeds the renewed man's desire to grasp and apply the truth, and also stems his unrenewed (natural) penchant for immediate and subjective reward. Psychologically, it combats the pietistic devaluation of the mind (and so, academics). It also encourages the student visually, in that he begins to see and understand the grammatical relationships which the diagram forces him to face and apply. With increasing practice something of the terror of the unknown trickles away.

Introducing Crucial Syntax. The above procedures foster the inductive method, whose integrity must be preserved by synthetic perspective. For the beginning exegesis class, therefore, the teacher should introduce/review crucial syntax categories as soon as possible. Otherwise, the above two procedures make little initial pragmatic difference to the student and his perception of the value of applied syntax tends to diminish. The broad categories which are *introduced*—and this is the key term—may be filled out as time goes on.

Since all this takes time, the teacher must hold to his aim to provide a *tool* by which the student will be motivated to study and apply the Scriptures for the rest of his life. The student primarily must learn to reproduce, else all is lost. Of course, this does not imply that little content is discussed, only that the teacher aims higher than the immediate.

The beginning exegesis class will usually spend the first three weeks introducing the categories and procedures described above.[30] Subsequently, each of our 75-minute class segments begins with a 25-minute section during which randomly selected individuals practice the orderly procedure of observing syntax as they translate. This stimulates the student's class preparation and, more relevantly, develops a *habit* of approach. It also enables the teacher to locate weaknesses and strengths, and to apply the fit word for the occasion. In the remaining 50 minutes, teacher and class syntactically exegete and apply portions of Scripture (e.g., Thessalonians, Galatians) during which the teacher demonstrates the procedures to the extent that time permits. When the external diagram/outlining projects are completed, class and teacher compare notes and insights within the class sturcture. This has proven to be a great joy; and also enables the teacher to assist the fledgling theoretician to develop his gift for the science and art of interpretative application.

Apart from class exegesis and the initial three-week introduction period, a number of segments are devoted to presentations that illustrate the importance of syntax using other portions of the New Testament which provide illuminating and interesting insights into the author's thought patterns. In this manner, we philosophically and psychologically appeal to the renewed man and attempt to attack any of the philosophically biased impediments which may have arisen.

Conclusion

Throughout this chapter we have attempted to show that the inestimable intrinsic value of the integration of faith and language suffers from extrinsic misunderstanding. This misunderstanding is a tragedy, since its overt objections confuse the importance of accidence with syntax and unfairly deliver the whole over to the unfounded charges of pedantry and/or relative inconsequence.

In large measure the responsibility for this belongs to those of us who teach the language. Somehow, in the midst of all our labors, our students miss the point. We teachers generally aim at scientific comprehensiveness but, through lack of time or space, miss the primary task of correlating syntax with living faith and practice. The latter failure, in turn, points to a defective or at least naive view of the implications of renewed (and renewing) human nature for education. In effect, Greek becomes a special study which, in many institutions, loses its place within the Christian curriculum.

The way back is to pedagogically honor the Christian philosophy of redeemed man, to conceptually dissociate the primary value of language from an overidentification with form (accidence), and to allow syntax to point us to Christ, the *plērōma* of deity. With the brush cleared away, it is not too much to hope that perhaps we may teach men to reproduce a fuller and thus more relevant portrait of our Lord.

Notes

1. M.L. Waugh, *The Preacher and His Greek Testament* (London: Epworth Press, n.d.), pp. ix–x.
2. Ibid.
3. In Marcus Ward, *Hidden Meanings in the New Testament* (Old Tappan, N.J.: Revell, 1969), p. 7.
4. The objection also assumes falsely that synthetic memorization is the sole method by which one grasps morphology. But see J. Lyle and Cullen I.K. Story, *Greek to me: An Easy Way to Learn New Testament Greek Through Memory Visualization* (San Francisco: Harper & Row, 1979).
5. Nigel Turner, *Grammatical Insights into the New Testament* (Edinburgh: T. and T. Clark, 1965), p. 1.
6. Cf. Ward, p. 4; Turner, p. 2; A.T. Robertson, *A Grammar of the Greek New Testament in the Light of Historical Research* (Nashville: Broadman, 1934/1976), p. x. For an illustration of the dangers of dynamic equivalence, and the value and limitations of translations, see the case study of Mark 1:1–15 and Galatians 3:1–14 provided by Lamar Williamson, Jr., "Translations and Interpretations: New Testament," *Interpretation*, 32 (Jan. 1978): 158–170. Also, Sakae Kubo and Walter Specht, *So Many Versions* (Grand Rapids: Zondervan, 1975), esp. p. 206.
7. See James Barr, *The Semantics of Biblical Language* (Oxford, 1961), p. 233, for enlightening examples and criticism of particular "word-book" conclusions and philosophy. Also, William Sanford LaSor, *Handbook of New Testament Greek* (Grand Rapids: Eerdmans, 1973), 1:viii, "The surest definition of any word will be gained by studying the word in the context in which it occurs." By their very nature, translations alter Greek thought patterns to English.
8. Turner, p. 1. Turner is familiar to many for his classic works on *Syntax* and *Style* in the 3rd and 4th volumes of J.H. Moulton's *Grammar of the New Testament Greek* (Edinburgh: T. and T. Clark, 1963).
9. Reprinted in English by Fortress Press, 1964. Cf. also James D. Mosteller, "Pietism," *Sacramentum Mundi*, ed. Karl Rahner et al. (New York: Herder and Herder, 1970), 5:24–26.
10. Harvie Conn, *Contemporary World Theology* (Philadelphia: Presbyterian and Reformed, 1973), pp. 100–105; Mosteller, col. 510; Lohff, 5:25.
11. Turner, *Insights*, pp. 1–2.
12. Col. 1:19. The position of "all" before "the fullness" (*pan to plērōma*) means "all without exception" and so "inexhaustible" is a deduction based on the NT

concept of God. Since some at Colossae evidently held Jesus to be less than fully God, the construction is precise and necessary. Cf. Jehovah Witness christological heresy.

13. *Institutes*, I, 15:4, 7. Cf. I, 15:8: "For the individual parts of his soul were formed to uprightness, the soundness of his mind stood firm, and his will was free to choose the good."

14. Traditional alternatives consist of idealism, realism, pragmatism, while the more contemporary modes have turned to existentialism and philosophical analysis. More recently the theories of progressivism and perennialism have come to the fore. See Gerald Lee Gutek, *Philosophical Alternatives in Education* (Columbus: Merrill, 1974).

15. Philip May, *Which Way to Educate?* (Chicago: Moody, 1975), pp. 3, 14. G.F. Kneller, *Introduction to the Philosophy of Education* (New York: John Wiley and Sons, 1964), pp. 2, 6–7.

16. Or relativism. The relativist's assumptions are (1) absolute values prohibit progress (moral, religious, rational, etc.) and (2) "progress" is inevitable. The difficulty is obvious—unless one denies (2). For then there is no measurement by which to gauge "progress."

17. *Phaedo* 85. Man's only hope is "if he cannot find some word of God which will more surely and safely carry him" through the limitations of human knowledge.

18. M. Howard Rienstra, "History, Objectivity and the Christian Scholar," *Fides et Historia*, 10 (Fall 1977): 8f.

19. We speak of overall design and of course not of random illustrative exceptions within the books which occur from time to time.

20. Turner, *Insights*, p. 2.

21. H.E. Dana and Julius R. Mantey, *A Manual Grammar of the Greek Testament* (New York: Macmillan, 1927), p. iii.

22. Turner, *Insights*, p. 2.

23. *An Exegetical Grammar of the Greek New Testament* (New York: Macmillan, 1960), p. vii.

24. *Biblical Greek*, trans. Joseph Smith, S.J., (Rome, 1963), Foreword.

25. Unfortunately, there are some serious pedagogical defects in his format and presentation: (1) There is no index of subjects and one sometimes searches in vain in the table of contents for clues, e.g., asyndeton. (2) Though Zerwick is aware of their importance (p. 36), there is no definite treatment of word and clause order. (3) Sometimes Zerwick assumes the student knows more than he does, e.g., what is the exegetical relevance of the particle *te*? (4) The nomenclature, e.g., case, is sometimes obscure; and (5) the section numbers are confusing.

26. *The Elements of New Testament Greek* (Cambridge, 1965/1976), pp. 1–15. H.P.V. Nunn, *A Syntax of New Testament Greek* (Cambridge, 1956), pp. 1–24, is more difficult, but more thorough than Wenham.

27. Howard Kuist, *These Words Upon Thy Heart* (Richmond: John Knox Press, 1947), pp. 59, 48.

28. Cf. F. Blass, A. Debrunner, and Robert W. Funk, *A Greek Grammar of the New Testament* (Chicago: University of Chicago Press, 1974), pp. 248ff.

29. We have outlined the procedure for the student working in English in *Handbook for Bible Study* (Grand Rapids: Baker, 1979), pp. 50–66. This book was coauthored by Grant Osborne. The procedure attempts to utilize the natural feel which students have for their own language so that it may be transferred to Greek.

Part Two

DIVISION OF
PROFESSIONAL EDUCATION

The Author

Clinton S. Foraker is the former director of the pastoral studies program at Philadelphia College of Bible and now serves as senior pastor at Perth Bible Church in Amsterdam, New York. He has served as guest lecturer at the California Graduate School of Theology from which he holds the Ph.D. degree, Winnipeg Theological Seminary, and the Word of Life Bible Institute. In addition to his Ph.D. Dr. Foraker has earned the B.S. from Philadelphia College of Bible and the M.Div. from Grace Theological Seminary. It was essential that we have a practicing pastor who could see the preparation of pastors within the academic realm and thereby connect the two phases of the discipline. It is obvious that Dr. Foraker meets those qualifications.

The Subject

Unpopular and maligned at the beginning of the last decade, the local church is now touted by many evangelical leaders as the place "where the action is" for the rest of the twentieth century. New efforts are being made to tie mission churches to mother congregations in developed Western nations. Internship programs at graduate and undergraduate levels are now mandatory in most accredited institutions. Seminaries are once again admitting hundreds of men each year who are convinced of their call to the pastoral ministry. Dr. Foraker speaks in this chapter to the undergraduate preparation of pastors in the Bible college setting.

4

PASTORAL STUDIES

Clinton S. Foraker

A pastor is a man of God, divinely called, prepared, and commissioned, in order to lead, feed, protect, and guide a local congregation; thus equipping them for the work of the ministry. From the divine perspective, the senior pastor of each local assembly has the most strategic position in his community. His influence in mobilizing and training the church is without peer. He should be the greatest catalyst for the establishment of godly living patterns in his community. There is no man in society who can do more to aid the citizenry in establishing high standards of public morality than the evangelical pastor. He is the symbolic conscience of the community.

Introduction

In essence, the curriculum of pastoral studies may be termed the discipline of pastoral theology. Dr. Thomas Murphy states: "That department of study whose object is to assist the Christian minister in applying the truths of the Gospel to the hearts and lives of men is called Pastoral Theology."[1] Dr. Jay Adams expands upon that definition by relating that:

Practical ministry can never be anything less than the ministry of the Word. That Word, understood exegetically and systematically, must permeate and motivate all practical work. The directions that one's practical activities take, the norms by which he operates and the motivation behind what he does must emerge from a biblical theological study of the Scriptures. The pursuit of Practical Theology, therefore must be seen as the study and application of the biblical means of expressing one's theology.[2]

Briefly, let us look at the term *pastoral theology*. It is pastoral because it pertains to the minister. The term *pastor* finds its meaning as we consider the Divine Shepherd or Pastor of the sheep. It is theological because the foundation and stimulus of our work, including our motives and the guiding of our goals, must be based on the sound exegesis of Scripture. Pastoral theology is, therefore, the putting into action of our systematic theology, in those ways which are most effective to reach lost people and build the body of Christ, the church, in a given culture and time.

The customary procedure for preparing a would-be pastor in our day is a college and seminary program that will enable him to perform the functions of a shepherd. Although some recommend a liberal arts college training in either a secular or Christian atmosphere, it is my sincere conviction that a Bible college is preferable. In every other professional field there is a specially arranged course of study that a student follows to prepare him for graduate training. For example: doctors and lawyers take very specialized undergraduate courses, in order to prepare for medical school or law school. A man preparing for the pastorate should pursue areas of study which will provide him with a basic, overall, comprehensive knowledge of the Bible; the ability to use the original languages; a sound theological system; the perspective of church history; the methodology of homiletics; and other necessary tools needed either for the ministry itself or for further training.

Historically, the genius of the Bible college program has been on-the-job training. In each semester of a student's collegiate career he must be involved in some type of Christian service. As a result, when he graduates, he knows how to conduct such pastoral duties as weddings, funerals, baptisms, board meetings, and leadership training programs. Many men have found that a four-year Bible college program has given them the know-how to perform successfully in the pastorate.

Biblical Foundation

Biblical sources for pastoral theology, although primarily rooted in the New Testament, span the whole Bible. The future pastor can learn many valuable lessons from the Lord as he observes and scrutinizes the lives of the Old Testament patriarchs, prophets, and other great personages, and how God dealt with them to accomplish His work in the world. The forgotten minor prophets are especially relevant to our day, as these men of God thundered out against the social evils and sins of the people in an attempt to call Israel and Judah back to God, and thus avert divine judgment. There is a desperate need in our Bible colleges and seminaries for an in-depth study of the prophetic office, demonstrating its parallels to the Christian preacher. Yet, because we are training "able ministers of the new covenant," the inspired text from Matthew to the Revelation is of particular concern.

Certainly every prospective pastor must trace the steps of the Lord Jesus Christ through the Gospels and become His disciple. Then, a careful exposition of Acts will unveil the principles for church growth that led the early believers to eventually "conquer" the Roman Empire. Furthermore, the pastoral office is so vital to the church era, that the apostle Paul wrote three epistles specifically with the Christian minister in mind—the Pastoral Epistles of 1 & 2 Timothy and Titus. Other New Testament writings provide the doctrinal foundations upon which all ministry must be based. Since the church is God's chosen instrument to carry out His program for this age, the key passages in the New Testament relative to the pastoral ministry are extensive, as would be expected. Therefore, we shall be very selective, choosing only those texts which speak directly of the pastor and his ministry.

Key Words

At the outset, it is important for us to clarify several terms. There are three major words employed in Scripture which refer to the minister. Each of these words properly presented adds to our understanding of the man and his position.

Elder. The Greek *presbuteros* (Titus 1:5) was a Hebrew term, probably coming "from the synagogue in which the chief officials bore this title."[3] The word itself connoted the blameless character of the man as well as the dignity of his position.

Bishop. The Greek *episkopos* (1 Tim. 3:1) comes originally from the Greek culture and identifies one who oversees, superintends, or administers. Ancient usage depicted an official commissioned and given authority to oversee and administer a Greek colony. The emphasis of *episkopos* is upon the function of the office.

Pastor-Teacher. The Greek words *de poimenas kai didaskalous* are often taken together because they "are named as one grammatical unit (by use of just one article in the Greek text)."[4] *Poimen* literally means a shepherd or herdsman, one who is to care for the flock. From its definition we get the purpose and function of the shepherd, which is to help, to feed, and protect the sheep. *Didaskalos* is used to describe the one holding the pastoral office as an individual who teaches or communicates the message of God from the Holy Scriptures, to his people. This term seems to be equivalent to the Hebrew "rabbi." *Didaskalos* was used in the Gospels of the Lord Jesus concerning His relationship to the disciples.

To summarize, we deduce that the minister, based on the previous descriptive words, has these characteristics:

1. He is dignified in his demeanor, blameless and mature in his character, and a master in the historic Christian faith.
2. He is given authority and is expected to use it in administering a local church.
3. He must guard the flock, protecting the sheep from spiritual and moral harm.
4. He feeds his flock the pure Word of God, being the instructor of the sheep in spiritual matters.

The terms *elder* and *bishop* are used inter-changeably as an examination of Acts 20:17 & 28 and Titus 1:5 & 7 reveals. Furthermore, since teaching is required of both the elder (1 Peter 5:1–2) and the bishop (1 Tim 3:2), we conclude that the "pastor-teacher" would be an acceptable, practical, synonym for either elder or bishop. To be sure, the New Testament teaches that all three of these terms refer to "ministry" and there are those who see a multiplicity of leadership roles in any given local congregation.

Key Passages

The key passages referring directly to the pastor's qualifications and responsibilities are these:

1. Matthew 28:17–20—Christ's commission to the church.
2. Acts 1–2—The founding of the church, its dynamic, and its priorities in ministry.

3. Acts 20:17–35—The pattern of Paul's ministry.
4. Ephesians 4:11–12—The purpose of the pastoral office.
5. 1 Timothy 3:1–7 and Titus 1:5–9—The qualifications for the pastoral office.
6. 2 Timothy 2—Instructions and warnings to the pastor in the midst of the conflict.
7. 2 Timothy 4:1–8—The aged apostle's last word to young pastors.

A detailed exposition of each of these texts would be a dissertation in itself; therefore, the following, of necessity, are merely brief comments in regard to pastoral training.

Matthew 28:17–20. Christ said to His church, "As you go," (not a command but an aorist participle, which in the context, carries the full weight of a divine expectancy) "preach the gospel to every creature." Then, our Lord commanded that we should teach and disciple those who would respond (Mark 15:16). It is tragic that so often the Great Commission is applied only to foreign missions. Here are the church's marching orders for this dispensation, and many pastors have no well-understood strategy or program to carry it out in their own communities. I believe the two greatest needs of the typical evangelical congregation are a proper understanding of the nature and function of the church and a well-defined strategy of accomplishing its goal of evangelizing the lost and edifying the body.

Acts 1–2. In Acts 1:8, the resurrected Christ stated the overall general game plan, and also related the dynamic for fulfilling the goals.

> But ye shall receive power after that the Holy Ghost is come upon you: and ye shall be witnesses unto me both in Jerusalem, and in all Judea, and in Samaria, and unto the uttermost part of the earth (Acts 1:8).

The church was instructed to begin carrying out the Great Commission immediately where they were, in Jerusalem, and then in an ever broadening circle into the entire world. The power of the early church came from the filling ministry of the Holy Spirit. Dr. Charles C. Ryrie makes this astute observation: "In every instance of the filling of the Spirit in the book of Acts, the filling of the Spirit, controlling the disciples in their service for their Lord, resulted in the salvation of souls."[5] Is it any wonder that the church in Jerusalem grew from 120 to tens of thousands in such a brief period of time?

The other marks of the apostolic church were fervency in prayer (Acts 1:14); powerful preaching (Acts 2:37); and the amazing ability to incorporate new converts into the life of the church (Acts 2:41–47) and take them on to spiritual maturity.

Acts 20:17–35. The characteristics of the apostle's ministry as exemplified in Acts 20 were threefold:

1. Humility in serving the Lord, v. 19.
2. Evangelistic burden for all outside Christ, vv. 21, 26.
3. Edification of every believer, vv. 20, 27, 31.

It is unfortunate that young men entering the pastorate may fail because of inadequate and unbalanced training. Either they emphasize evangelism and ignore teaching, or they believe teaching to be their sole responsibility and are content to shepherd the same fifty people forever, with no burden to evangelize their "Jerusalems." Would to God that every Bible-college-trained pastor could say with Paul at the conclusion of each pastorate: "Wherefore I testify unto you this day that I am pure of the blood of all men" (Acts 20:26).

Ephesians 4:11–12. This crucial text is in the midst of a context which explains how the resurrected Christ gave gifts to His church: "And he gave some, apostles; and some, prophets; and some, evangelists; and some, pastors and teachers" (Eph. 4:11). The word "perfecting" comes from the Greek *katartismos* meaning to fit or prepare fully, to equip. From *katartismos* we get our English words "artist" and "craftsman," indicating that the purpose of Christ's gifts to the church (in the form of apostles, prophets, evangelists, and pastor-teachers) is to train and equip the saints to do the work of the ministry. This equipping begins with an expository preaching ministry, but must also include the pastor's use of on-the-job techniques to train his people in methods of Sunday school teaching, personal soul winning, family devotions, etc. Consider the inadequate alternatives.

First, there is the pastor who thinks he gets paid to do all the work of ministry for his church. Secondly, there is the minister who exegetes the Word and believes his job is completed. He never applies the Word to his hearers' lives and never trains his people in evangelism. Both extremes are deadly: the former kills the minister and the latter kills the church.

1 Timothy 3:1-7 & Titus 1:5-9. In these passages, every young man aspiring to the pastoral office must be confronted with the twenty-two different Greek words which present the biblical qualifications for the pastoral office. Such an in-depth study should serve to confirm (or cancel) one's supposed call to the ministry. The qualifications divide naturally into the following four categories:

1. Personal character and conduct.
2. Family life.
3. Interpersonal relationships (with both saved and unsaved).
4. Spiritual and doctrinal matter.

The staggering list of qualifications should serve to impress upon the minds of these future ministers the sacredness of the pastoral office and the greatness of the ministry.

2 Timothy 2. The minister's obstacles and pitfalls are many—discouragement, the temptation to quit, infidelity, laziness, lack of self-discipline—all are things any pastor might face. Therefore, in these verses Paul counsels Timothy to

> endure hardness, as a good soldier of Jesus Christ. No man that warreth entangleth himself with the affairs of this life; that he may please him who hath chosen him to be a soldier. And if a man also strive for masteries, yet is he not crowned, except he strive lawfully. . . . Consider what I say; and the Lord give thee understanding in all things (2 Tim. 2:3-5, 7).

It is imperative that all pastoral students get a realistic picture of some of the negative aspects they may face in the ministry.

2 Timothy 4:1-8. Paul's parting word to all pastors is twofold: (1) preach the Word, (2) do the work of an evangelist. However, these are two of the weakest areas in many pastoral studies curricula.

First, Timothy is told to preach the Word (v. 2). Here the Greek word *kērusso* is employed, for "preach" means to herald and proclaim. The message he is to proclaim is the Word, the Bible, referring to all of Divine Writ from Genesis to Revelation. Instruction is even given as to the manner in which the proclamation is to be made, for v. 2 says the delivery must be diligent, involving reproof, rebuke, and exhortation.

The apostle's second exhortation is to "do the work of an evangelist, make full proof of thy ministry" (v. 5). We have often failed to prepare future pastors with sufficient expertise in evangelism. The average Bible college curriculum has a mere one to three hours in personal evangelism. No wonder the growing church is such a rarity. Every pastor needs at least one comprehensive course in local church evangelism in which a professor who has worked faithfully in a local congregation can share his know-how concerning every conceivable way to legitimately reach the lost with the Good News of Christ. This will include evangelism in the Sunday school, pulpit, home Bible studies, camping, visitation, forms and letters, crusades, busing, media, and literature. Along with church growth, the growing shepherd must learn to evaluate the church's evangelistic effectiveness. With these tools, any young Timothy can confidently enter a church and lead its believers to establish a strategy that will result in the evangelizing of their community and the edifying of that local body of believers.

The pastoral ministry is an essential part of God's program for this age because Christ has ordered the evangelization and discipleship of the world through His church, of which the pastor is the overseer. The greatness of the ministry requires a man convinced of his call, filled with the Holy Spirit, and assured theologically that Christ is building His church "and the gates of hell will not prevail against it" (Matt. 16:18).

Practical Application

Pastoral Studies Curriculum

A pastoral theology which leads to a proper curriculum is established on the premise that a pastor is essentially a shepherd who leads, guides, protects, and feeds his sheep. Therefore, by parallel, our curriculum should reflect courses which instruct a pastor to fulfill his biblical role in equipping the saints to achieve the goals of the Great Commission, to evangelize and disciple all nations.

Homiletics. Since above all else a pastor is the feeder of the sheep, our curriculum should include several courses in sermon preparation and delivery. Ample time should be given for laboratory experience of preaching numerous kinds of expository messages, ranging from the normal verse by verse treatment to biographical, doctrinal, and topical expositions.

Poimenics or Shepherding. Several courses must be dedicated to training the prospective pastor in the following areas:

Pastoral Leadership
- Qualifications
- Administrative responsibilities and authority
  - Management
  - Pastoral community service
  - Church polity

Pastoral Functions
- Weddings
- Funerals
- Visitation
- Biblical stewardship

Pastoral Counseling

Graduates should be comfortable in assuming any and all pastoral functions.

Pastoral Evangelism. Based on a general course in personal evangelism, this advanced class should be comprehensive instruction covering how to lead a church in fulfilling its biblical obligation to evangelize its community.

Pastor and Ministries. Each pastor-to-be should receive a survey of each of the other local church ministries of missions, music, and Christian education. This will enable the minister to provide intelligent leadership in these vital areas of the church.

Such a curriculum would meet the minimal needs of aspiring pastors, in preparing them to fulfill their biblical roles in the local church context.

Professionally Prepared Personnel

In preceding generations, throughout several free church traditions, a prospective pastor received his vocational training by becoming an apprentice to an experienced pastor. Quite obviously, this method has the weakness or strength of being limited to one man, and no individual can excel in all areas. However, integration was natural; it was a part of daily life, since everything was learned on the job, and thus immediately incorporated into ministry.

Eventually, Bible colleges came into being. At first, these colleges brought together in one faculty, men who had excelled in a given academic area or ministry, so as to expose theological students to a resident expert in each division of professional studies. In the beginning, most professors came right from the ranks of vocational Christian workers, most often the pastorate. This precipitated and enhanced practical application, based on the proven experience level of the resident faculty.

With the pressures of accreditation and academic development, an increasing number of faculty, even in the professional disciplines, have little or no ministerial background. Obviously, a purely bookish approach to the study of parish ministry creates great disadvantage in the application and integration of truth to ministry. It is often forgotten that the great theologians such as Paul, Augustine, Luther, Calvin, and Wesley were not men who taught in an academic vacuum. They were all vitally involved in preaching, evangelism, and other pastoral functions. The situation has become acute in recent days, creating an unbiblical dichotomy between the theological and the practical. Bible colleges committed to serious pastoral training must take immediate steps to remedy the unfortunate deficiency.

Although it is somewhat idealistic to hope that every professor in a Bible college will have had some "good" experience as a pastor, Christian education director, missionary, etc., it certainly is not too much to ask that faculty in the professional disciplines, such as pastoral studies, be qualified not only academically but also practically. Granted, it is difficult to secure the services of the successful pastor of a growing church, but it is not impossible. Often such ministers are outstanding communicators with a deep burden to preach. A wise Bible college administration will arrange to schedule the pastoral studies department chairman in special conferences and meetings in order to allow for the use of his spiritual gifts, and to enable him to maintain personal freshness and continuing contact with the pastorate. Also, the department chairman should be intimately involved in the planning of chapels and the overall spiritual tone of the campus. This is not a job description, only several suggestions to get and keep a strong pastoral figure at the college.

However, when we consider the necessity of building a department, an even more creative approach must be taken. One approach is to develop a core of faculty whom I would designate as pastor-professors. These would be active clergymen who have excelled in some aspect of ministry, and whose theology and philosophy of ministry are in harmony both with the college and its constituency.

It would take some innovation within the curriculum to incorporate such team teaching, but it could be done.

This procedure could be employed to supplement the expertise of the department chairman in areas where he believes there are men more qualified to share. Therefore, counseling, administration, missions, Christian education, evangelism, etc. are all subjects where experts could add greatly to the educational process of training pastors. Established men could be brought to the campus for a week, or could teach a whole course over an entire semester, depending upon the visiting pastor-professor's schedule and proximity to the college. Such a program is already being used effectively at a well-established university dental school in the East, where a heavy percentage of the faculty teach part-time, while maintaining successful and growing dental practices of their own. The visiting professor's approach would also serve to promote better understanding and close relationship between Bible colleges and the churches they serve.

Life-Related Teaching Methodology

Those teaching in pastoral studies must not only be theologians in their own right, but must also have the ability to continually relate eternal truth to contemporary situations in church ministry.

Perhaps it is important to state that experience alone is not sufficient to make a good practical theology teacher. Twenty years of mediocre experience is not a positive legacy to pass along to succeeding generations. Instead, we need to search out those who have done well in leading their churches in spiritual and numerical growth, who can share genuine case studies, both in teaching and testing. The case-study approach is widely employed in law schools in order to teach young barristers how to think independently, so as to apply and integrate the law to specific situations. The most proficient and sought after lawyers are not just those who have the highest grade point average, but rather those who have developed the genius of relating what they have learned to life, and then communicating it.

In pastoral studies, the professor will have to do extensive reading in the bibliographic field and in professional journals in order to supplement his own background, so as to effectively communicate how key pastors, presently and in former years, conquered formidable odds in accomplishing their biblical goals. The key in the case-study approach is to offer as broad and diversified a spectrum as possible, within the limits of our theology. Case studies can also be used in testing by creating problem situations that the student must solve, utilizing the integrative learnings acquired in and out of the classroom.

Pastoral Internships

The medical profession has found that an intensive one or two year internship is absolutely essential in preparing physicians of the body. During their grueling internship, young doctors actually perform the tasks of the physician, but under the scrutinizing eye of an established doctor. They also observe their mentors to see how the job is to be done properly. The value of medical internships is quite apparent and the ministerial parallel is evident: if a doctor of the body needs such an internship before entering medicine on his own, how much more does the doctor of the soul need a practical internship before launching into his first church.

The idea of internship is not a new concept, but finds its roots biblically in the schools of the prophets in the Old Testament, and the training of the Twelve by our Lord in the New Testament. As previously mentioned, in bygone eras extended internship was the only way to train pastors. However, somehow we have drifted away from such programs, both on college and seminary levels. The need to redevelop the concept of internship is made obvious by the tremendous popularity of "how-to-do-it" seminars dealing with practical aspects of the ministry. Without question, the seminars are filling a gap for pastors concerning areas for which their previous education has failed to equip them.

The two keys of a good internship program are *coordination* and *personnel*. Careful coordination of the ingredients of the program is essential, along with sufficient time allowed for the internship itself, so as to accomplish and fulfill one's goals. The internship could be done over a summer, or during the regular school year. If possible, the young men should live near the churches where they are interning, in order to get the feel of that particular church's ministry. The student must be given the privilege of watching the senior pastor in actual ministry situations, such as preaching, board meetings, counseling, weddings, funerals, administration, visitation, hospital calls, celebrating the ordinances, etc. Then the intern should be given opportunity to participate as much as possible in all these varied ministries.

Next, personnel both at the college and on the field must be chosen very selectively for their spiritual tenor and professional ability. This program should fall under the supervision of the pastoral studies department chairman. A man of broad pastoral experience, who has performed with excellence, should be secured to head up the internship ministry under the department chairman. This position will necessitate a good bit of correspondence and travel, since communication with the field pastor and personal observation will be important. The cooperating pastor must be a very special kind of man, who is being greatly used by God, and who has the desire and gifts to properly disciple a young Timothy.

The college should have an internship manual which specifically indicates what the school expects of the cooperating pastor and church, and how the school and intern will serve the church in return. I strongly suggest a contractual arrangement, which contains ample provision for regular and detailed reports to be submitted by both the intern and the field pastor. As in student teaching, a stipend should be given the cooperating pastor. Unless the guidelines are clearly drawn up ahead of time and agreed upon, with strict accountability expected from all the parties, the program will fail.

Projects and Reports

The integration of theology into ministry can be enhanced by assigning term projects and reports that necessitate independent and creative thinking regarding integration. Although such a process would come primarily from the pastoral studies department, it certainly should not stop there. In fact, unless integration to ministry is encouraged in theological and expositional courses, students will fail to get a Pauline approach to doctrine and practice. To illustrate: a report assigned in soteriology could require the students to research a paper on "The Theological Foundation for Evangelism." The Bible and theology departments, in consultation with the pastoral studies department, could also assign work that would grapple with contemporary issues of abortion, euthanasia, homosexuality, capital punishment, etc., to stimulate the student's mind to think critically and biblically as he plans for a need-meeting ministry.

Naturally, the pastoral studies department will give work requiring integrative ministry. For example, after a unit on principles of church growth, future pastors can be given a term project, using the principles learned, to evaluate the evangelistic effectiveness of their churches. Remember that the results of such a project can be frightening. In our research carried out over a three-year period with one hundred churches, we discovered 75 percent were either stagnant or declining, with 20 percent showing some limited growth, and only 5 percent actually experiencing an annual growth rate of better than 10 percent. We also found that very few of these churches had any strategy whatsoever toward fulfilling the Great Commission in their Jerusalems.

Special Speakers and Conferences

A ministry which blends biblical theology with contemporary life can be learned from positive models. Guest speakers and conferences can aid the process of integration as they make a significant impact on students' lives. It is absolutely imperative in pastoral studies to continually be exposing our men to inspiring and powerful models who represent a variety of ministerial philosophies. This variety is demonstrative of how God uses different types of men to do His work, and should also serve to encourage each future pastor to be himself. Contact with these men coming right from the field makes integration live in reality.

Faculty Discipleship

As professors take students along to minister in churches and conferences, the added dimension serves to teach, stimulate, and excite them about the ministry. Actually seeing their teacher minister brings it all together. Inviting students into our homes is another way for them to observe firsthand the harmony of mature biblical truth within the family context. Many students may come from broken and/or unsaved homes, without having had opportunity to observe a biblical model.

Faculty testimonies in public services such as chapel are helpful to demonstrate how teachers are winning souls and discipling as well as edifying the believers. Students become easily disillusioned when they are required to share their faith regularly, but see little or no evidence that the faculty and administration are setting the pace.

Conclusion

It is interesting to me that a heavy percentage of the pastors in large and expanding works have had only Bible college training. In most cases the colleges they attended placed much emphasis on church growth, with the philosophy that Bible college was, for most students, terminal education. The fact remains that far too many of our evangelical churches, pastored by "well-trained" seminary men, are simply not growing. It is not the *level of education* but the *quality of reality* in ministry that counts.

Historically, the emphasis of the Bible college movement has been biblical education, coupled with professional expertise, to equip students for careers serving Christ. If the local church is central to God's program for this age, then the office of pastor is absolutely crucial to the Father's strategy. Therefore, the teaching of pastoral theology is foundational to every other major. Without churches and pastors, the other professional fields could not properly function.

Nevertheless pastoral studies faculty members exert less influence than they should on the college as a whole. The logic seems to be that pastoral studies majors will automatically proceed to seminary or graduate school; therefore we need to do less for them in undergraduate theological education. The response to this is as obvious as the complaint. First of all, students who do go on to graduate study and seminary need the very best possible foundation. Secondly, there will always be some students who do not go on to seminary and whose Bible college preparation is terminal for the ministry. It is essential that the Bible college provide for these people a complete program of training which, while recognizing the limitation of four years, still offers a well-rounded ministerial background in Bible, theology, the languages, homiletics, church history, apologetics, Christian education, counseling and church administration. It is a tall order but hardly one from which we can turn away.

Notes

1. Thomas Murphy, *Pastoral Theology* (Philadelphia: Presbyterian Board of Publication, 1877), p. 13.
2. Jay Adams, *Shepherding God's Flock*, vol. 1 (Nutley, N. J.: Presbyterian and Reformed, 1974), p. 2.
3. Joseph Henry Thayer, *Thayer's Greek-English Lexicon of the New Testament* (Grand Rapids: Zondervan, 1965), p. 535.
4. Homer Kent, Jr., *Ephesians* (Chicago: Moody, 1971), p. 72.
5. Charles C. Ryrie, *Balancing the Christian Life* (Chicago: Moody, 1973), p. 121.

The Author

The founding director of the Canadian Church Growth Centre and professor of Missiology at Canadian Bible College, Canadian Theological College, and Ontario Theological Seminary, Dennis Oliver is currently serving at Morningside-High Park Presbyterian Church, Toronto. He holds the B.A. from the University of Victoria; the B.D. from Knox College, University of Toronto; and the D.Miss. from Fuller Theological Seminary.

The Subject

Few fields of study are more in harmony with the historic commitment of Bible colleges than the one which Dr. Oliver addresses. Concern for the salvation of others and involvement in the sharing of the Good News is a part of each school's Christian service thrust as well as an essential component of the academic program. The chapter therefore speaks to an issue which should be foremost in the minds of academic deans and curriculum committee members as well as the faculty who actually teach in the field of evangelism.

5

EVANGELISM

Dennis Oliver

Few things are more essential to wholesome Chrisitan living and responsible church membership than evangelism. At the heart of God's purpose for the world, and at the core of His calling for the church, is the presenting of His Good News. Directly or indirectly, the whole of the Bible relates to the Lord's saving purposes. Throughout the Old and New Testaments we find material explicitly related to our subject.

Historically, the Bible college movement has placed evangelism in the core of its curriculum. This course has served the church well, by orienting and activating scores of thousands in their mission to their near neighbors, as well as to the farther mission fields. In this era of blossoming evangelistic concern and flourishing evangelical scholarship, the instructor has access to dozens of solid studies concerning the theology and practice of evangelism, biographies of evangelists, and case studies of evangelizing congregations. Never in the history of the church has this subject been so fully developed as an academic discipline. And never has the need for effective evangelism been so great, with over three billion persons separated from any form of the Christian faith and over half even on the North American continent clearly needing a first, or a fresh, commitment to Jesus Christ.

We should resist oversimplifying our concept of evangelism. It is as all-encompassing and as deep as the love of God. It relates both to

His mercy and His judgment. It involves what we say about our Lord, but (even more) the living out of our faith and our Christian character. Yet the word is simple enough. *Euaggelizesthai* ("to evangelize") means to announce good news. The image of a herald returning home with news of a battle won comes to mind. The richness of our subject comes from its content (God, in Christ, reconciling the world to Himself) and from its consequence (life and death, in eternal perspective). The constraint of the gospel adds to its depth: it demands repentance and in-depth discipleship from all who hear it or speak it. As they are evangelized, men and women are "cut to the heart" (Acts 2:37, NIV). The evangelist is also moved by the message, crying out, "Woe to me if I do not preach the gospel" (1 Cor. 9:16, NIV). Ours is not a course to take or teach lightly. Yet it need not have an air of heaviness, since evangelistic fruit brings with it the deepest joys known to men or angels (Luke 10:17; 15:10; Acts 8:8; 13:48,52).

Introduction

Recognizing the depth and the complexity of our subject, we can still provide a basic definition, understandable by every Christian. The following has proved instructive to Christians around the world for over half a century. It was formulated by the Anglican Archbishops' Committee on Evangelism, under the direction of William Temple:

> To evangelize is so to present Christ Jesus in the power of the Holy Spirit, that men shall come to put their trust in God through Him, to accept Him as their Savior, and serve Him as their King in the fellowship of the Church.[1]

With this Christ-centered, Spirit-centered, and church-centered definition, we and our students can begin plumbing the depth of our subject.

Even if the ideal were realized, and evangelistic concerns were evident in every Bible college course, a special course in evangelism would still be merited. Besides summarizing and integrating the relevant data from biblical studies, theology, literature and the social sciences, we must provide consideration of and training in evangelistic practices. The unmet needs of those outside the church, joined with the too-prevalent introversion and self-concern of Christians more than justify our course. Moreover, the ever-changing nature of congregations and their communities requires an ongoing, disciplined evaluation of the subject.

The focus of evangelism is, at best, the local church. But it is almost impossible to sufficiently relate our course to the ongoing life, work, and discipline of Christian congregations. In this era of congregational pluralism and multifaceted renewal, the instructor will do well to assess carefully the Christian motives and understandings of his or her students. What have they absorbed (often unconsciously) concerning the Christian faith, church fellowship, spirituality, and the ministry? In their Christian pilgrimage how far have they traveled, and how well? An amazing variety of students may exist in a single class: keen converts from unchurched backgrounds, mature children of the church, and nominal Christians who themselves need a conscious commitment to Christ. In this course we may well be privileged to evangelize some of our students. Since we can all be deepened and renewed in our appropriation of Christ's salvation, expect that many in the class (including the instructor) will be spiritually enriched by this study.

Just as students and their churches represent many realities, the communities from which they come and in which they will be living contain a rich plurality of challenge and opportunity. Regions have their particular profiles and predispositions (both religious and secular). The great cities of North America contain an amazing variety of ethnic and social groupings, with dazzling differences in mentality. Effective evangelism requires a sensitive understanding of the world, as well as of the church and her Lord.

Evangelism is best considered a multifaceted, complex *process*, rather than an isolated, single event. Even in its simplest and most essential form, one-to-one witness, the process includes *contact* (between the believer and the unbeliever), *bridging* into faith, and *assimilation* into the church. Students probably tend to underestimate the value and importance of preevangelism and follow-up ministries. In contrast, the wholesomeness and effectiveness of evangelism within the context of established contact must be stressed, together with the importance of nurturing an initial acceptance of Jesus Christ into fruitful Christian service.

Biblical Foundation

Realizing that our subject is so thoroughly biblical that it is informed by almost every book in both Testaments, from Genesis to

Revelation, we dare not attempt an exhaustive identification of relevant passages. Some books deserve special mention. The gospel of John was written, "that you may believe . . ." (20:31) and is an excellent source of instruction regarding the basic truths of saving faith (for the evangelist as well as new or potential converts). John 4 contains a paradigm of Jesus' evangelism. Luke-Acts contains an account of basic Christianity including many illustrations of the first evangelists, Jesus and His apostles. Romans provides essential passages regarding justification. Jonah is concerned with missionary motivation.

Those seeking a scriptural definition of our evangelistic message have several passages to research. The title of Mark's gospel (1:1) reminds us that the Good News is "about Jesus Christ," an essential fact confirmed by Old Testament prophecy and the entire New Testament. An evangelism class may wish to compare and contrast the church's earliest evangelistic speeches: Acts 2:14-39; 3:12-26; 13:16-41; 17:22-31, etc. Although some were to Jews and others to Gentiles, and although some related to specific circumstances, common elements in the evangelism of Peter and Paul form the core of the original Christian proclamation. First Corinthians 15:1-6 and Romans 1:1-6 both contain summaries of "the gospel."

The Motive

The motive for our evangelism, found in Scripture, involves both inward and outward dynamics: the *compassion* for the lost which is a natural part of our regenerate nature, and our response to the *commission*, by which we are made responsible to share our spiritual riches with others. In His resurrection appearances Christ repeatedly commanded His followers to "make disciples of all nations" (Matt. 28:19), to "be witnesses" to our neighbors, near and far (Acts 1:8), and to "preach the gospel to the whole creation" (Mark 16:15).[2] The church (every congregation and every member) is under orders to share the faith, not hoard it; the latter is gross disobedience. Jesus would have us identify with His mission to the world (cf. John 20:21), not only as His dutiful followers but also as those who share His life and His love for the lost.

The Methods

The New Testament illustrates a rich variety of evangelistic methods and approaches. Since evangelism and witness involve Christian living in the fullest sense, we do well to learn from the

example of Jesus and that of the early church. Two descriptive
statements about our Lord's public ministry are found in Matthew
9:35–38 and Luke 4:14–44. Acts 2:42–47 provides us with the pattern
of church life in Jerusalem, immediately following Pentecost
(Luke's paradigm for a healthy congregation). Acts 1:8 makes explicit what is implicitly true of Jesus' evangelizing: our efforts to
share the faith are effective when they reflect the life of the Spirit.
Evangelism has a prerequisite pneumatological dimension, which is
more essential to effectiveness than methodology (programs and
techniques). This explains why the resurrection commissions to "go"
are complemented by a caution to "wait" for the promised Spirit
(Luke 24:49), and why the disciples were enjoined to "receive the
Holy Spirit" when they were sent out into the world (John 20:21–22).

From the scriptural data we are impressed that there was no single
pattern or method by which the good news was shared. Word and
deed (life and lip) were conjoined in the Christian witness. Verbal
sharing was essential (the New Testament presents no models of
wordless witness). But words were joined to lives that demonstrated
the love and power of God. Peter's first evangelistic act was scripturally oriented *preaching* (Acts 2); his second was *healing* (Acts
3:6). But note that the healing was done "in Jesus' name," and was
followed by an explanatory address (verses 12–16). Words about
God's love were linked to demonstrations of His loving concern for
the whole man, and the contemporary calls for "holistic evangelism"
are hardly unbiblical. Besides declarative preaching, teaching is a
method by which both Jesus and His apostles communicated the
evangel (e.g., Matt. 9:35; Luke 24:45–49; Acts 8:30–35; 17:11;
19:8–10).

The Message

The good news of God's redeeming love is the essential biblical
theme, and it is hardly limited to the New Testament. We find an
evangelical perspective on life in the beginning chapters of Genesis.
Our God is the universal Lord and Creator (1:1). All that He made
was "very good" (1:31); including man (1:26), who was created in
His image and likeness (1:26–27); capable of relating to Him in a
wholesome way (cf. 3:8–11); and of living a fruitful life (1:28–29).
However, Adam and Eve were vulnerable to temptation; they fell
from the freedom and fulfillment of their original innocence (3:1–7).
As a consequence, both they and the tempter received divine judgment (3:14–19), affecting them and their posterity (all mankind).

A disappointing and depressing story! But classical theology has recognized that God was gracious, giving reason for hope even as He judged the first disobedience. In Genesis 3:15 we find a promise, which has been termed the protoevangelium (the foreshadowing of good news): the woman's seed shall bruise the serpent's head. Note that the serpent (which is biblically identified as Satan) has a continuing existence through the generations of mankind, while Eve's posterity is involved. In this we recognize Jesus' victory over the evil one: evil shall be defeated, and the tempter's work shall be terminated. The defeat of evil is made progressively clear, especially in Revelation 20:10. Genesis 3:21 tells how, after He judged them, the Lord clothed Adam and Eve. His continuing care for His errant children is again demonstrated in the divine guarantee of Cain's protection (Gen. 4:14–15).

The opening chapters of Scripture establish understandings which inform our reading of the whole Bible (and are confirmed by the wider biblical data). God is the fundamental, controlling reality. He is for us, loving us as a father favors His children. Our sin separates us from this love, and incurs judgment. But God reaches out to us, beyond our sinful separation, offering final hope and continuing concern. This message unfolds with increasing clarity in the Old Testament, culminating in the New Testament message that in Jesus Christ "God was reconciling the world to Himself" (2 Cor. 5:19) and offering eternal life to all who believe in Him (John 3:16). "Biblical realism" has a world view which speaks of both divine love and divine judgment, of human dignity and human sinfulness. In this mix the divine overshadows the human (promise proves victorious), but only when joined to repentance and faith (see below). Clearly, to borrow from a well-known contemporary translation, we have a "Good News Bible"—from Genesis to Revelation.

Important Bible passages relevant to our course can be grouped around various subjects. Regarding man's condition, we have fallen from a state of innocence and favor (Gen. 1:26–31; 3:1–19; 1 Cor. 15:22), and we are all sinners (Isa. 53:6; Rom. 3:23; 5:12), deserving and facing the penalty of sin which is death (Gen. 2:17; Ezek. 18:20; Rom. 6:23) and eternal punishment (Isa. 66:24; Luke 16:19–31; Rev. 22:14–15). But God, in His love (John 3:16–17; Rom. 5:8; 1 John 4:9–10), sent His Son, Jesus, to die willingly for our sins, and thus satisfy His justice (Isa. 53:4–5; Rom. 3:24; 5:9–10), resulting in the forgiveness of our sins (Luke 24:46–47; Acts 10:43; Col. 1:14) and new life, abundant and eternal (John 11:25–26; Rom. 5:21; Rev. 21:6).

It is Christ alone who gives salvation (John 8:24; Acts 4:12; Rev.

5:9), by His death and resurrection (Luke 24:46; Rom. 6:5; 1 Cor. 15:3–4). He frees us from our bondage to sin and Satan (John 8:34–36; Acts 26:18; Col. 1:13), gives us His indwelling Holy Spirit (John 14:16–17; Acts 2:38; Rom. 5:5), enabling and demanding a new life of holy obedience (John 14:15; Rom. 6:1–2; Eph. 2:10), and resulting in the assurance of salvation (John 6:37; Rom. 6:5–6; 1 John 4:4,13). Salvation is a gift from God's gracious hand (Rom. 3:24; Eph. 2:8–9), but applied by our response to its offer (Acts 13:48; Rom. 10:12–14). We receive this gift by repentance (Acts 2:38; 11:18; 2 Peter 3:9) and faith (John 1:12; Acts 16:31; Rom. 10:14). God saves us by His sovereign act, yet not apart from responsible human involvement (John 10:27–29; Acts 13:48; 1 Cor. 3:6). The biblical vision of salvation is universal in scope (Gen. 12:3; John 1:9; Phil. 2:10–11), but not without urgency, lest unredeemed sinners die in their sins (Luke 16:31; John 4:31–38; 2 Peter 3:9).

This brief summation of God's good news in Christ, and these few quotes cannot but begin exploring the multifaceted message and context of evangelism. Our subject is broader and deeper than any summary . . . or even a multivolume theology!

Philosophical Concerns

A major issue in evangelism is our relationship to the surrounding culture. The philosophic base to our popular culture includes rationalist idealism and existentialism. If the pragmatist believes, "whatever works is true and good," the idealist asserts, "whatever is conceived as true is in fact ultimate," and the existentialist holds, "whatever I will to assert is right is my proper reality." Many of our students are radically touched by the idealist and existential moods of our day. They naively assume that their limited concept of the human situation, and of God's solution to it, will meet the felt need and self-conception of all they meet. But real life is more complex and complicated than most of us can conceive; our conception of reality does not really comprehend all that life forces us to encounter. Therefore, we must encourage our students to remain sensitive listeners, even as they speak the Word to a needy world. Disregarding all others is dangerous, and destructive of a proper evangelistic dynamic.

Basic to our concern for God-honoring evangelism is the issue of manipulation in the decision-making process. Care must be taken lest our human persuasiveness (which is quite effective for the "natural leaders" and "born salesmen" among us) not be allowed to stifle the free, wholehearted, and understanding response that God desires from the unconverted. Our pragmatic North American culture emphasizes achieving the desired end, often at the expense of less tangible values. As we seek to build God's kingdom, and lead others in so doing, we must be very sensitive to the need for giving God, the Holy Spirit, room to do His work. Contemporary analysts of social movements, such as Jacques Ellul and Eric Hoffer, demonstrate that our society is fraught with manipulative decision making. In our enthusiasm to win decisions for Christ we must be cautious.

Another major issue evangelism departments will face is their relationship to the local church. We are living in an era in which evangelism is rightly linked to church growth. Decisions for Christ are meant, in God's plan, to flow into worship, fellowship and service within the context of congregational life. The "electronic church" (TV religious programming) is a temptation for new converts, if they are led to feel that they can nurture their new-found faith apart from the local church. Isolated converts will tend to be victimized by non-Christian religions and sub-Christian cults. Although we want to coordinate with local congregations, it is often extremely difficult to do so, even for denominational schools. However, it is possible, and well worth the effort. At the very least, practical assignments in the evangelism department should be done in consultation with the church leaders of the constituency, especially those in the local community. At the very best, students work alongside congregational members, who are then able to follow through on the converts and other contacts.

Yet, the above issues notwithstanding, our courses can be effective in maturing our students through sensitive and prayerful interaction with the unchurched around them. Departments of evangelism combine academic expertise and missionary zeal as they prepare students to concentrate on the mandate of world evangelization.

Practical Application

In structuring departmental curriculum we should begin with basic concepts and orientations, move on to particular methodologies, and then develop wider and deeper areas of the subject. Assignments should include both academic study and personal engagement.

Since fewer than one-fourth of all the Bible colleges in North America have fully developed majors in evangelism, I have chosen to concentrate on the basic foundational course, often mandatory for every student. The development of a major or even minor in the field would include additional courses in such areas as the use of media in evangelism, evangelism with modern religions and cults, contemporary cultural issues related to evangelism, evangelism in the local church, and several interdepartmental studies with the missions program.

Foundational aspects of the preliminary course include a descriptive definition of evangelism, relating to both contemporary and biblical data, and an initial statement of what the gospel is. Not only the model of the early church in Acts, but the gospel writers' portraits of our Lord, the great evangelist, are rich scriptural data which will vitally engage our students.

The process of student integration takes place as he brings into focus three crucial areas: the biblical and theological content which must make up the message of evangelism; the varied cultural surroundings in which that message must be communicated; and the methodology by which this is carried out. Perhaps there is some merit in further detailing this third ingredient.

Evangelism Methods

It is important that the students be helped to realize that there are a variety of valid approaches to the practice of evangelism. If their training includes experience with but one approach, it is especially needful that other options be mentioned. No one method or approach will suit every student, but the presentation of a rich variety of evangelistic strategies and programs will demonstrate that there is some means of faith-sharing that every member will find attractive and appropriate.

Bible study evangelism uses scriptural content in a study/discussion motif. While such study can be done alone or between two people, it also lends itself to the small group context. Bible correspondence courses and pulpit teaching are different ways to use this method. (Those with teaching gifts can thereby bear evangelistic fruit as well as upbuilding the saints.)

Friendship evangelism stresses the importance of establishing a trusting, knowledgeable relationship with those we hope to win for the Lord. Such an approach, in corporate context, has been called "fellowship evangelism" (through a camping or coffee house program). With this methodology is often linked the concept of "natural witness," sharing our faith by word and deed in ordinary interactions. Service evangelism emphasizes the demonstration of Christian love in deed as well as (but not excluding) verbal expression. Even our joyful worship can witness to the reality and desirability of the Christian life.

Evangelism is linked in many minds to *visitation* ("door knocking"). Systematic neighborhood visitation is one way to gain a wide exposure for our Christian concern. It can be linked to a low-key friendship approach (perhaps including an invitation to some church program), or to a very direct confrontation with the claims of Christ. Questionnaires and surveys have been developed to help the evangelist make contact with those at home, leading to some form of witness.

Course Structure

Most commonly, a course on evangelism will have the students prepare a *personal testimony* of Christ's work in their own lives. This need not relate to the experience of salvation (not always clear, especially for those whose parents were part of the household of faith). It can include relating the difference Christ has made at any decisive point in the student's pilgrimage. The form and emphases of such a story telling should be controlled by the kind of gospel presentation that will follow it, and by nature of the audience. Small group in-class interactions with these assignments are useful mutual learning/mutual instruction times.

Another common element in our course is *Scripture memorization.* The more verses committed to memory, the better able a student will be at sharing his or her faith in life's regular encounters with the world. Ten to twenty verses is not much to ask in the course of a semester or quarter.

The academic aspect of this course can include *major papers*: "The Role of the Holy Spirit in Evangelism" (Acts); "Contrasting Evangelistic Methods in Acts"; "Comparing and Contrasting the Great Commission Passages"; "Jesus as Model Evangelist" (Mark); "Jesus' Theology of Evangelism" (John); or "Divine Sovereignty and Human Responsibility in Evangelism" (the possible topics are inexhaustible). Word studies (using a concordance or theological dictionary) are a rich source of theological education. Besides *evangelism, salvation,* and *redemption* (and their cognates), students could explore *grace, faith, judgment, baptism,* and any other appropriate Bible words. Instruction in word study technique may be necessary, unless the students have previously been introduced to this approach.

Prayer is a proper, and major, focus for our course. Our subject is a natural one in which the students can grow in their ability to relate to their life-changing God. Because our course provides such a natural context for the maturing process (sanctification), the instructor should be prepared to counsel in this area, as well as offering classroom guidance in such subjects as walking in the Spirit.

Another ingredient of a foundational course in evangelism is *active student participation* in evangelism. To decide whether, and in what way, the students will be active in evangelism calls for sound judgment. The tradition in most schools is for students in the basic class to evangelize those in their community (or a nearby area). Usually this work is done apart from (or only tangentially related to) local churches. Such activities have both dangers and benefits.

On the positive side, it seems appropriate to provide the opportunity to demonstrate that what we are teaching is essential for wholesome Christiantiy. To send our students out to the unchurched and unsaved also underscores the urgency of the world's need. Many of our students, even freshmen, will be spiritually ready for this ministry. The fruits from their evangelistic efforts will be encouraging, and proof that it is possible to share our faith. Finally, applied ministry is appropriate to such a program as ours, especially in the context of a faith that emphasizes "doing" the truth.

We must, however, realize the possible dangers in sending our classes into the community for such ministry. Some will not be spiritually prepared for such work. Others will not have sufficiently digested the instruction prerequisite to this ministry. Many will have difficulty approaching strangers with diplomacy and discernment. When we realize that we are dealing with matters of eternal import, some measure of caution is merited. Will some of our students' efforts tend to dishonor the name of our Lord? Will they needlessly offend some, causing problems for the congregations in our community? Will the students have the discernment to know when to press for a decision, and when to ease off?

In the first year of teaching most professors want to follow the past course pattern. This writer, who has led many freshman classes in evangelistic activities, has always allowed those students who sense themselves unprepared for such ministry (or who have sincere and conscientious questions about the particular approach involved) to opt out of the practicum, providing prayer support for the others.

(Such an option, if employed, should be exercised through personal counseling with the instructor.) If those experienced in evangelism (perhaps upperclassmen) could team up with the uninitiated, the discipling aspect of Christian education would be enhanced. The above reasons for caution in involving immature students might argue for placing our course in the third or fourth year of the curriculum. This would not only give the class more maturity of age; it would eliminate one year students and sophomore drop-outs.

Finally, *observation of models* is a vital aspect of the course. Students should be exposed to those who have a demonstrated gift and wisdom in the subject. By inviting a number of pastors and lay people to share their experiences in evangelism, the instructor will be able to supplement his own limited experience. As well, individual classes and, at times, the entire student body will hear firsthand about the way Christians are sharing their faith, and with what results.

Conclusion

In developing courses in evangelism the instructor must face certain basic issues, about which sincere Christians will have differences. Besides his initial judgments, the instructor will develop reasoned and experienced convictions throughout his years of teaching evangelism ... leading to a philosophy about how the various subjects can best be taught.

It is hard to imagine another course which demands the integration of theory and practice to such an extent. The potential for changing lives (of the students, of those they will meet, and of the teachers as well) is immense. With Paul, we wonder, "Who is adequate for the challenge?" and with Paul we reply, "I am, through Christ who strengthens me!"

Notes

1. J. I. Packer, *Evangelism and the Sovereignty of God* (London: Inter-Varsity, 1961), p. 19.
2. Note that the authenticity of this passage is being questioned by evangelical New Testament scholars. It is not found in the earliest manuscripts.

The Author

Timothy Warner is a veteran leader in the Bible college movement, having served as academic dean and president of Fort Wayne Bible College and also vice president and president of the AABC. He holds the A.B. degree from Taylor University; S.T.B. from New York Theological Seminary; M.A. from New York University; and Ed.D. from Indiana University. Before serving at Fort Wayne Dr. Warner was a missionary in Sierra Leone and in 1980 he was named the director of the School of World Missions at Trinity Evangelical Divinity School.

The Subject

Like evangelism, missions has been at the heart of the Bible college movement since its very inception. Several of the earliest schools were known as "missionary training" institutions and that emphasis must still characterize our colleges. It is a simple fact that the majority of North American missionaries serving around the world had their training in Bible colleges. Dr. Warner offers a biblical base upon which to construct and operate an effective department of missions in today's complicated society.

6

MISSIONS

Timothy M. Warner

Missions has been a part of Bible college programs from the very beginning. Even the European antecedents of the more highly developed American Bible college movement gave strong emphasis to the training of missionaries. The first schools founded in this country had the preparation of missionaries as one of their primary objectives.

Introduction

In the minds of many, "missions" includes everything the church does in fulfillment of the Great Commission—from personal witnessing to the most demanding pioneer missionary effort, from being salt and light in one's own cultural setting to becoming involved in the meeting of social and economic needs around the world.

For the purposes of this study we will limit the definition to those evangelistic and church planting activities carried on by persons sent from a well-established church to a people in a different culture where the church is not yet well established. While this includes evangelism as part of such missionary activity, evangelism as carried on within one's own culture is not included since it is covered as a separate discipline in chapter 5. The same is true for what we may call *church extension* or *church planting* within one's own society.

A widely accepted manner of looking at this difference is the use of the terms E-1, E-2, and E-3 types of evangelism. E-1 evangelism is that which takes place within one's own language and cultural area. E-2 evangelism is that which takes place in a subcultural area or a closely related language group. E-3 evangelism is that which takes place in a distinctly different cultural milieu and/or an entirely different language group. In this chapter we are concerned primarily with the E-3 situation.

The cross-cultural nature of the missionary's task requires a much broader spectrum of studies than would be the case for a person ministering within his or her own culture. The subject matter of the discipline begins, of course, with a mastery of the biblical message and of the biblical principles for the dissemination of that message. It also includes many of the areas of training appropriate for witnesses or ministers anywhere. Of necessity, however, it must incorporate the insights of the social sciences—cultural anthropology, sociology, and linguistics in particular.

Basic missionary problems include motivation, identification, communication, and indigenization. The *motivational problem* is essentially spiritual in nature and is answered by a careful study of and response to the Scriptures. The *identification problem* is learning to think like the people to whom one seeks to minister so that the message can enter meaningfully into their lives. It is fundamental to establishing a relationship of trust across which the message may flow. The *communication problem* is the challenge of putting the message into a language the target audience can understand. Such a complex task involves the nuances of pronunciation, grammar, word meaning, and idiomatic expression.

The fourth problem is *indigenization* which assumes that the aim of the missionary is to plant the church so that it will be functionally related to the culture of which it is a part, that is, "indigenous." This involves a biblical identification of the essential characteristics of a church and an equally clear understanding of those elements of church structure and life which are culturally rather than biblically determined.

A related problem receiving considerable attention recently is *contextualization*. Here the process seeks to define the relation of all theology to the cultural context in which it is being studied and lived out. Different cultures provide their own unique perspectives on and insights into theology, but this most be done without changing the absolute nature of the truth under study.

The discipline of missiology, then, is a cross-disciplinary study. It needs the input of the theologian, the anthropologist, the missiologist, the linguist, the educator, and the expert in psycho-social ministries.

Except for the fact that tradition does not establish validity one would be tempted to require a rationale for *not* including missions in the Bible college program. A central theme of the Bible is the plan of God for the establishing of His kingdom among men. The Great Commission forms the marching orders for the church, and the characteristic activity of the church in the time between His first and second comings is to be missionary activity. When that task is completed, the Lord will come again. Missionary studies would not seem to be an option for a Bible college, but a necessity.

Biblical Foundation

Identification of Passages

The Bible is preeminently a missionary book. To remove the idea of world evangelization and church planting would be to destroy the essential fabric of the Scriptures. There are, however, certain passages which especially emphasize this message.

The missionary idea is inherent in the opening statement of the Bible, "In the beginning God created the heavens and the earth." Knowledge of the God who created the world in which we live places upon the one who has this knowledge the responsibility to share it with any who do not know the Creator. Perhaps even more compelling is the need to declare and vindicate the glory of God among those who have forsaken Him to worship gods of their own making.

The unique linguistic problems confronted by missionaries (as over against evangelists in general) have their roots in what happened at Babel (Gen. 11:1-9). God's plan to deal with those problems is immediately revealed in the call of Abraham and the establishing of the nation of Israel (Genesis 12:1-3). The missionary idea in the Old Testament probably reaches its zenith in the Servant passages of Isaiah (42:1-9; 49:1-9a; 50:4-11; 52:13-53:12).

The New Testament imperative for and pattern of missionary activity is found initially in the incarnation of Christ (John 1:14) and His earthly ministry (John 17:4). It is stated more explicitly in the statement we know as the Great Commission (Matthew 28:18-20; Mark 16:15; Acts 1:8). Passages in Luke 24:46-48 and John 20:21 also fit in this category.

The whole Book of Acts is the account of the missionary expansion of the early church and thus forms a basic study document for the missionary enterprise. The Epistles are letters written by missionaries to missionary churches and must be studied in this light. The Revelation pictures the climax of this process when the twenty-four elders sing "You are worthy to take the scroll and to open its seals, because you were slain, and with your blood you purchased men for God from every tribe and language and people and nation. You have made them to be a kingdom and priests to serve our God, and they will reign on the earth" (5:9–10, NIV).

Explanation of Passages

While volumes have been written on the biblical basis of missions and/or the theology of missions, it is appropriate to point out here how the passages identified apply to the teaching of missions. First of all, it must be remembered that missions is, in the first instance, God's business. He has initiated the process; He is the central figure in missionary activity at any point in history; and it is He who will signal its conclusion by the return to earth of His Son. This needs to be kept in view lest the missionary enterprise be humanized to the point where it degenerates into human theories, strategies, and programs.

We have noted that the basic problems facing the missionary are motivation, identification, communication, and indigenization. The motivational problem began with the Fall (Gen. 3), and the solution will be seen at numerous points in the outworking of God's plan. The next two problems both have their root in the deliberate disobedience of the people at Babel. God's command was to "be fruitful and multiply, and fill the earth" (Gen. 9:1, NASB). The people at Babel said, "Come, let us build ourselves a city, with a tower that reaches to the heavens, so that we may make a name for ourselves and not be scattered over the face of the whole earth" (11:4, NIV). God's judgment on this rebellion was the confusing of the languages and the consequent beginning of the many nations or ethnic groups found in the world today. These divisions based on different languages and different cultures are the reason for the cross-cultural problems faced by the church in carrying out its missionary task.

God immediately demonstrated that His plan still included the redemption of men in all of those diverse groups. He did this by choosing one of them, namely Israel, to be the channel through which He would send His message to the others. When He called Abram to be the first leader of this nation, He promised him that "all peoples on earth will be blessed through you" (12:3, NIV). So, in the rest of the Old Testament God is seen to be at work revealing His glory and working out His purposes through Israel, sometimes with their cooperation, but often without it.

The point to be noted, however, is that training for missionary service must still address these two problems through the diligent study of cultures and languages. Cultural anthropology and linguistics are relatively new as academic disciplines, but the need for such study is as old as the Tower of Babel.

It is in the New Testament, however, that the context for contemporary missions is found. The church replaces Israel as the primary instrument through which God is carrying out His purposes in the world, and its marching orders are clearly spelled out in the pages of the New Testament.

In His incarnation, Jesus demonstrated how a missionary copes with the basic problems we have identified. His relationship of love (John 14:31) and obedience (John 5:30) to His Father provided the right motivation. His becoming man and taking the form of a servant (Phil. 2:6–7) is a model of identification with those one seeks to win. His careful delineation between the principles involved in the laws of God and the traditions of men which had been added to them comes right to the heart of the problem of indigenization (Matt. 5:21–48; 15:1–9). It is interesting to note that this last problem was the occasion for the first serious controversy in the early church and was the topic of discussion at the Jerusalem conference in Acts 15. The question was, "Do Gentile Christians have to adopt an essentially Jewish lifestyle in order to be acceptable to the church?" The answer was clearly negative.

Missionaries are constantly faced with distinguishing between those things which are essential for the church at all times and in all places and those things which are cultural expressions of the absolutes. The inability to make such distinctions has resulted in the church looking like a foreign (especially a Western) institution to people in non-Western societies with accompanying resistance to the gospel. The gospel message is always life-changing, but such dramatic revolution of life needs not traditions developed by a particular church within some other cultural context.

The statement in John 1:14 provides a helpful commentary on the Incarnation and its connection with the Old Testament. The verse reads, "And the Word became flesh, and dwelt among us, . . . full of grace and truth" (NASB). The "Word" clearly refers to Christ, but to a Jewish reader there would also be a ready connection with the expressions found so often in the prophetic writings (e.g., "The word of the Lord which came to . . ."). God has always had a

message of love and redemption for man. He has sought to deliver
that message in different ways at different times. In Christ, the
message—that "Word of the Lord"—became incarnate in a Person;
and Christ came not only to *deliver* a message, He came to *be* the
Message.

When Jesus had completed His missionary trip to earth, had
finished the work of redemption, and had given us the example of
how life is to be lived to the glory of God, He gave the church its
marching orders in the Great Commission. The several statements of
the commission give us the following perspectives on the missionary
enterprise:

The Commissioner—The risen Christ (Matt. 28:18)
The Authority—That given by God to the risen Christ (Matt. 28:18)
The Commissioned—The disciples, then and now (Matt. 28:16; cf. 2
                Tim. 2:2)
The Commission—Make disciples (Matt. 28:20)
The Provision—The power of the Holy Spirit (Luke 24:49, Acts 1:8)
The Methods—Witness (Luke 24:48; Acts 1:8)
                Preach (Mark 16:15)
                Teach (Matt. 28:20)
The Scope—All nations (Matt. 28:19; Luke 24:47)
                All the world (Mark 16:15)
                Every creature (Mark 16:15)
                The end of the earth (Acts 1:8)
The Duration—The end of the age (Matt. 28:20)
The Promise—"I am with you always." (Matt. 28:20)

It is significant to note that the Great Commission is never quoted
later in the New Testament as a reason for missions. The motivation
was assigned to the Holy Spirit. The relation of the Holy Spirit to
missions is therefore an imperative study.

In the Old Testament it was always made clear to Israel that they
could not claim the promised land by their own military might or
strategy. God's power would always be the difference between
them and their enemies. So in the New Testament, the church was
told that the margin of victory in the spiritual claiming of the world
for Christ would always be the power of the Holy Spirit. Thus the
original band of disciples was told to tarry in Jerusalem until they
were endued with this power; on the mount of ascension they were
told very clearly, "You will receive power when the Holy Spirit has
come upon you; and you will be my witnesses in Jerusalem, and in
all Judea and Samaria and to the ends of the earth" (Acts 1:8, NIV).

This is a statement, not a command. When the Spirit of the resurrected Christ lived in them He would provide both motive and power for this global witness. A humanistic approach to missions is ultimately as fruitless as the efforts of Israel to conquer their enemies without the supernatural intervention of God.

To say that methods and strategy will not guarantee success in missionary work apart from the operation of the Spirit is not to say that they are unimportant or unnecessary. However, such methods need also to be studied in the light of Scripture, and the Book of Acts in particular. The limits of this study do not permit an exposition of that subject, but it should be said that one's biblical search must center upon the identifying of basic principles of missionary work rather than an attempt to copy the particular methods used by Paul on his missionary journeys.

Systematization of Passages

It is evident from even a cursory look at the biblical passages relating to missions that every area of theology is vitally related to this discipline.

Theology Proper. Missions is the God-ordained program of the church. His message is to be delivered in His way with the result that His church will be established in every tribe and nation. A concern for His glory in the world is a fundamental motivation for missions.

Bibliology. The Scriptures are the fundamental textbook of the missionary enterprise. They are the source of the evangel to be delivered and the truth to be taught. They are an essential guide for the church to be established. Apart from the Bible there would be no missionary enterprise.

Christology. Christ is at once the heart of the missionary message and the model of missionary activity. As the risen Lord, He is the Commissioner of the church—the One on whose authority missionaries dare invade territory held by the enemy.

Pneumatology. The launching of the New Testament missionary movement came with the gift of the Spirit on Pentecost. He is the source of power for effective witness and preaching. He is the inner motivation for the discipling of the nations. He is the One who provides guidance for those involved in planning missionary strategy and determining places of ministry.

Anthropology. The fallenness of man on a universal basis is one of the key concepts undergirding the global scope of the Great Commission. Ministry to persons is at the heart of missionary ministry and the biblical teaching about man is fundamental to effective ministry.

Soteriology. Without the message of salvation, the rationale for the missionary movement would change dramatically if it did not disappear altogether. The clear definition of the essentials of soteriology as over against the cultural rules and taboos which may be practiced by saved people in any given place is one of the basic studies in a missions curriculum.

Hamartiology. As with other aspects of theology, the definition of sin must be understood clearly in order not to confuse it with cultural concepts of evil which are often quite different from the biblical concept.

Ecclesiology. This is an essential study for anyone who is to be involved in church planting. The establishing of an indigenous church requires the careful distinction between that which is to be true of the church at all times and in all places and that which may change with changing cultural contexts.

Eschatology. It is the clear teaching of Scripture that the completion of the missionary task and the Second Coming of Christ are closely related. One hermeneutic suggests that the eschatological motive for missions is that we are to pray sincerely, "Even so come quickly, Lord Jesus," and that we must be diligent about completing the discipling of the nations as the condition for His return. The depth of our desire to see His return will depict the depth of our commitment to missions.

Volumes have been written on the relationship between theology and missions or, as it may more properly be stated, the theology of missions. It is therefore impossible to be more than suggestive of this area of study in this brief paper.

Philosophical Formulation

The move from theology to philosophy in the field of missions is almost imperceptible. Missions is rooted so deeply in theology that one seldom encounters any reference to a philosophy of missions, at least none which does not use theology as its basis.

The area of epistemology may raise some significant ideas for consideration, however. It certainly is necessary to begin with a basic philosophical premise of Christian education, namely that all truth is God's truth. Since missions study draws so heavily from other disciplines, especially the social sciences, it is essential to recognize that a correct observation of the way God has created things and people is valid regardless of the faith of the observer.

On the other hand, the fact that a person has made some significant observations in the natural realm or that he has understood and correctly restated the findings of others does not qualify him to also speak in the area of values. *Thus it is necessary for the person instructing in an area which is "nontheological" as it comes from the minds and hands of the experts in that field to distinguish between the items which are objective scientific facts and those which are theories or judgments based on a secular value system.*

The valid data of the particular discipline should be fully utilized as resources for the accomplishing of the missionary task. They should not be rejected just because they come from a source which does not share our theological position. If a statement is true, it is true because God made it that way, and the discoverer of that truth does not change its validity or usefulness.

A similar approach may be taken to understanding the Bible. There are, for example, men who do not share our theology but who have become experts in the history of Bible times. Their background information may be crucial to the interpretation of some biblical passages. The truth of their information is not changed by their theology. All truth is God's truth regardless of who discovers it.

A further factor to be considered in the area of epistemology is the ability to distinguish between the principles which God has established for our life and work and the particular application of those principles at any given time or place. These principles are revealed in the Scriptures, but they are not always stated in theoretical form. We see them in some particular application and must reason back to the principle.

For example, Jesus did not teach any one form of church government. In the Book of Acts we see a church develop, and we see church government emerge. The natural tendency is to try to copy the structure of historical New Testament churches. The basic lesson to be learned, however, is that church government should develop as there is need for it and in patterns which the people who will practice it know how to operate. If the principle is missed, the missionary may well fall into the trap of trying to superimpose an episcopal form of church government on a group of people who operate their own society through a council of elders, or vice versa.

Implicit in much of the preceding discussion are elements of axiology. The missionary will constantly be dealing with value judgments in a cross-cultural situation, and it is imperative that he clearly understand the basis for a Christian value system. The tendency is to substitute rules for values. Rules come from the personal application of absolute values to a particular cultural situation. It is essential to identify the value in its pure form so as to apply it to changing cultural situations without falling into the opposing traps of a complete relativism on the one side or legalism on the other.

Practical Application

Curriculum Integration

By this time it should be clear that the Bible is the starting point for the study of missions, and therefore the problems of correlation are not what they would be if the materials of the discipline were drawn largely from nonbiblical sources.

There is the danger, however, that one may approach the area of missions with preconceived ideas, from whatever source, and may attempt to superimpose those ideas on the Scriptures. There is also the danger of approaching the study of missions with a low view of Scripture. In such cases, humanism and relativism readily take over as the primary considerations, and the Bible is used as only one source book among many, no longer viewed as the authoritative Word of God. In such a situation, there may be negative correlation between the teaching of the Bible and the ideas of those involved in the missionary enterprise.

Such a situation is virtually unthinkable in a Bible college. The commitment of the Bible college movement to the authority of the Scriptures is one of the primary reasons it has also had a strong commitment to missions. Indeed, if negative correlation emerges in the teaching of missions, the teacher had better review and reaffirm his theological underpinnings.

The one subject area where the greatest problem is apt to occur is cultural anthropology, taught under the general area of the social sciences. But in most Bible colleges the course is offered principally for students majoring in missions and is therefore appropriate for inclusion under this heading.

Most anthropology textbooks are written from a secular viewpoint. They assume varying degrees of relativism in the area of values, thereby challenging the Christian teacher to help the student clearly identify such nonbiblical ideas without rejecting the many valid and valuable insights to be gained from anthropological studies. Fortunately, there are now many significant writings by Christians in the field of anthropology which assist in this process. The use of biblical illustrations and the application of biblical principles by the teacher are important ingredients in this learning process.

Another potentially problematic sub-category is non-Christian religions. This is, of course, related to cultural anthropology because religion is an aspect of culture. It has its own distinctive literature, however, and in that literature one encounters points of view ranging from pure relativism (making each religion as valid as the next) to an open condemnation of all religious systems which differ from that of the author as fabrications of Satan to deceive men. A corollary of the latter view is that these other religions are not even worthy of study.

Effective communication with persons of differing religious systems would seem to require some understanding of what they believe and how they arrived at that belief system. Examples of how the apostle Paul used his knowledge of the religion of the people to whom he was seeking to minister will help to establish the biblical approach to a study of such religions. During the study, student and teacher should constantly be looking for points of contact with persons embracing a given religion and for bridges across which communication of the gospel could take place with greater understanding than would be the case if one had no knowledge of the belief system of the hearer.

Classroom Integration

The Bible college philosophy and program are ideally suited to the kind of integration of learning with which we are concerned. It cannot be assumed, however, just because a student has a major in Bible and theology, that such study has included a significant missionary perspective. Nor can it be assumed that the student has come out of that major armed with the necessary biblical principles to apply in cross-cultural situations. All too often Bible study is used to justify the church structure and personal life style of the teacher or sponsoring church. The best learning takes place when students are constantly challenged to find the underlying principles involved in the Scriptures being studied and to see how they have been applied (or perhaps misapplied) at various times and places through history. The desirable result then is a growing harmony of truth and life.

It would be most desirable if missionary applications could be made in each Bible or theology class. It is probably too much to hope, however, that every professor will have sufficient missionary insight or that such application will have high priority in the use of time allotted to each class. It will therefore be necessary for the missions professor to make the applications. This will be done on a fairly constant basis in each of the courses taught, but it may also be done in a special class on "Missions in Biblical Context" or the "Theology of Missions."

Another way to achieve integration and also help the student to see how it works is through team teaching utilizing a theologian and an anthropologist in the same class. The dialogue generated in such situations dramatizes the integration process for the student.

Inductive Bible study is also much more likely to get the student involved in the pursuit of basic principles and of finding the points of integration with contemporary situation. Admittedly this is more difficult for both student and teacher, but it is also calculated to produce more significant long-range results both in terms of the impact of what is learned at the time and in the ability to continue the learning and integrating process throughout the rest of life.

Overall Integration

There is perhaps one final and overriding consideration in the achieving of the integration of faith and learning with which we are concerned, and it is found in the overall purpose of education. In general terms, this purpose may be stated as the overcoming of provincialism and ignorance, through a comprehenisve knowledge of the Word of God and a broad acquaintance with the world of men, ideas, and things. The natural tendency on the part of man to feel insecure in the midst of so many threatening unknowns often leads to an inordinate grasping after a few anchor points in familiar and timetested realms. This tends to develop into a stranglehold which prevents further learning.

The Bible college program should provide the necessary balance between that solid place on which to stand based on revelation, and the incentive to explore at the frontiers of one's knowledge in the various disciplines of learning. The one provides security; the other involves risk. In proper balance they are the essence of genuinely Christian education. If they are separated, they tend to produce an anti-intellectual, superspiritual stance on the one side, or a super-intellectual, antispiritual stance on the other. Both curriculum-building and instructional philosophy need to be approached with this in mind.

Conclusion

The department of missions in a Bible college exists primarily to train those who will participate in the cross-cultural expansion of the church. Nothing could be more appropriate to a Bible college and no other major field of study will use a broader spectrum of studies from the college curriculum in order to prepare a graduate adequately for this demanding task. *The more skillfully these many elements of curriculum are brought together within a biblical context, the more adequately the student will be equipped for his mission.*

It should be pointed out, however, that teaching personnel in the field of missions should also serve as catalysts to see that a missionary perspective is maintained in the totality of school life and in all areas of the curriculum. The fact is, that which is farthest removed from our experience and our view tends to be lost sight of first. Missions seems to suffer from that sense of distance. The planting of the church on the frontiers of missionary expansion, however, is still the primary task of the church in this period between the first and second comings of Christ. If that perspective is lost in any of the areas of church life and ministry, an element essential to the church's vitality will be missing. The motivation for maintaining this integration will normally not come from other departments. The missions department may therefore help achieve integration by being a catalyst in the opposite direction.

The teaching of missions offers one of the broadest challenges posssible to the application of biblical principles to life and ministry. It is particularly the cross-cultural aspects of the discipline which introduce this breadth. Happy are professors and students who accept this challenge.

The Author

Having looked at church education from three angles—local church ministry, the college classroom, and the editor's desk—Wesley R. Willis brings to this chapter varied as well as long-term experience in the field. After completing undergraduate work at Philadelphia College of Bible he went on to earn the Th.M. in Christian education at Dallas Theological Seminary and an Ed.D. in Educational Administration at Indiana University. He has taught church education at Washington Bible College and has taught and was academic vice-president at Fort Wayne Bible College. He presently serves as senior vice president at Scripture Press Publications in Wheaton, Illinois.

The Subject

Church education is a theological discipline. Dr. Willis approaches it by looking through the threefold lens of the home, the church, and the para-church organization. He emphasizes the role of the church education professor as one who must guide students into spiritual maturity through a cognitive and experiential knowledge of the Word of God. In its practical application, Dr. Willis suggests several types of courses which lead toward education in biblical truth with a professional area of Bible college study.

7

CHURCH EDUCATION

Wesley R. Willis

Introduction

The educational function of the church is an essential aspect of its ministry. Without education the church is unlikely to become the dynamic living organism that Christ intended. God has provided basic educational principles to guide both parents and church leaders. This is not to say that the New Testament commands Christians to establish departments of church education. The term itself appears neither in the Old Testament nor the New. However, God expects both the home and the church to contribute toward helping persons come to spiritual maturity and developing their ministry skills to help others grow. The common designation of this field of study in most Bible colleges is still "Christian education." We use "church education" in this chapter to differentiate our subject from the rapidly increasing Christian school movement also referred to as "Christian education."

Phase I—Personal Growth

First the home and later the church were assigned the responsibility of helping individuals to become what God intended them to be. These institutions were established by God to help persons come to maturity.

When children are born into a family, they progress through successive stages of maturing. As they mature, they require less and less assistance by parents and others. At some point they reach a level at which they are able to take responsibility for themselves.

The same principle applies to spiritual growth. One of the primary responsibilities of the church is to assist the home in promoting such growth. Persons must be born again. And once they have been spiritually reborn, they progress through successive stages of spiritual maturity. They require less and less assistance, and finally are prepared to assume primary responsibility for their own spiritual welfare.

It is important to recognize that the first phase of Christian education includes both salvation and spiritual growth. Gaebelein described this phase as consisting of two aims: "The first aim of Christian education may be defined in terms of evangelism, remembering that evangelism includes more than public meetings in which appeals for decisions are made."[1] He recognized that evangelism includes home atmosphere, teacher counsel, study of the Word, and other elements. "The second function of Christian education is that of nurture. Christ's analogy of entrance into the kingdom as new birth is an exact one. Infants need to be fed."[2]

Phase II—Helping Others Grow

There also is a second phase in which both home and church contribute to individuals. As persons mature and take increasing responsibility for themselves, they also must discover and develop ministry skills that will enable them to help others mature. In the sphere of the home, children grow up and become parents. Instead of being the recipients of parenting, they become the source. As maturing takes place, parents must insure that their offspring are prepared to become responsible parents themselves.

The church's contribution, likewise, is to equip believers to assume responsibility for ministering to others. Those who are more mature must develop ministry skills (spiritual gifts) so that they, in turn, can help those who are maturing or developing ministry skills.

These two phases of home and church ministry accurately describe the focus of church education—helping individuals to mature and to develop ministry skills so that they in turn can minister to others. Paul admonished Timothy to ". . . be strong in the grace that is in Christ Jesus. And the things which you have heard from me in the presence of many witnesses, these entrust to faithful men, who will be able to teach others also" (2 Tim. 2:1–2, NASB). The first part of this admonition described Timothy's personal maturity. The second part of the admonition focused on the need for Timothy to develop ministry skills in order to serve God faithfully.

Agencies of Christian Education

Dr. Lois LeBar wrote, "In God's economy, the Christian home rather than the church agency is the the primary educational unit. Whatever the church does ought to reinforce the home, rather than vice versa. Parents have the first claim and responsibility for their children."[3] Dr. LeBar has clearly identified not only the two main agencies of Christian nurture, but she has placed them in their proper order. The home is the primary agency of Christian education, but God also has established the church to provide assistance in the personal growth and development of ministry skills.

A third organizational category might be added—that of the para-church organization. In recent years a myriad of organizations has emerged to assist the home and church in accomplishing their mission. The church education department must build its curriculum around the proper relationship of home, church, and para-church organization, equipping students to minister in and through them as effectively as possible.

The Function of the Church Education Department

The *function* of the church education department can be defined simply as helping students to develop as lay persons and/or professional leaders who are equipped to help others mature and develop ministry skills.

The *purpose* of the church education department is defined by the American Association of Bible Colleges.

Professional Christian Education . . . has as its function the preparation of students for church-related educational ministries, first, through subject matter concerned with principles and practices of the teaching-learning process, and with the organization and administration of educational agencies; and second through learning experiences that develop requisite skills and Christian maturity for effective service.[4]

While the *curriculum* of the church education department includes some emphasis on personal growth and maturity, generally these elements are included elsewhere in the Bible college curriculum. The church education curriculum concentrates on helping students to develop ministry skills. These skills include how to assist others in growth through activities such as teaching and counseling. But the curriculum must also include instruction in the criteria of effective homes, churches, and para-church organizations, and how to organize and administer these so that they function as efficiently as possible.

Biblical Foundation

As with other departments in the Bible college, the church education department must build upon a strong biblical base; it is in very essence a theological discipline.

Element I—Life-Changing Knowledge

If the church educator is going to guide others into spiritual maturity, he must be aware of what it means to become spiritually mature, and to be progressing well toward maturity. Thus, the student must acquire an intimate and personal knowledge of the Word of God, since it is the Bible that is the source of growth: "Like newborn babes, long for the pure milk of the word, that by it you may grow in respect to salvation" (1 Pet. 2:2, NASB). Endeavoring to lead others into spiritual maturity with an inadequate knowledge of the Word is unthinkable.

But *cognitive* learning alone is inadequate. Professors must also stress *affective* learning that results in behavioral change. Professors must expect more than mere verbalization. Lois LeBar admonishes, "We haven't been changing life. We've merely been playing at the game of life. We've repeated words, and more words. We've insisted that our pupils repeat words. We seldom fathom the depth of ignorance and unreality over which we skate on a film of words."[5] Students must not only recognize biblical truths and give intellectual assent to them, but they also must internalize and act upon them. Larry Richards comments, "The Bible teacher must teach in such a way that his students, understanding the truth of God, discover and are led to make an appropriate life response to the God who speaks to them through His Word. Only thus learned can God's Word transform."[6]

As students allow the Holy Spirit of God to apply those biblical truths to their lives, they become children of God through faith in

Jesus Christ and become increasingly like Him. Then students are in a position for God's Spirit to use them in ministering to others, so that others also can grow spiritually.

Element II—Knowledge of Home and Church

The second element in the base is the biblical teaching concerning the place and function of both the home and the church.

Shortly after the creation of man, God evaluated Adam's situation. In Genesis 2 God reported that Adam was functioning alone and that condition was not good. Therefore He created a wife for Adam, thereby establishing the first family unit. Periodically through the rest of Scripture, additional and explanatory guidelines were given to instruct in the proper biblical order to be expressed through the family unit. Passages such as Deuteronomy 6:1-25, Psalms 127 and 128, numerous Proverbs, Song of Solomon, 1 Corinthians 7, Ephesians 5:15-6:9, Colossians 3:18-4:1, 1 Peter 3:1-7, and many other Scriptures give specific commands or guidelines for the effective functioning of family units. In addition to specific hortatory passages there are countless examples, both positive and negative, which can be equally instructive.

God also has provided guidelines for the other facets of Christian education in the church. Matthew 16:13-20, Matthew 18:15-35, Matthew 28:18-20, Acts 1:8, Romans 12, 1 Corinthians 12-14, Ephesians 4, Philippians 2:1-11, 1 Timothy, Titus, Hebrews 13, 1 Peter 2, and 1 Peter 5 are but a few of the more obvious passages that give specific directives to the local church.

Element III—Biblical Basis for General Courses

There is a third element in the biblical foundation. It is imperative that church education professors begin with revealed truth in building all courses in the departmental curriculum. Naturally some units will draw more heavily upon revealed truth than others, depending on the extent of Scripture dealing with those subjects. As has been suggested, an abundance of materials deal with the proper functioning of homes and churches. But other subjects in a church education curriculum afford fewer passages as biblical base, making the task of foundation building more difficult, but no less necessary.

For example, a course on methods of teaching should draw heavily upon revealed truth. Many precepts that apply to teaching are found in the Bible. First Timothy 4 gives instruction not only on the personal life of the teacher, but on elements to be included in teaching. Second Timothy 2:1–3 describes discipling, a basic type of teaching in which the teacher personally builds himself into the life of the student. Jesus Christ demonstrated the process of discipling throughout the Gospels. An entire unit appropriately could be built upon the examples of effective teaching methods employed by Jesus Christ. A book such as *Jesus: The Master Teacher*, by Herman H. Horne, would be a valuable resource in studying this subject.[7]

In other courses, the scriptural basis might be less explicit. In these courses it is important to seek to establish principles of revealed truth upon which to build. While at first glance a course in understanding children would seem to have a minimal biblical base, there is much to draw upon. Many of the Proverbs describe children and what they need in order to mature appropriately. Passages such as Ephesians 5:1, Ephesians 6:1–4, 1 Thessalonians 2:7–12, 2 Timothy 1:5, and 2 Timothy 3:14–15 give specific commands or principles that help to demonstrate how God views childhood. Illustrations from the life of Christ, Moses, Jacob, Noah, and others demonstrate normal and abnormal childhood.

A word of caution is in order at this point. By no means should church education classes draw their content exclusively from the Bible. Professors must be free to integrate all truth and freely incorporate the best that man can learn and know into all classes. *But courses must be designed with the presupposition that where the Bible, by precept or by illustration, addresses itself to a topic, that is to be the point of reference.* When a professor knows what God has revealed concerning a subject, he is in a much stronger position to draw upon other sources. These sources must be tested both by biblical teaching on that subject, and by the whole testimony of . Scripture. Richards states that "the Bible communicates that which is objectively true. It describes accurately events which really happened. It shares feelings men of God really had. It communicates in words revealed information about God and from God to which we have no other access."[8] This third element demands that, to the greatest degree possible, revealed truth from God must comprise both the base and the integrating factor in all courses.

Element IV—Biblical Perspective on Para-Church Organizations

The fourth and final element in the biblical foundation is functionally related to the second element. Since the two basic agencies of Christian nurture are the home and church, all teaching that relates to para-church organizations must demonstrate how such organizations complement the ministry of the home and church. If students are preparing for ministries concentrating on the church, they must understand how para-church organizations relate to local congregations. But even more importantly, when students are preparing for ministries in para-church organizations, whether ministering to children, to youth, or in other special interest organizations, they must understand how such organizations carry out biblical priorities. A biblical foundation demands that the biblical agencies of Christian education have priority. All other organizations, including Christian elementary and secondary schools, and Bible colleges and seminaries, must strengthen and reinforce the home and the church.

Philosophical Formulation

At no point is the church education department more vulnerable than when the transition is made from the biblical/theological base to the practical outworking of the curriculum. Grievous though it may be, and incongruous as it seems, some church education courses are little more than secular education which has been "baptized." Specific Bible colleges could be cited that have denied their biblical/theological commitment by offering courses with a totally secular orientation. Students cannot be guided effectively into a biblical philosophy of instruction while employing curriculm materials which contradict the biblical view of man.

Courses in church administration built upon uncritical acceptance of popular American values, pagan to the core, are not only useless, but actively dangerous. Management principles that accept secular philosophies of leadership without subjecting them to biblical analysis easily fall into the category of the philosophy of the "rulers of the Gentiles" that Christ so graphically contrasted to the "servant leader" model in Matthew 20:20–28.

Adequate philosophical criteria comprise the missing link between biblical/theological commitment and the practical outworking of the curriculum. These criteria are imperative to insure that curriculum decisions indeed grow out of theological convictions. In this way *curriculum becomes theology incarnate.* Gaebelein observed that "we need teachers who see their subjects, whether scientific, historical, mathematical, literary, or artistic, as included within the pattern of God's truth."[9] Such a perspective demands that philosophical parameters be established upon the base of absolute truth. These parameters then provide criteria by which to make judgments. And it is imperative to make judgments about which concepts and systems are worthy of inclusion in a church education curriculum.

Epistemology

The most obvious philosophical dimension is *epistemology*, or the study of truth and how it can be known. As stated earlier, a curriculum is built not upon theory or speculation, but upon the revealed truth of God. Without God's Word, educators would be groping in darkness without a candle. "The core of Christianity is the confidence that our Creator God is, that He has acted in Christ Jesus to redeem, and that He has revealed both Himself and Truth to us in the written Word."[10]

Having access to the mind of God contributes a significant dimension to the formulation of curriculum. Instead of debating the merits of speculative systems, educators are able to build upon the base of revealed truth. In addition to propositional truth, God's Word provides examples to guide leaders today.

Normative truth provides the base for philosophical assumptions upon which to build both the curriculum and also personal and professional guidelines for the faculty. Some have accused those who believe in normative truth of closing their minds to the search for truth, of operating with a limiting ceiling over their heads. In reality, rather than being limited by a ceiling, Christian educators are characterized by stability because they have a solid base upon which to stand. By providing a reliable base, absolute truth freely allows one to seek additional facts from all fields of human endeavor.

Anthropology

Accurate perception of the nature and needs of humanity, as well as the goals of the educative process, grow out of a distinctly bibliocentric view of man. If one were to examine outstanding educational philosophers, it would become apparent that each one's view of humanity is the significant element in determining his philosophy of education.

If an educator sees man as inherently good (as did Rousseau in the 1700's, or A. S. Neill, the founder of Summerhill, in the 1900's), then an internally coherent philosophy of education dictates that the best an instructor can do is to stay out of the way and permit the natural goodness in the child to ultimately triumph. A. S. Neill writes, "My own way is Summerhill, or rather the idea behind Summerhill: The belief that man is originally good, that, for reasons no one so far knows, man kills his own life and the lives of his children by harsh and antilife laws and morals and taboos."[11]

However, in contrast to such secular speculation, knowing that man who was made in the image of God has fallen and naturally follows the base instincts of his carnal nature will lead to a conviction that regeneration is imperative for a person to achieve his true potential.

The value of persons and the interrelationships between persons, as well as the very nature and needs of those persons, are clearly established by God in His Word. It is this perception of the actual worth and estate of humanity that enables Bible college leaders to design curricula which help students prepare for effective ministry. The effectiveness of a student's future ministry will be enhanced because he has grasped the essence of humanity, and has cultivated ministry skills for service.

Axiology

At this point—the value of persons—the field of anthropology merges with that of axiology.

Again it is the normative revelation of God which provides a stable reference point. Since the focus of the church education department is equipping students to minister, the growth and development of persons is the end result of genuinely Christian education. Biblical revelation enables professors to comprehend both the dignity and value of man, and also to understand the fallen state in which unregenerate man exists and his potential when born again.

When the base of a church education department is theologically sound, the primary element in its programs has been appropriated. But that does not automatically transfer to curriculum design. The tie between the theological and the practical is the philosophical formulation. It is these philosophical propositions that link the biblical foundation with its practical implementation in the curriculum.

Practical Application

The courses of study, and the interrelationships that develop through the teaching/learning process, must build upon and accurately reflect the convictions that the Bible college educator affirms. The purpose of the curriculum is to help the student develop both understanding and skills. In order to achieve this purpose there should be several categories of courses within the church education curriculum.

Since the two basic agencies of Christian nurture are the home and the church, these logically form the starting point for the curriculum. Following an introductory course in which the entire field of church education is summarized, *in-depth analysis of these two agencies is warranted*. It would seem appropriate to have courses in the curriculum dealing with each of these two fields. One course could deal with God's pattern for the home and how that pattern can be implemented in the lives of believers. A second course might deal with the nature of the church and how effective church ministries can be designed and administered.

A second category of curricular emphasis includes courses to help students *understand the nature of those to whom they minister*. This includes both developmental psychology and the techniques by which various sub-groups can be ministered to effectively.

One approach to teaching these concepts is to design a series of courses in which both of these dimensions are addressed. The church education department might offer a course entitled "Christian Education of Children," in which the student examines the characteristics of children and means of effective ministry. There ought to be similar courses focusing on youth and adults.

An alternative preferred by some department chairmen is to have the student enroll in courses, such as child development or adolescent development, taught by professors in other departments. In these courses the basic characteristics of special groups are learned. Following these basic developmental courses, the student enrolls in departmental courses that focus specifically on designing ministries to those sub-groups that have been studied in the developmental psychology courses. This interdisciplinary approach affords a broader view.

Courses in the third category of curriculum should teach students *the basic ministry skills needed to help persons develop*. Foremost in this category is understanding the teaching/ learning process and the related skills required for effective teaching. Closely related to this course is another focusing on instructional technology. Counseling is another field where a level of understanding and skill is required for all who desire to teach effectively.

This third category encompasses a variety of courses that might be offered to assist students in organizing and administrating parachurch ministries. A field such as Christian camping would probably require a series of courses to equip a student for such specialized ministry. Many students are interested in day care or preschool ministries. A series of courses could be offered in such fields. One caution: it is counterproductive to attempt too much specialization at the undergraduate level.

Courses in the fourth category of curriculum emphasize the *personalization and application* of what is being learned. The student must develop his own personal philosophy of Christian education. This means that the student must weigh what he has learned in various courses, and he must incorporate it into a unified, biblically based, philosophically coherent, personalized system. This will be accomplished theoretically in an academic course such as "History and Philosophy of Christian Education." But opportunities must also be provided for practical implementation. A student training for professional ministry ought to study in a practicum where the curricular elements are integrated through experience. A student who participates in a field study or internship will understand better the relevance of classroom instruction. He will also be more specific in formulating a philosophy of Christian education that will prove invaluable as a guide for a lifetime of ministry.

Conclusion

The field of Church Education draws freely upon many other disciplines. While biblical theology is the base, other fields such as developmental psychology, sociology, educational psychology, and organizational administration contribute greatly to the course of study. But the theological base is that starting point. It is this base that guides in the philosophical determination of what fields to draw upon, and how they ought to be incorporated into the overall curriculum.

Education is neither dragged in nor superimposed upon the church. Christ's instruction to His disciples at the end of His ministry provides a solid foundation for Christian education. "Go therefore and make disciples of all the nations, baptizing them in the name of the Father and the Son and the Holy Spirit, teaching them to observe all that I commanded you; and lo, I am with you always, even to the end of the age" (Matthew 28:19-20, NASB).

The mandate to the church is spelled out clearly. The Greek

grammar in this passage indicates that Christ issued one command: "Make disciples." That is the mission of the church. That is the mandate for church education.

And in this passage there are three verb forms describing how the activity of making disciples is to be done. These are the three participles, which are subordinate to the finite verb of command: *going*, *baptizing*, and *teaching*. The implication of the first participle is that Christians are to be making disciples while they are going, wherever they are going.

But while "going" wherever God directs, Christians should concentrate on two specific activities. The first is baptizing. In the New Testament the act of water baptism was the extrinsic demonstration of a new relationship with God through Jesus Christ. It was a testimony to all that a person had been born into the family of God. As was stated earlier, the growth process begins with being born. Spiritually, growth begins when a person is born again, and baptism is the visible statement that this new birth has taken place. There is also a relationship, however defined, between water baptism and membership in the local body.

The third participle in this passage describes what must happen to these believers after they have been born again. Progress toward maturity is imperative. *Teaching* is the word Christ used to describe the ongoing process. Christians are to make disciples (1) by being available to God wherever they go; (2) by leading persons to make a personal commitment to Christ; and (3) by teaching them all things that have been commanded.

Even as Christ promised His disciples, so Christian professors today can expect His support as they minister to students. And students can expect that same support as they, in turn, minister to others. "And lo, I am with you always, even to the end of the age" (Matthew 28:20, NASB).

Notes

1. Frank E. Gaebelein, *Christian Education in a Democracy* (New York: Oxford, 1951), p. 30.
2. Ibid., p. 31.
3. Lois E. LeBar, *Focus on People in Church Education* (Old Tappan, N.J.: Revell, 1969), p. 165.
4. American Association of Bible Colleges, *Preparing Bible College Students for Ministries in Christian Education* (Wheaton: American Association of Bible Colleges, 1973), p. 10.
5. Lois E. LeBar, *Education That Is Christian* (Old Tappan, N.J.: Revell, 1958, p. 120.
6. Lawrence O. Richards, *Creative Bible Teaching* (Chicago: Moody, 1970), p. 73.
7. Herman Harrell Horne, *Jesus: The Master Teacher* (Grand Rapids: Kregel, 1964), p. 212; also published as *Teaching Techniques of Jesus.*
8. Richards, p. 49.
9. Frank E. Gaebelein, *The Pattern of God's Truth* (New York: Oxford, 1954), p. 23.
10. Lawrence O. Richards, *A Theology of Christian Education* (Grand Rapids: Zondervan, 1975), p. 309.
11. A. S. Neill, "Can I Come to Summerhill?" in *Readings in Educational Psychology Today* (Del Mar, Cal.: CRM Books, 1970), p. 6.

The Author

Ronald P. Chadwick is chairman of the Department of Christian Education at Grand Rapids Baptist Theological Seminary and a regular member of the summer faculty at the Institute for Christian School Administration, held annually at Winona Lake, Indiana, under the joint sponsorship of Grace Theological Seminary and the Association of Christian Schools, International. He holds the B.A. from Bryan College, the Th.M. from Dallas Theological Seminary, and the Ph.D. in Educational Administration from the University of Missouri. Before going to Grand Rapids, Dr. Chadwick served on the faculties of Arizona Bible College and Calvary Bible College. He is currently under contract with Mott Media to design and write an elementary curriculum package for Christian schools.

The Subject

Christian school education is one of the greatest challenges facing the Bible college movement today. Many faculty at the elementary and secondary levels of the Christian school movement have been trained in Bible colleges. Rightly so, for teaching in a Christian school is a distinctly Christian vocation and preparation of such a teacher is a distinctly theological discipline. Dr. Chadwick has given as much consideration to the subject of integration as any author in the book and his charts are particularly helpful as they can be related to almost any field of study.

8

CHRISTIAN SCHOOL EDUCATION

Ronald P. Chadwick

Introduction

What is education and how do we more specifically define Christian education? *Education is both the process of acquiring significant learning experiences as well as the product of a desired change of personality and behavior.* While education may be classified as both formal and informal, and more recently even "nonformal," the test of education is not how much the student knows, but what kind of person this educational process produces. If no observable character change is evident in the one who is supposedly involved in the educational process, then the entire effort may be said to be woefully lacking. In genuine education, personal change (process) and personality development (product) are both essential. This is achieved through guided, graded experience which meaningfully involves the learner. Change is something that the learner must experience in order to grow and develop.

Today educators recognize that the goal of education is the integration of a personality within a world view. Thus it may be concluded that education is the complete development of a personality for complete living consistent with a world view.

The guided, graded process presupposes three essential elements: a teacher, a learner, and an environment in which learning may successfully take place. This guided, graded, ongoing process must assist the student in making the learning experiences his own so that he may develop as a person, acquiring what he needs as an individual to achieve his full potential.

Nowhere is character or behavioral change and vital personal development more essential than in Christian education, elementary or secondary. The learner must exhibit outwardly what has taken place inwardly. He must give living, demonstrable proof of the power and strength of individual commitment. Apart from this the processes of his educational experiences have apparently failed and the product is merely a substitute for the real commodity, a genuine Christian. It is tragic that so many have been able to *verbalize* their Christianity without ever being able to *actualize* it, to put it to work in flesh and blood. This is where the principle of John 1:14 must become a reality in Christian education, the Word must become flesh.

Negative Description

Christian education is not an alias for *evangelism*. It must be recognized that Christian education in the context of the school is not primarily in the business of producing Christians. Though it is true (especially during the younger grades) that many children are brought into vital relationships with the living Savior, the Christian school is not an intellectual counterpart to the revival meeting. True Christian education can never take place until the student is indwelt by the One who guides us into all truth (John 16:13). Prior to this time the student is only receiving an education in a Christian atmosphere.

Also, Christian education is not just having a *faculty or student body composed of Christians*. Though it is true that, apart from these two prerequisites Christian education cannot exist, it does not follow that their presence provides a guarantee. When Robert Louis Stevenson was informed by his wife that the maid was a good church girl, he is alleged to have replied, "Then I would like some Christian broth." Just as a church girl could not make Christian broth, so the combination of a Christian teacher and student does not guarantee that the education is distinctively Christian. Even compulsory attendance at chapel services or other religious exercises does not produce Christian education.

The *sponsorship of the school* is not the deciding factor in whether the education is Christian. Many traditionally Christian colleges controlled by denominational groups have long since passed off the stage of Christian education. In some the apostasy was caused by allowing on the faculty, people who did not fulfill the first qualification of Christian teaching and this failure came because of theological indifference in the governing body. It would be easier to attempt Christian education with a Christian faculty in a state school than it would be on the campuses of these so-called Christian schools.

In addition to these, *the inclusion or exclusion of any course from the school curriculum* does not provide Christian education. In other words, just because the Bible is taught in a school does not make the education Christian, nor does its absence as a separate course of study make the education secular. Neither content nor subject matter alone can exclusively determine whether or not a school is engaged in education that is distinctively Christian.

Positive Definition

The apostle Paul gave a comprehensive principle of life when he wrote of the Lord, "He is before all things, and by him all things consist [hold together]" (Col. 1:17). The apostle John also stated an underlying principle of Christian education when he declared, "All things were made by him, and without him was not any thing made that was made" (John 1:3). Jesus Christ ought to have the preeminent place in all subject matter if it is true that in Him "are hid all the treasures of wisdom and knowledge" (Col. 2:3). The basis for Christian education is found in the Scriptures. In a very real sense, education, like every subject of the Bible college, is first a biblical or theological discipline and therefore must be firmly built on the foundation of biblical theology.

A complete definition of Christian school education at all levels would emphasize the following: Christian education deals with the process of teaching and learning, conducted by a Christian teacher from a Christian perspective. As both teacher and student are controlled by the Spirit of God, He brings all truth into a living relationship with the truth of the Word of God for the purpose of integrating the whole of the student's personality with the Word-centered, Christian, theistic world view, thereby enabling man to better serve and glorify God.

Biblical and Philosophical Formulation

A biblical philosophy of education emphasizing the theocentric view seeks to formulate a unified and coherent concept of God and

His Word in relationship to the creation and nature of man. This theistic philosophy becomes the central integrating core in Christian education. If such be the case, the educational process should develop the complete man of God, completely fitted for every good work for the glory of God. The measure of this complete man will be the stature of Christ, who is the core and integrator of the totality of Christian education.

This process of education will produce individuals who are not only capable of being functioning members of society, but also capable of being functioning members of the body of Christ, "unto the measure of the stature of the fullness of Christ" (Eph. 4:13).

Because Christian education is not merely an emphasis upon teaching precepts or concepts but rather communicating life, it has as its goal "the perfecting of the saints, for the work of the ministry for the edifying of the body of Christ" (Eph. 4:12), so "that we may present every man perfect [complete] in Christ" (Col. 1:28) and "in order that (*hina*) . . . we may grow into him in all respects" (author's translation of Eph. 4:14–15).

Philosophy of Teaching–Learning

What is a distinctly biblical philosophy of teaching and learning? Is the teacher's role primarily that of a disseminator of information or is it primarily the role of a facilitator of learning?

Educators generally are in agreement that teachers teach as they were taught. The Scripture gives us some interesting insight along these lines in Luke 6:39–40 as well as in Matthew 10:24–25. Literally translated the Luke 6 passage says, "Can one blind person guide another? Shall they not both fall into the ditch? A disciple is not above his teacher, but everyone having been perfected will be as his teacher." The Scripture is saying to us that as the teacher is, so the student will become.

Are there any specific passages of Scripture that can provide for us a model for the teaching-learning process? In Deuteronomy 6 Moses outlines the steps involved in ultimately producing the desired result: the Word of God becomes the controlling factor in the actions and attitudes, the private and public life of an individual. Matthew 28 and the words of our Lord emphasize that teaching should be done in such a way that the people might be able to observe the lesson in the life of the teacher.

Probably 1 Thessalonians 1 is one of the most complete passages dealing with the subject of the model teacher and model teaching. It provides for us some valuable insights. Paul begins in verse 2 by emphasizing the necessary preparation as he stresses making mention of his students unceasingly in his prayers. In verse 5 he emphasizes that the gospel came "not unto you in word only, but also in power, and in the Holy Ghost, and in much assurance; as ye know what manner of men we were among you for your sake." Then Paul says that they became followers, literally imitators, of him and as a result, even of the Lord and welcomed the word in much affliction with joy of the Holy Spirit. The result of this is seen in verses 7 and 8 where he says that they have become a model, example, or pattern to all of the ones believing in Macedonia or Achaia, and "also in every place your faith to God-ward is spread abroad so that we need not to speak any thing." Apparently, Paul is emphasizing that we must be concerned not only with the content that is being taught, but even how it is being taught, as well as the life of the individual who is actually doing the teaching.

In both 1 Thessalonians 1 and Colssians 1 the apostle Paul is trying to stress for us that true learning begins with the facts about God and ends with an increased knowledge of God, but *the real goal is to produce godliness in life.* True learning begins with information about God's plan and purpose and ends with the knowledge of His person, but again, the ultimate goal is to produce a "perfect" man. According to the Bible, learning for the sake of learning, to amass knowledge, is not acceptable. True learning is for living. This is even seen in Hebrews 5:11–13 where the writer says:

> Concerning whom we have much to say and hard to interpret since you have become dull in your hearings. For indeed because of the time you ought to be teachers you have need that someone teach you again the rudiments of the beginnings of the oracles of God and you have become as those having need of milk and of solid food. For everyone partaking of milk is without experience of the Word of righteousness for he is an infant (author's translation).

Verse 13 in the Authorized Version says that they were unskillful in the word of righteousness and this is often interpreted to mean that the individual did not have the ability to properly understand, interpret, and teach the Word. Even though this may be involved, the true meaning of "unskillful" is that they were lacking (were without experience) in relationship to the Word of righteousness. In other words, they knew the truth but were not experiencing it in their daily lives.

There are at least two dangers we always face in our teaching-learning situations. One is the danger of leading students to only verbalize their Christianity. We must recognize that verbalizing (expression) is the test or proof of teaching but actualizing (living) is the proof of real learning. Our goal should not be to simply lead students to verbalize their Christianity but to actualize it in their lives on a day-to-day basis. The second danger is to lead people to have only an experience or an emotional catharsis in relationship to the Word. The goal of Christian education as given to us in the Word is not just to know the truth but to implement the truth, to become truth. Moses says *teach* to *observe* to *do*; Jesus says *teach* to *observe*; while Paul emphasizes the fact that we should *teach* in order that people might be able to *walk* in a manner that is *worthy* of their calling.

Though it is true that John 1:14 refers specifically to the person of the Lord Jesus Christ, there is a sense in which the principle of this verse must still be applied in teaching-learning today. "The Word became flesh." Our educational system and approach to teaching-learning must be solidly based upon and centered in the Word, both Written and Living. Let us never forget that the ultimate test of Christian education is not academic excellence (as important as that is) but Christ-like character change. In Christian education true teaching-learning always aims at the purpose of living that is more Christ-like.

Philosophy of Curriculum

The word "curriculum" is derived from the Latin, *currere*, which means "to run" and in ancient Rome referred to "running or a race course." Traditionally the course or curriculum was considered the body of the content that the student covered in his educational progress. More recently the term connotes the activities of the student as he is engaged in various experiences which involve content.[1]

A traditional philosophy of curriculum, such as that espoused by Friedrich Herbart, emphasizes the outer factors of the student and therefore becomes teacher-centered. In Dewey's progressive education, the inner factors are stressed with the result that the education becomes student-centered. For years Christians were content to buy up whatever educational ideas were popular at the time, whether Herbart and traditionalism, or Dewey and progressivism. But Christian education is distinctive and will not allow the same integrating factor as would be found in a man-made system.

Is it not sufficient to have a God-centered or Bible-centered education? Certainly if God and the Bible are not at the center of the curriculum it can never be Christian. In reality, however, God never meant the Written Word and the Living Word to be separated. The *integrating factor in the student's Christian life* obviously should be the Living Word, Jesus Christ, who is the "same yesterday, today, and forever" (Heb. 13:8). With Jesus Christ there is a nonterminating core and all of life is integrated around a Person who never changes.

But the Living Word can only be known through the revelation of the Written Word; this is the *integrating factor in Christian education* for discovered truth. A God-centered or Bible-centered approach is not incorrect but it does not clearly show the unity of Jesus Christ the Living Word and the Bible, the Written Word. The statement "educational philosophy is Word-centered" shows the balance between the outer and inner factors, the Bible and Jesus Christ.

Thus, the center of Christian education, and specifically the integrating principle of curriculum, does not change with every new idea on the educational market, nor is it centered in sinful human life, but rather in Life Himself; fulness of life; eternality of life; the Living Word revealed in the Written Word. It is not the book but the Person revealed in the book who gives the dynamic and vitality needed in a distinctive Christian philosophy of curriculum at any level of education.

Christian education must be a balance of both content and experience, truth and life. Apart from the Written Word (content) the Living Word (experience) can never be known. The concept of a God-centered, Bible-centered approach is best drawn together, then, in a clear concept of the Word-centered approach. No other concept can compare in immutability, vitality, and power. The concept-competence curriculum, from a Christian perspective, therefore, is an attempt to integrate the student's cognitive development with the development of his total personality in relation to a thoroughly biblical world-and-life-view for the purpose of producing character change that demonstrates maturity in Jesus Christ. This approach to curriculum is solidly based in and dependent upon God's revelation yet reasonably and rationally ties it to reality.

Model For Integration

Much of Christian education in the past has been secular education with a coating of Christianity. Too frequently morning devotions, prayer, or Bible reading were expected to exert a hallowed influence upon the work of the day. Even the inclusion of a Bible course in the curriculum often did no more than add "religion" to an essentially secular content.

Historically the word *Christian* always referred to a world view based upon the Bible. To attempt Christian education by adding a Christian frosting to a cake of man-made and man-centered philosophy is neither consistent with Christianity nor is it distinctive. All four basic areas of curricular content—abstract science, social science, physical science, and fine arts—must be interpreted and integrated within a recognized world view and therefore, for the Christian, it must be a Christian theistic world view.

What then is integration? Probably much of what has been attempted in the past in the area of *integration* in Christian education would better be described as *correlation*. To correlate means to "have a common relation," to "show a causal relationship to two things." It directly implies that two things are complementary to each other, such as husband and wife. To correlate two concepts common to each other is simply to show their common relationship. To integrate these concepts, however, would be to unite them into a single unit which may be expanded as a result of the union. *Integration is the bringing together of parts into a whole.* In Christian education it is not only the living union of concepts with concepts, or truth with truth, but the living union of the subject and the life of teachers and administration as well as students. The eternal, infinite pattern of God's written truth must be woven together with all of truth and all of life.

What kind of model is necessary for implementing integration? Model 1 illustrates the implementing of integration. The first component is *truth with truth*—the revealed truth and discovered truth. The second is a *biblical philosophy of teaching-learning* which stresses the importance of the student's need to be stimulated to learn and then guided into the truth which is so essential in teaching and learning. God has purposed that we be taught in such a way that we will want to act upon His teaching. It is this attitude teachers and parents ought to have when instructing children. What is needed in our approach to teaching and learning is to communicate concepts in a meaningful way and then to apply and utilize the concepts and skills learned, developing competency or mastery.

The third element, *biblical theology*, provides for us the *structure* or basic principles and concepts, the framework which holds all the Bible together. Based on an adequate exegesis of Scripture we are then able to develop the doctrinal threads. It is these doctrines, principles, or concepts which are actually supra-, trans- or cross-

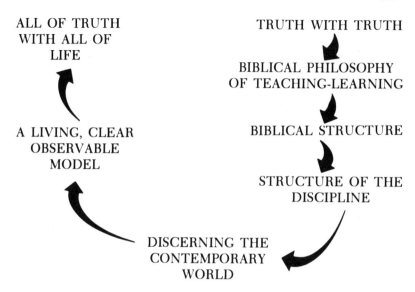

ALL OF TRUTH
WITH ALL OF
LIFE

TRUTH WITH TRUTH

BIBLICAL PHILOSOPHY
OF TEACHING-LEARNING

A LIVING, CLEAR
OBSERVABLE
MODEL

BIBLICAL STRUCTURE

STRUCTURE OF THE
DISCIPLINE

DISCERNING THE
CONTEMPORARY
WORLD

Model 1. Implementing Integration

cultural and provide us with the ability to relate biblical truth to the subject area or discipline we are dealing with.

The *structure of the discipline* is the framework for the subject area or the principles or concepts without which we could not design a particular subject area or discipline. The structure for the discipline never changes and the structure for any given discipline (when properly discerned as principles apart from interpretation or application) is exactly the same for Christian and non-Christian.

Discerning the contemporary world (life-awareness and life-relatedness) is crucial because our goal in Christian education is to equip our students not only to be functioning members of the body of Christ, but functioning members of society. We and they must have an awareness of what is happening in the world around us. It is possible for us not to be fully apprised of what is going on in the contemporary world. As a result we are not only incapable of communicating to the needs of the world today, but even more tragically, are incapable of equipping our students to be able to relate biblical truth and thus be able to minister to the needs of a world lost without Jesus Christ.

A *living, clear, observable model* is the final element in the process of implementing integration. Christian education understands the necessity of demonstrating a clear, observable model of the reality of the person of Jesus Christ, and it demonstrates the feasibility of the practical implementation of this concept. Teachers and professors must provide for students clear models of the reality of the revelation they attempt to communicate both in and out of the classroom. As young people grow up they often find and seek to emulate individuals who seem particularly attractive. The young child may begin this process of identification with his mother, following her around the house in an attempt to imitate her behavior.

Later other persons become objects of identification. This process is one of the ways people learn, and with a variety of constructive personalities available, the outcome can be positive including the acquisition of attitudes, values, and interests, as well as skills and practices. However, in some of our schools, the range of constructive personalities close enough to the student to permit attraction and emulation is much too narrow, so that many young people find no one on the faculty enough like them to encourage identification. Instructional planning should seek to use all the important resources, especially the human resources, that can possibly be provided for learning.

The apostle John states, "The Word was made flesh and dwelt among us and we beheld his glory" (John 1:14). Essentially John was saying he saw Him, he touched Him, he saw Him operate, he saw Him reflect the realities of what He spoke, and he saw consistency not only in the words Jesus spoke but in the life He lived. What our students need to see so desperately today is a clear, observable model of the reality of Jesus Christ and a communication both by words and life that it is absolutely feasible to live a life of faith. This is not only the integration of truth with truth but *truth with truth with life*.

Model 2 illustrates concept integration. It shows the process of the concept of the discipline (C.D.) with the biblical concept (B. C.) from biblical theology to arrive at the biblically integrated concept (B. I. C.) The movement is from the C.D. to the B.C. to the B.I.C.

Model 3 illustrates life integration. Teachers are often required to teach abstract concepts, both in biblical as well as practical areas of the curriculum. In order to make the abstract more meaningful we go to a concrete illustration from the natural realm and use it to make our teaching more life-related. At this particular point the process is neither correlation not integration. True integration actually takes place at the step we call life application or life integration.

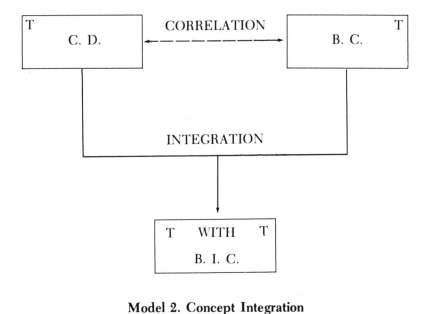

Model 2. Concept Integration

CONCRETE
NATURAL
ILLUSTRATION

"LIFE
RELATED"

ABSTRACT
BIBLICAL
CONCEPT

TRUTH	TRUTH	TRUTH	TRUTH
WITH	WITH	WITH	WITH
LIFE	LIFE	LIFE	LIFE

Model 3. Life Integration

Actually there are two different aspects of the process of integration. The first is the academic or the theoretical type of integration where concept is integrated with concept. But there is also (wherever possible) the need for applying these concepts practically in terms of real life application. Model 4 shows the correlation. In some areas the theoretical aspect of integration is not capable of being accomplished, as in the areas of vocational work or even in some aspects of physical education. Then the integration step is actually a life integration or a practical rather than theoretical aspect of integration.

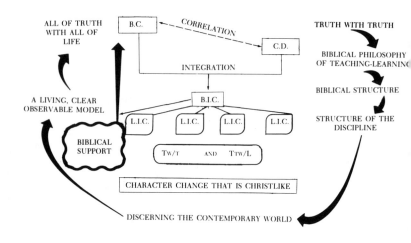

Model 4. Correlation-Integration

Summary

I believe that it is possible to summarize the crucial subject of integration but not necessarily to draw final conclusions. It appears that the principle to be drawn from our brief look at the subject is that learning is most effective when that which is learned is integrated with all of truth and all of life. Ideally, this is a never-ending process. Even when you have taught a group to be honest, the task is not complete until the individual student is able to bring the concept of honesty into every area of his life. Rather than learning truth in isolation, this is an attempt to learn truth in relationships: truth with truth, and ultimately, truth with life. True integration means that ideas learned in one situation should not just be correlated (shown to be complementary) with another situation, but they should be vitally united and in this way transferred to other areas and even to other cultural settings. If we are truly dealing with principles or concepts, then these principles or concepts will always have the capacity of being trans- or cross-cultural.

To the extent that the truths presented are integrated with the truth of the Written Word, and then transformed into experience both in and out of the classroom, to that extent maturity in Christ is developed and the ultimate goal of Christian education is reached. Christian education evaluation is dependent upon integration. As Paul wrote in Colossians 3:17, "Whatsoever ye do in word or deed, do all in the name of the Lord Jesus, giving thanks to God and the Father by Him."

Notes

1. Lois E. LeBar, *Education That Is Christian* (Westwood, N.J.: Revell, 1958), p. 203.

The Author

Samuel Hsu is an accomplished piano artist as well as classroom teacher and well qualified to prepare our chapter on the teaching of sacred music in the Bible college. He serves on the music faculty of Philadelphia College of Bible. His professional preparation includes both the B.S. and B.Mus. degrees from Philadelphia College of Bible and a Ph.D. in music from the University of California at Santa Barbara. He has also studied privately with Mme. Rosina Lhevinne at the Juilliard School.

The Subject

Dr. Hsu raises a crucial question in his first paragraph: "How much value do Christians place upon music?" He then proceeds to show the role of music in the total milieu of Christian worship and service with special emphasis on the development of the biblical preparation to serve God in music ministry. The chapter bears the imprint of a theologically sensitive artist whose concern for the Bible college transcends the boundaries of his own discipline. His consideration of David, Paul, Luther, and Bach as proponents of music used to the glory of God lays a good foundation for the encouragement of creativity in composers and performers.

9

SACRED MUSIC

Samuel Hsu

George Santayana offers an incisive definition of music when he says; "Sound readily acquires ideal values. It has power in itself to engross attention and at the same time may be easily diversified, so as to become a symbol for other things."[1] Thus, music is both an artistic discipline in its own right and a symbol for life's many experiences. We use music to express love, to inspire heroism, to instill piety; we welcome the presence of music for all it can offer. Furthermore, we acknowledge the importance of talent and training in the production of good music; and to the degree that we value music, to that degree we encourage the cultivation of musical talents. This brings me to the crucial question: *How much value do Christians place upon music*? The justification for music in the Bible college curriculum and the process of integrating that musical learning with biblical faith depend entirely on an accurate answer to this question.

Some pastors believe that music is merely a supplementary aspect of church ministry. They suggest that a neglect of music is to the gain of ministry in the Word of God. A well-known speaker advised a gathering of Bible college students, "Since the vast majority of Americans listen to country and western music, the church should concentrate its efforts on this style." Apparently one can have a clear vision of music as a tool for evangelism, yet disregard any aesthetic implications of the formula. To understand the function of sacred music, we need to look for a better rationale.

Introduction

Martin Luther and Johann Sebastian Bach are two names that quickly come to mind whenever there is a discussion of sacred music. In Luther we find the ideal spokesman, a theologian who was not afraid to accord to music all the privileges of service in the life of the believer. In Bach we have a great church musician whose large body of compositions stands as a brilliant testimony of what sacred music can be. Paul Nettl explains the significance of their joint contribution to the music of the Christian church:

> The jubilant faith of Luther, his joyful experience of God, his teaching of salvation by grace, caused him to break out in exultation before his God, and his feelings could find expression only in music. . . .
> The objective piety of the Middle Ages has given way to an eminently subjective one—salvation by faith. Here grace, devotion, comfort, and joy are personally experienced, and find their expression in music that stems from the innermost heart of man. Bach's melodies reflect his personal experience. For Bach, like Luther, received his inspiration from the Bible with its impressive language, and he approached his God without the mediation of the Church.[2]

To understand Luther's theology of music therefore is to have a clear rationale for sacred music and to possess the needed justification for its inclusion as a scholarly discipline in a Bible college program. To listen to Bach is to witness Luther's theory put into practice.

Music, says Luther, "is an endowment and a gift of God. . . . I place music next to theology and give it the highest praise."[3] He insists that "before a youth is ordained into the ministry, he should practice music in school."[4] Luther recognizes God as the source of music and expects every minister to study music. Music is not an option for Luther, it is "an essential ingredient for the life of the spirit and soul. . . . a power for life and order."[5]

Three important aspects of music's ministry must take place in our lives if we are to experience what Luther and Bach experienced. First, we must learn to appreciate music for its own sake; for, it is a gift from God to charm our spirits and to soothe our tattered nerves. "It also drives away the devil and makes people cheerful," says Luther.[6] Bach's large output in instrumental music attests to his commitment to the art of music aside from any textual consideration. In the Goldberg Variations, for example, Bach's brilliant pupil Goldberg was in the employ of the Russian baron, Count Kaiserling who was afflicted with insomnia. To relieve the misery, the count solicited Bach for some musical medicine which Goldberg would administer nightly. The end result was a work of surpassing brilliance and beauty, a work universally acknowledged to be the crowning summation of the Baroque variation technique. Such is Bach's respect for the power of music not only to delight but also to heal.

Secondly, we must discover those powerful musical impulses which, in cooperation with the sacred text, will awaken us to the truths of the Scripture. "Bettered and strengthened in the faith through His holy Word, driven into the heart with sweet song" is how Luther puts it.[7] To this end Bach wrote numerous motets, passions, and hundreds of cantatas. They were meant for the edification of the saints, even as preachers' sermons are.

Thirdly, we must transcend the healing and teaching aspects and enter the realm of worship in our music. "Sing joyfully to the Lord, you righteous; it is fitting for the upright to praise him. Praise the Lord with the harp; make music to him on the ten-stringed lyre. Sing to him a new song; play skillfully, and shout for joy" (Ps. 33:1–3, NIV). It always pleases the Lord when His people offer as a sacrifice what He has graciously given to them in the first place. The same applies to music. The more we allow music to heal us and teach us, the more it will assist us in our worship. "A new miracle deserves a new song," says Luther.[8]

Should not the daily ministry of the Holy Spirit in our lives result in a daily worship in music? When we listen to the "Credo" from Bach's Mass in B Minor, we hear not only a vivid portrayal of the text from the Nicene Creed; we hear not only a glorious demonstration of Bach's compositional skills: we hear Bach in worship; we hear him expressing to God his own feelings and convictions for the truth and grandeur of the text. When we can appreciate music this deeply, we have allowed this gift from God its fullest ministry in our lives.

We must not deprive ourselves of this comprehensive musicianship in our church life or in our Bible college preparation. Each of the three aspects meets a vital need in our spiritual lives. The first points to the *nature of music* itself. The right sound of music can set the mood, ease the mind, and prepare the heart for the entrance of the Word of God. This is called *musical therapy.*

The second aspect deals with the *biblical content* itself. How often have our hearts been stirred in recalling our hearing of Handel's *Messiah* when any of its scriptural texts is cited in sermon or in conversation? Is this not *musical theology*, the embodiment of biblical truth in aesthetic form? The third touches on the whole *purpose of redemption.* Are we not redeemed from our sin in order that we may live and worship God forever? But must we wait until we get to heaven to do that? Is not God pleased when we employ all our musical resources to tell Him how much we love Him? Yes, this is music at its best. This is *musical theopathy*!

Biblical Foundation

The Bible abounds in musical references. From Genesis to Revelation God's people live, move, and have their being musically. Music marks their joy, their sorrow, their faith, their doubt: in short, music embraces the whole spiritual experience. "Where morning dawns and evening fades you call forth songs of joy," says David (Ps. 65:8, NIV). From this vast source of music in the Bible, I have chosen to examine three areas which together provide a biblical norm for music: (1) the career of David, (2) the ministry of the Levitical musicians, and (3) the experience and instruction of the apostle Paul.

The Career of David

Just as Luther and Bach stand out in church history, David stands out in biblical history as God's musician *par excellence*. We have a description of his musical ability (1 Sam. 16:18), a sizable repertoire of his creative output (the many psalms of David), and numerous accounts of his musical activities (eg., 1 Sam. 16:14–23; 2 Sam. 6:12–22).

In 1 Samuel 16:18 (NIV) we find David's qualifications: he is skilled ("knows how to play the harp"); he has a good character ("is a brave man and a warrior"); he has a commanding presence ("speaks well and is a fine-looking man"); and most importantly, he is spiritual ("the Lord is with him"). What awesome requirements they are for God's musician.

Today we read the psalms mainly for their literary content; but, each psalm was originally conceived as an artistic composition in which music and poetry 'together communicated aspects of God's greatness to the listeners. The musical instructions which accompany the psalms indicate a considerable degree of sophistication in structure and instrumentation. I am especially fascinated to observe that some of the psalms were written for tunes already composed for other purposes. The melodies for "The Death of the Son" and "The Doe of the Morning" became "hymn tunes" of David's psalms.

Likewise, in our own repertoire, Hans Leo Hassler's love song "My Peace of Mind Is Shattered by a Tender Maiden's Charms" became the German chorale "O Sacred Head Now Wounded"; and George Frederic Handel's secular operatic duet formed the basis of the chorus "For Unto Us a Child is Born" in his sacred oratorio *Messiah.* In these we witness modern examples of *contrafactum* whose roots go all the way back to David's psalms.

Besides the technical references which suggest a rich and lively musical practice in David's court, there are the biographical references which tell us that the psalms were a natural outgrowth of intense encounters with God on the part of David and the other psalmists. To cite two examples: Psalm 3 was written when David fled from his son Absalom, and Psalm 51 when David repented from his sin of adultery.

Our psalmist may address issues of theology proper, christology, soteriology, or eschatology; but he always speaks through a beautiful musical composition and in a highly personal language. Anne Ortlund poses a probing question when she asks: "Would you agree that a worship service is man's highest art form?"[9] If we answer in the affirmative, we are also obliged to acknowledge that the music we bring before God must represent our supreme artistic effort and reflect our genuine spiritual life. C. S. Lewis says that the psalmists "in telling everyone to praise God are doing what all men do when they speak of what they care about."[10] Can the world know how much we care about God by our music? More importantly, can God?

Like his psalms, David's life shows how much he cared about God. Two events in particular are worth mentioning here because of the lessons God's musicians can learn.

The first is the story of David playing his harp for King Saul. David's music calmed Saul's hostile disposition. This should tell us something about the awesome power of music. And I have no doubt that David's playing was polished and appropriate for the occasion. But we have only half the story if we fail to realize that David was performing a spiritual service. Saul was out of fellowship with God because of his disobedience and was afflicted by an evil spirit as a result. David was called upon to bring healing to Saul by means of music. It was therefore not a mere harp recital which David was performing. It was a ministry of comfort rendered on behalf of a tormented man who was nevertheless God's anointed one. And God honored David's service, for the Bible says: "Whenever the [evil] spirit from God came upon Saul, David would take his harp and play. Then relief would come to Saul; he would feel better, and the evil spirit would leave him" (1 Sam. 16:23, NIV).

On the surface our second story from David's life seems to have little to do with music, though it carries even greater significance for sacred music. It is the occasion of the ark's entrance into Jerusalem during which we are told that "David, wearing a linen ephod, danced before the Lord with all his might, while he and the entire house of Israel brought up the ark of the Lord with shouts and the sound of trumpets" (2 Sam. 6:14–15, NIV). It was a moment of great joy for Israel. The return of the ark signifies the return of the shekinah glory, the visible symbol of God's presence. David's response is instructive for all of us. There was already music accompanying the celebration; but, David, who was so overwhelmed by the fact that full fellowship and blessing had been restored to Israel by the return of the ark, found even the greatest music to be inadequate for the occasion. So, with all the might of his physical and spiritual being David danced before the Lord. It was a visual alleluia. It was David's greatest psalm. It shows us that spiritual joy can and must have a physical response. The joyful impulse in turn is translated into a rhythm which forms the basis of a spiritual dance, a spiritual song. Susanne Langer says it perfectly: "The commanding form of a piece of music contains its basic rhythm, which is at once the source of its organic unity and its total feeling."[11]

Finally, it should not surprise us to note that the story of David's dancing (2 Sam. 6) is followed by the account of David's desire to build the temple of the Lord (2 Sam. 7). There is a correlation between these two events which goes beyond their textual affinity. We need to see David's motivation for service (chapter 7) in light of his deep love for the Lord (chapter 6). This is the strongest case for sacred music. For music not only helps us come to grips with our love for God, but it also leads us to perform spiritual tasks which are apropos to the love we have declared to God.

The Ministry of the Levitical Musicians

"Your procession has come into view, O God, the procession of my God and King into the sanctuary. In front are the singers, after them the musicians; with them are the maidens playing tambourines" (Ps. 68:24–25, NIV). If David was God's virtuoso soloist, the Levitical musicians were God's symphony orchestra. The impulse which prompted David to creative heights individually was also at work in the Levitical musicians corporately. Let us look at two such instances.

Second Chronicles 7 records the dedication of the temple under King Solomon. God showed His love and approval by filling the temple with His shekinah glory. Like David, the musicians re-

sponded with expressions of great joy. They made music and pro-
claimed: "His love endures forever." Psalm 30, a psalm written for
the dedication of the temple, says: "You turned my wailing into
dancing; you removed my sackcloth and clothed me with joy, that
my heart may sing to you and not be silent. O Lord my God, I will
give you thanks forever" (vv. 11–12, NIV).

Second Chronicles 20 describes an entirely different setting for
their musical ministry. It is the military conflict of Judah and King
Jehoshaphat against her heathen neighbors. The centerpiece of this
drama is the amazing ministry of the musicians. The Moabites and
Ammonites had declared war against Judah. The Lord assured
Jehoshaphat: "The battle is not yours, but God's" (v. 15).
Jehoshaphat responded in faith. "After consulting the people,
Jehoshaphat appointed men to sing to the Lord and to praise him for
the splendor of his holiness as they went out at the head of the army,
saying: 'Give thanks to the Lord, for his love endures forever '"
(v. 21).

This was no victory celebration *after* the war. This was a victory
proclamation *before* the war. How it must have thrilled God's heart
to hear such music. And their faith was not misplaced; God kept His
promise and delivered Judah from her enemies. This is sacred music
at its best. This is *bona fide* theopathy.

The Experience and Instruction of the Apostle Paul

The intensity of music-making in the Old Testament was not
diminished in the New Testament. Christ's death and resurrection
have assured us victory over our enemy, death. "Where, O death, is
your victory? Where, O death, is your sting?" says Paul (1 Cor.
15:55, NIV). This is both theology and theopathy, and in each case it
calls for an expression commensurate with its true significance. Paul
declares: "I will pray with my spirit, but I will also pray with my
mind. I will sing with my spirit, but I will also sing with my mind" (1
Cor. 14:15, NIV). In Ephesians 5:18–20 and Colossians 3:16 Paul
explains what it means to sing in the spirit and to sing with the mind.

I will sing with the spirit. Ephesians 5:18 commands: "Do not get
drunk on wine, which leads to debauchery. Instead, be filled with
the Spirit" (NIV). And what are we to do when we are filled with the
Spirit? Verse 19 answers: "Speak to one another with psalms, hymns
and spiritual songs. Sing and make music in your heart to the Lord."
Music-making is the direct result of the filling of the Holy Spirit. We
are to let music permeate our entire lives, "always giving thanks to

God the Father for everything, in the name of our Lord Jesus Christ" (v. 20). If I understand these verses correctly, Christians should be the most musical people in the world.

I will also sing with my mind. We have already observed that, in the Old Testament, much of God's Word was clothed in music. The same idea is found in Colossians 3:16: "Let the word of Christ dwell in you richly as you teach and admonish one another with all wisdom, and as you sing psalms, hymns and spiritual songs with gratitude in your hearts to God" (NIV). So, as we grow in the knowledge of God, let us make sure we have not only pure doctrine but also a musical theology.

In ending this brief biblical survey I cannot resist referring to Paul's own musical testimony in Acts 16:25–34. Paul and Silas were in the Philippian prison because of their Christian witness. Instead of feeling sad, they sang hymns of praise to the Lord and to the hearing of their fellow prisoners. God applauded their performance by loosening all the locks and chains in the prison and by giving the gift of salvation to the Philippian jailor. This was true evangelism in music. It was music that reflected the power and majesty of God.

Philosophical Formulation

The brief biblical survey clearly shows that God loves to see His saints give their emotion the fullest expression in music. Why, then, do we find Bible teachers who are so reluctant to embrace music as a fullfledged partner in the ministry? Perhaps because the preacher who finds music negligible has strong support from the early church fathers. Clement of Alexandria says it best: "We need . . . the word of adoration only, not harps or drums or pipes or trumpets."[12] Lee Olson points out that such an attitude was the result of a world view heavily influenced by Platonism, a philosophy which enthrones the invisible realm of ideas while minimizing the visible realm of God's creation.[13] Perhaps Christians have borrowed the Platonic model and have rightly enthroned the Word of God, but wrongly minimized the sanctity and power of God's creative gifts. He who despises music despises a precious gift whose Giver is none other than God Himself.

Then, we have some who are interested in music only for its usefulness in evangelism. Any style that does not effectively serve the purpose is discouraged. This too does not harmonize with the biblical teaching on music. It is a form of aesthetic utilitarianism. Such people do not so much despise music as abuse it.

What, then, should our attitude be? What, then, is the proper Christian aesthetic? Very simply, we must respect God's creative order and recognize that man is both privileged and obliged to express himself by means of his God-given creativity. This is a concept at once simple and profound. God, who is before creation, reveals Himself in creation. Man, who has been created, reveals himself by creating works of art which reflect his needs, desires, personality, and in the case of a Christian, his experience with the Lord.

In recent times a number of authors have given eloquent expression to the subject of Christian aesthetics. Dorothy Sayers advocates a Trinitarian aesthetic based on Christ's incarnation as opposed to a unitarian one derived from Platonism. As Christ is the express Image of the Father and not a mere copy, "the true work of art, then, is something new."[14] The aesthetic experience which each work of art communicates must necessarily be something new. "The poet himself did not know what his experience was until he created the poem which revealed his own experience to himself."[15]

H. R. Rookmaaker is equally emphatic in his plea for a Christian commitment to the arts. Citing the paintings of Rembrandt and the music of Bach as examples of Christian influence in the past, he urges Christian artists of today to strive for a renewal of our culture through a consecrated pursuit of the arts. "Weep, pray, think and work" is his advice.[16] He warns against utilitarianism, even evangelistic utilitarianism. "Art has too often become insincere and second-rate in its very effort to speak to all people and to communicate a message that art was not meant to communicate."[17] This may sound harsh to some, but it shows Rookmaaker's respect for the arts and his yearning to see the arts become all that God wants them to be in the life of the believer. "The Christian's art must be Christian in a deep sense, showing the fruits of the Spirit in a positive mentality and with excitement for the greatness of the life we were given."[18]

Harold Best, dean of the Wheaton Conservatory of Music, is probably the leading proponent of this philosophy among Christian musicians. In a lecture given for the National Association of Schools of Music in 1976[19] and in a subsequent interview in *Christianity Today*,[20] Best called for a comprehensive musicianship in Christian education based on a theology of creativity. He sees the practice of music within the creative mandate established by God the Creator and argues that the believer's relationship to God the Creator should be greater and not lesser because of his new birth. He blames the insipid quality of so much of our contemporary church music on the church's failure to recognize this creative mandate. "We have concluded that the best way to reach others is with familiarity. So our witness in music or art is based on what the world is already doing—and really invented—in the first place. We borrow it and give it back second-rate and second-hand."[21]

Church music, according to Sayers, Rookmaaker, and Best, should not only be as good as the world's music but better. We can no longer hide behind Platonic piety and consider the practice of music unworthy of Christian involvement. We can no longer raise the banner of evangelistic utilitarianism and make excuses for our aesthetic myopia and our artistic inferiority. If these authors have taught us anything, it is that every musician who names the Name of Christ has the obligation to develop his talent to the fullest and to confront the church and the world with music that is technically unashamed and spiritually indicative of his personal relationship with God.

The implication of such a philosophy is that while the Christian shares with the world the common bond of creativity, he is nonetheless distinguished from his non-Christian colleagues on account of his salvation. What, in actuality, are these similarities and differences?

Obviously, there is a common fund of technique from which all artists draw to produce their works. Each artist will be judged by his talent and his craftsmanship. What Igor Stravinsky says of himself is true of all artists, whether or not they wish to acknowledge it: "I take no pride in my artistic talents; they are God-given and I see absolutely no reason to become puffed up over something that one has received."[22] By the same token, when he told the students at Harvard how he composed, he was indicating a creative process common to all composers, Christian or secular:

> All creation presupposes at its origin a sort of appetite that is brought on by the foretaste of discovery. This foretaste of the creative act accompanies the intuitive grasp of an unknown entity already possessed but not yet intelligible, an entity that will not take definite shape except by the action of a constantly vigilant technique.

> This appetite that is aroused in me at the mere thought of putting in order musical elements that have attracted my attention is not at all a fortuitous thing like inspiration, but as habitual and periodic, if not as constant, as a natural need.

The premonition of an obligation, this foretaste of a pleasure, this conditioned reflex, as a modern physiologist would say, shows clearly that it is the idea of discovery and hard work that attracts me.

The very act of putting my work on paper, of, as we say, kneading the dough, is for me inseparable from the pleasure of creation. So far as I am concerned, I cannot separate the spiritual effort from the psychological and physical effort; they confront me on the same level and do not present a hierarchy.[23]

But there is also a Christian distinctive in the arts. Jacques Maritain's remark is illuminating: "The content of the poetic intuition is both the reality of the things of the world and the subjectivity of the poet, both obscurely conveyed through an intentional or spiritualized emotion. The soul is known in the experience of the world and the world is known in the experience of the soul."[24] Now, there should be no argument that the spiritualized emotion which inspires a Christian must necessarily differ from that which inspires a non-Christian.

We need not look very far for instances of non-Christian inspiration. Many contemporary artists are avowedly non-Christian and view their lives in existential terms. The creative process becomes a way of authenticating an otherwise meaningless existence. Summarizing the *raison d'être* of poetry as articulated by Archibald MacLeish, Rollo May says: "The poet's labor is to struggle with the meaninglessness and silence of the world until he can force it to mean; until he can make the silence answer and the Non-being be."[25] Quoting a Chinese poet, MacLeish himself says it even more poignantly: "We poets struggle with Non-being to force it to yield Being. We knock upon silence for an answering music."[26] We too struggle, we too knock, but not against the meaninglessness and silence of the world. The psalmist who asks "Why are you downcast, O my soul?" also reassures: "Put your hope in God, for I will yet praise him, my Savior and my God" (Ps. 42:11, NIV). The apostle Paul who exhorts us to work out our salvation with fear and trembling also reminds us that it is God who works in us both to will and to do of His good pleasure (Phil. 2:12–13). Francis Schaeffer calls them the minor and major themes of the Christian arts. "Man is fallen and flawed [minor theme], but he is redeemable on the basis of Christ's work [major theme]. This is beautiful. This is optimism."[27] We struggle against sin, but we also triumph through the Lord Jesus Christ.

Practical Application

It is clear from what has been said so far that music is both a precious gift and a demanding profession. It originates in God's creative order and flows into spiritual ministry. It is not only God's greatest gift next to theology, it is also to be used in cooperation with the ministry of the Word.

In an essay addressing Bible college personnel and the membership of the National Church Music Fellowship, J. C. Macaulay made a simple but essential point which we will do well to heed. "Church music is music. Therefore the minister of music should be a musician both by native ability and by training."[28] To provide such training is the mission of Bible college music departments. We must provide the best training possible. We must produce students who possess comprehensive musicianship. Their equipment, compositional skills, performance abilities and knowledge of music history must be unquestionably excellent. Not realizing that this is precisely what our Bible college music departments are attempting to do and not being familiar with our curricula, many gifted young musicians in our churches have gone to secular conservatories for their training and have thus failed to avail themselves of an educational opportunity specially designed for them. We must make them realize that their music does not suffer when they opt for a Bible college education. Instead, they will get the best in both fields: Bible and music. Our churches are blessed with a large number of people who have expertise in either the Bible *or* music. What we need are more individuals who can handle the Bible *and* music with equal competence. This is the aim of music education in the Bible college.

More importantly, we must recognize the ministry of the Holy Spirit. Sacred music, by definition, is sanctified music, Spirit-filled music. "Spiritual force is an empowering which is far more essential than natural skills, understanding and inspiration," says John Wilson.[29] In 1 Chronicles 25 we are told that some were set apart (sanctified) for the ministry of music. They were all trained and skilled in music for the Lord. Young and old, student and teacher, they all cast lots for their duties. Likewise, a music department in a Bible college is more than a place of learning. It is a place of spiritual ministry for teacher and student alike. "Spiritual preparation for service is essential," says Alfred Lunde. "We must remember the principle that *sin and service do not mix.*"[30] And he is speaking to Christian musicians. Let us not forget the psalmists' lament during their exile in Babylon: "How can we sing the songs of the Lord while in a foreign land? If I forget you, O Jerusalem, may my right hand forget its skill. May my tongue cling to the roof of my mouth if I do not remember you, if I do not consider Jerusalem my highest joy" (Ps. 137:4–6, NIV). If we are out of fellowship with God, we are also out of sacred music. In the final analysis, we can achieve total integration of faith and learning only by the power of the Holy Spirit. For only the Holy Spirit can anoint our learning and stir our creativity to turn everything we have learned into a vehicle of praise.

Having established the biblical and spiritual foundations for sacred music, we nevertheless need to understand something of its educational procedures. Johann Nikolaus Forkel, the first biographer of Johann Sebastian Bach, made two profound statements about Bach the music educator. First, he says that "to teach well a man needs to have a full mind. He must have discovered how to meet and have overcome the obstacles in his own path before he can be successful in teaching others how to avoid them."[31] Obviously, Bach qualified. Second, Forkel observes that "as long as his pupils were under his instruction Bach did not allow them to study any but his own works and the classics. The critical sense, which permits a man to distinguish good from bad, develops later than the aesthetic faculty and may be blunted and even destroyed by frequent contact with bad music."[32]

The lessons are simple: (1) The young musicians under our charge have no other models but us. Let us be the best we can, even if it is only for our students' sake. (2) The repertoire we choose for them to study will invariably inform their minds and shape their aesthetics. Dare we compromise on the quality of music we teach?

It should sober us to realize that our students copy us daily. They copy our technique; they copy our musicianship; they copy our spiritual attitude. If we strive to improve the current state of church music, they too will join our ranks, even if at times they seem to rebelliously revel in the status quo. If we condone and wallow in mediocrity in the name of being "with it," they too will be happy to settle for less than the best. What Frank Gaebelein said in 1954 still needs to be said today:

> There is a great deal of music in favor among evangelicals that justly falls under condemnation; cheap, vulgar, and aesthetically false, its use for good ends does not alter its character. The fact is that American evangelicalism urgently needs to progress to a higher level of music. In the recognition of this need and in doing something about it, Christian education faces a great challenge.[33]

Bible colleges cannot meet this challenge alone. Our churches must help. Great church music has always come out of strong church patronage. Our evangelical churches must understand their God-given duty to be the patrons of sacred music. First, they need to encourage talented musicians to create music with all their might, solely for the glory of God. *Music motivated by consumerism must be replaced by music motivated by the love of God.* Secondly, churches must encourage their young musicians to seek careers in the music ministry. Thirdly, churches must urge and assist them to receive their necessary training in Bible colleges. And when they finally do enter Bible college, we who teach them must make sure that we are indeed models worth copying and that we give them a musical diet that will enable them to become comprehensive musicians.

Conclusion

The process of integration goes on in all fields, including sacred music. We want to show our students those aspects of music study and ministry which correlate positively with distinctly biblical theology. At the same time we want to show them where there is a doctrinal dissonance, an incompatibility between something musical and something theological. The combination of Luther and Bach is the most obvious example of positive integration.

Like Luther and Bach, let us seek God's music with all our hearts and minds. God's music always begins with the voice of His people singing praises; but it must grow until it embraces the whole realm of musical experience. Karl Geiringer states that Bach's sacred compositions "received their decisive impulse from the Protestant church song, the *chorale*, as it is commonly called. Its basic significance for the new forms of worship was recognized by Luther himself."[34] But Bach brought to the chorale every conceivable musical influence: French court music, Italian opera and concerto grosso, and the instrumental and choral traditions of his native Germany. It is a sacred music that reflects comprehensive musicianship and divine majesty. We too can have glorious church music. We too can cherish our treasury of hymns and build on our hymns a magnificent structure using all the resources of our musical heritage from Gregorian chant to George Crumb. Dare we pray that God will send to our Bible colleges many new Bachs who will turn this dream into a reality? Let us so teach our students, believing that they are the instruments God will use to give us a new revival of music in His church.

Notes

1. George Santayana, *The Life of Reason* (New York: Scribner's 1905), p. 315.
2. Paul Nettl, *Luther and Music*, trans. Frida Best and Ralph Wood (New York: Russell and Russell, 1948), pp. 2–3.
3. Martin Luther, *What Luther Says: An Anthology*, compiled by Ewald M. Plass (Saint Louis, Mo.: Concordia, 1959), p. 980.
4. Ibid.
5. Friedrich Blume, *Protestant Church Music: A History* (New York: Norton, 1974), p. 6.
6. Luther, p. 980.
7. Ibid., p. 981.
8. Ibid., p. 982.
9. Anne Ortlund, *Up with Worship* (Glendale, Cal.: G/L Publications, 1975), p. 95.
10. C. S. Lewis, *Reflections on the Psalms* (New York: Harcourt Brace Jovanovich, 1958), p. 95.
11. Susanne K. Langer, *Feeling and Form* (New York: Scribner's, 1953), p. 129.
12. Quoted by Karl Geiringer, *Instruments in the History of Western Music* (New York: Oxford, 1978), p. 42.
13. Lee Olson, "Church Music," *Christianity and the World of Thought*, ed. Hudson T. Armerding (Chicago: Moody, 1968), pp. 290–95.
14. Dorothy L. Sayers, "Toward a Christian Aesthetic," *The Whimsical Christian* (New York: Macmillan, 1978), p. 83.
15. Ibid., p. 85.
16. H. R. Rookmaaker, *Art Needs No Justification* (Downers Grove, Ill.: Inter-Varsity, 1978), p. 25.
17. Ibid., p. 30.
18. Ibid., pp. 30–31.
19. Harold M. Best, "Church Relatedness, Music, and Higher Education," *Proceedings of the 52nd Annual Meeting, National Association of Schools of Music, Atlanta, Georgia 1976* (Reston, Va.: NASM, 1977).
20. Harold M. Best, "Music: Offerings of Creativity," *Christianity Today*, 6 May 1977, pp. 12–15.
21. Ibid., p. 13.
22. Vera Stravinsky and Robert Craft, "Stravinsky's Early Years," *Ovation*, 1 (May 1980): 20.
23. Igor Stravinsky, *Poetics of Music* (Cambridge: Harvard University Press, 1942), p. 51.
24. Quoted by Albert Hofstadter, *Truth and Art* (New York: Columbia University Press, 1965), p. 27.
25. Rollo May, *The Courage to Create* (New York: Norton, 1975), p. 79.
26. Ibid.
27. Francis A. Schaeffer, *Art and the Bible* (Downers Grove, Ill,: Inter-Varsity, 1973), pp. 56–57.
28. J. C. Macaulay, "The Ministry of Music," *Accrediting Association of Bible Colleges Newsletter*, 16(Fall 1972): 9.
29. John F. Wilson, *An Introduction to Church Music* (Chicago: Moody, 1965), p. 18.
30. Alfred E. Lunde, *Christian Education thru Music* (Wheaton: Evangelical Teacher Training Association, 1978), p. 7.
31. Johann Nikolaus Forkel, *Johann Sebastian Bach: His Life, Art, and Work* (1802; reprint ed., New York: Vienna House, 1974), p. 93.
32. Ibid., p. 99.
33. Frank E. Gaebelein, *The Pattern of God's Truth* (Chicago: Moody, 1954), pp. 76–77.
34. Karl Geiringer, *Johann Sebastian Bach: The Culmination of an Era* (New York: Oxford, 1966), p. 109.

Part Three

DIVISION OF
GENERAL EDUCATION

The Author

A Ph.D. candidate at Bowling Green State University, Samuel Canine brings to this important chapter the heart of a pastor and evangelist as well as academic experience at Moody Bible Institute where he serves as assistant professor of evangelism and pastoral training. He has earned degrees from Cedarville College (B.A.), Dallas Theological Seminary (Th.M.), and Bowling Green University (M.A.).

The Subject

The rapid influx of evangelicals into the mass media has created a new arena of ministerial training for Bible colleges. In addition to the radio communications programs of earlier decades we are seeing new offerings in television, journalism, drama, and other forms of communication. These aspects of the field are often identified as professional studies while communication theory and practice belong to the general education in speech required of every student. Thus this chapter connects the third section of the book with what has come before.

10

SPEECH/ COMMUNICATIONS

Samuel Canine

"Revelation"—"disclosure"—"communication" is in the very fiber of our existence. Toffler declares, "all human groups, from primitive times to today, depend on face to face, person to person communication."[1] Countless verbal and nonverbal messages are sent and received every day of our lives. Fisher points out the term *communication* may refer to (1) a process, (2) media, (3) an event, (4) state of connectedness, (5) mutual understanding, or (6) a discipline.[2] The fact that the term *communication* has so many different definitions simply underscores the central role it plays in each of our lives.

Introduction

The need for communicative studies both in the general education curriculum and as a discipline in the professional studies division is required by the phenomenal increase in Christian ministry opportunities in various media. This need is seen in the increasing complexity of our day and in the nature of man and of learning.

The Complexity of Our Day

Probably the greatest evidence of communicative need is demonstrated by the proliferation and power of mass media. Our global community possesses an awareness which has greatly accelerated in the last two generations. The sophistication of knowledge in our day is incredible. At the present rate our available information doubles every five years.[3] With this kind of knowledge explosion, we must comprehend the communication process to ascertain the world in which we live.

The Nature of Man

From the beginning God declared it was not good for man to live alone (Gen. 2:18). Companionship was a primary purpose in the creative action of God. Within the human family, communication is a given. Families are predicated upon a communicative foundation. The cooperative unity expected within the filial context demands effectiveness in communication. Since man is social by nature, communication should be studied, improved, and taught so that human beings might find greater fulfillment in their creative purpose.

The Nature of Learning

In the contemporary world, learning seems to be associated with some change of behavior. This experience-oriented concept has what Jaarsma calls "reference to the interaction of a subject and an object in which the subject undergoes a change such that a new relationship is established between the two."[4] This interactive notion is a mutual matrix of learning and communication. Just as learning is impossible without interaction, so genuine communication demands interaction with a new relationship as the outcome.

Biblical Foundation

Every time an individual picks up the Scriptures or looks at creation there is an implicit reminder of the God who communicates. Communication is written into the very foundation of our physical and spiritual existence. However, within the broad context of the self-communicating God, some specific passages stand out as underscoring this discipline.[5] For our purposes we will consider Psalm 19 and John 4 from a communicative perspective.

Psalm 19—A God Who Reveals Himself

This piece of Hebrew poetry begins by depicting a revelation of God in nature (Ps. 19:1-6). The question could well be asked, "What does a person learn from the revelation of God in nature?" "What evidence has He presented?" God has communicated at least five characteristics of Himself through His work.

A God of Power (v. 1). A continual message is being sent by God to man. This uninterrupted message is clearly seen in the rendering of verse 1, "The heavens are telling of the glory of God and their expanse is declaring the work of His hands" (NASB). Any message sent from one individual to another reflects the personality of the sender. The vastness of God's creative power is imbedded in the physical world around us. Throughout the Scriptures the physical universe is viewed as accomplished by a God with tremendous power.[6]

A God of Consistency (v. 2). Speech and knowledge consistently pour forth from God's revelation in nature. Congruency is an essential trait for any communicator. With the Supreme Communicator, perfect congruency is a reality. In any human communication distortion (noise) may exist in the sender, the channel or the receiver. In man's communication, the greater the degree of congruency, the better the fidelity of the communicative transaction. However, with God, no noise exists in the sender. Some distortion will be recognized on the channel because sin has affected the material as well as the human creation. Unfortunately, most of the message garble surfaces in the receiver, man.

A God of Universality (v. 3). Most communication originating in the human cadre has definite restrictions resulting from the finiteness of man. But when God's communication through nature is considered, no limits exist in His voice to humankind. It would be difficult indeed to cite an example of a human message universally communicated. Strong limitations exist in our power to transmit and receive. But God's natural revelation is genuinely universal. No human being has ever lived who has not been sent this message.

A God Who Appreciates Beauty (vv. 4-5). Even in a sin-scarred world, much beauty still surrounds us. The picture of Psalm 19 is one of anticipation, joy, and beauty as a bridegroom would emerge on his wedding day. Even so the sun rises, brightening everything in its path. Its light and warmth affect everything exposed to its power. The sun as God's creation reflects the personality of the One who brought it into existence. Every time the flower opens to the sunlight and the grass greens at its rays, a reminder is flashed to all intelligent creation that a God exists who has designed beauty.

A God of Endurance (vv. 6-6). The strong runner who runs the race must be characterized by endurance. The sun seemingly moves across the heavens never stopping but completing its course until it sets in the western sky. Each day is always completed. Basic to the nature of God is His ability to always finish what He begins. This should greatly encourage every individual in his struggle against sin and for righteousness. The sun in the sky is a visual aid declaring to us the endurance of God.

The heavens keep informing humanity of God's glory but the law of the Lord must reveal God's converting power. It is through the written Word of the Lord that intimacy with our self-revealing God is known. The God of nature communicates at one level but the Lord of the written Word establishes a personal relationship with man. At this level God may be known in a more personal way as:

A God who changes people (v. 7a)
A God who makes one wise (v. 7b)
A God who produces joy (v. 8)
A God who satisfies (vv. 8–10)
A God who warns and rewards (v. 11)
A God who can solve the sin problem (v. 12)
A God who grants acceptability in His sight (v. 13)

In verses 1 through 6 our God communicates *what* He does; in verses 7 through 13 it is far more *who* He is. The closeness of the Psalmist to his Lord is highlighted in the second half of the chapter. Interestingly, in the first six verses, "God" (*Elohim*) is the name ascribed to the communicator. "Lord" (*Yahweh*) is the term employed in the last eight verses suggesting the close covenant relationship sustained with the Lord. The revelation of God through His works and His Word is followed by a proper response of the Psalmist (v. 14). The outer response, "words of my mouth," and the inner response, "meditation of my heart," indicate more than linear communication. A cyclical pattern surfaces when the writer refers to these being "acceptable in Thy sight." The sequence, God reveals—

man responds—God evaluates, enlightens the astute reader as to the mutuality present in all communication. Simply regarding communication as sender-receiver is far too narrow to be a significant approach to communicative studies. Even in public address via mass media, verbal or nonverbal, messages are sent from audience to speaker as well as speaker to audience.

John 4—A God Who Interacts

A classic example of such mutuality in the interpersonal context is apparent in the encounter of Jesus Christ with the Samaritan woman (John 4). At least six communication transactions (i.e., both Jesus and the Samaritan woman addressing themselves to a given topic) can be identified in the passage.

Communication Topic	Christ	Woman
1. water, nationalities	v. 7	v. 9
2. living water, physical identity	v. 10	vv. 11-12
3. quenching of thirst	vv. 13-14	v. 15
4. husband	vv. 16, 17b-18	vv. 17a
5. worship	vv. 21-24	vv. 19*-20
6. coming Messiah	v. 26	v. 25*

*she initiated

From a communicative perspective, that which transpired between Jesus and the Samaritan woman was part of an on-going mutually interactive process in which each participant affected and was affected by what the other party said.

Communication Theory

An accurate view of communication must provide for a multiplicity of variables. This requires a mutuality in relationship between the sender and receiver. In *Communication Yearbook 3*, Seral comments that the linear view of communication

> tends to conceive of communication as originating in a vacuum and continuing in isolation and ignores the multiple, multidimensional contexts which continually contribute to the richness and complexity of all communication experiences.[7]

Communication, i.e., the sending-receiving-responding to messages, transpires at many different levels. The following model demonstrates a conceptual visual representation of communication at various levels. (See Figure 1.)

This fivefold level of communication is so designed to indicate the foundation of communication and what should be built upon it. No one level can stand independently of the other four and succeed in producing effective communication.

Theologically as well as theoretically the veracity depicted in this model is strong. For example, the individual must know "who" God is before he can comprehend "what" He has said (1 Cor. 2:14). The relationship established by the new birth (John 3) must be true before the content of the Bible can be adequately grasped. Even in the believer's life, the child of God who is *walking* with God will understand the Word of God more precisely.

The tragedy existing in many Christian schools is that we have been satisfied to simply be technicians of our craft. Like the Sophists of old our speech courses instruct in *content* with a heavy dose of *methodology*,[8] but little or no concern is given to the more foundational levels of communication. If communication curricula are

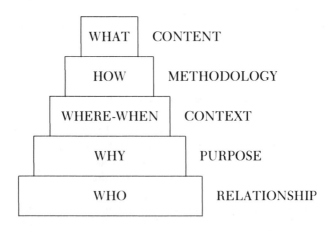

Figure 1. Levels of Communication

effective in the long run, the *relationship level* must be considered as well as content and methodology.

In every facet of our lives more and more *small group communication* is occurring. In community, church, family, and employment being part of a small group is a way of life. Monroe and Ehninger correctly observe that "the need to become a skilled communicator in the small group situation is more important today than at any earlier period in history."[9] A group's survival becomes jeopardized when communication loses its effectiveness. Brooks has informed us, "when there is no relevant interaction and cohesiveness, groups disintegrate."[10]

Small group communication was utilized throughout the earthly ministry of Jesus Christ. His training of the twelve apostles involved group work.[11] Many of His miracles were performed as small groups interacted with the Creator.[12] Jesus subdivided the Twelve by bringing Peter, James, and John to the Mount of Transfiguration (Matt. 17:1–8). Today, effective small group communication in the Christian community happens more by accident than design. Our speech curriculum should put emphasis in this area—particularly such variables as small group leadership, cohesiveness, roles, environmental arrangement, and size.

Interpersonal communication should also receive adequate attention in any Christian college approach to communication. Interpersonal communication is understood as dyadic or two-person communication. According to Brooks and Emment, dyadic communication is the most frequent form of communication, and the most influential. For it is through the dyad "that group and cultural communication comes into being."[13] When we consider the hours spent in counseling, interviewing, and planning over lunch, we begin to comprehend the maximum usage of interpersonal communication in each of our lives. And yet, how much focus on interpersonal communication is there in a Bible college curriculum? Somehow, it seems to be lost in the shuffle of our notes for public address. Communication must be viewed from this perspective if any degree of holism is to characterize our speech training.

Throughout the Old and New Testaments, dyadic communication is mentioned. From Adam and Eve to John conversing with God's messenger on the isle of Patmos the context of many communicative events is undeniably interpersonal. Our approach to teaching communication ought to mirror what we find revealed in Holy Scriptures.

Finally, our communication theory must be based on biblical presuppositions. One of the dangers affecting much of our Christian education involves humanistic infiltration. When a philosophical position asserts that man is the measure of all things, the resulting product is antibiblical. In the field of communication this becomes obvious as communicologists chase one new theory after another.

The professor of Christian communication should not be caught in the most recent theory discussed in the current journals, but rather he should take responsibility for the theistic interpretation of any advancement in scholarship.

One way to measure a presuppositional base is to examine the illustrative materials in textbooks and journal articles. Theory at times is obtuse but examples and illustrations often clarify most existing ambiguity. Another telltale sign of faulty presuppositions often appears in the preliminary materials, or front matter of a text. The preface and introductory chapters should be carefully studied if we are to understand the foundation of the author's thought.

Practical Integration

If the approach to communication suggested in this chapter is valid, how can we practically implement this type of communication in our individual situations?

Of all of the studies contemplated in our academic experience few can boast *the transdisciplinary nature of communication.* Speech communication literally cuts across all departmental lines. When the student advances in his communicative skills, the history department benefits when this student gives his *oral* report. A greater awareness of communication by faculty in other departments needs to exist. In a sense the benefits of what we do must be "sold" to other faculty in our institutions. Our work should assist them in a mutual quest for excellence in education.

For communication to be positively integrated with other subjects is impossible without the ministry of the Holy Spirit. Since He is the One who guides us into all truth (John 16:13), a regular dependency on His ministry is absolutely essential. The teacher as well as the student must consciously receive and respond to the working of God the Spirit for lasting education to be realized.

Integration will be more positively achieved when we work toward a more effective *transference from classroom to outside world.* To accomplish this carry-over to the real world the classroom must assume a laboratory setting. Students should engage in trial communication under supervision so that their speech skills can develop. Involvement is crucial to the acquiring of expertise in communication. Perhaps other disciplines can maintain a purely cognitive stance but communication cannot be understood or taught if student participation is denied. Therefore, it becomes a learning-by-doing situation. Correction and further development through careful assistance should characterize the classroom as a laboratory. This presupposes a tension-free atmosphere so the student can afford the luxury of making mistakes and benefiting from them. Ego-centered, theatening comments must be minimized. The student needs to sense a teacher-student cooperative endeavor which works on what the student is doing without attacking who the student is. We will maximize pedagogical potential if we conscientiously take time to make the classroom a laboratory.

Our studies in communication should also be marked by a *multiple view of themes*. Some topics in communication traverse many different contexts.[14] For example, conflict could be studied as a separate topic which cuts through public address, small group, and interpersonal communication. When we synthetically recognize the role of conflict in these different settings we begin to make progress toward a holistic view of our discipline. This inductive approach has many benefits to offer. Accuracy is improved if we have all the pieces of the puzzle before displaying the picture. Both positive and negative traits start to emerge when a given topic is thoroughly researched. For example, in studying the topic of conflict, the students will find that the entire concept of corrective church discipline so clearly taught in Scripture and so seldom practiced by churches would suggest that conflict be instigated so as to help a brother deal with sin (Matt. 18:15–20; 1 Cor. 5:1–13).

We also desperately need a return to *utilizing the Bible* for examples and principles to ascertain what is effective in communication. The apostle Peter on the day of Pentecost provides an excellent example of sermon building (Acts 2). His inductive approach building to the climax, "Therefore let all the house of Israel know for certain that God has made him both Lord and Christ—this Jesus whom you crucified" (Acts 2:26, NASB), is totally different from Paul's deductive message on Mars Hill (Acts 17:22–31). Yet both are effective ways to speak and preach.

The Bible should serve as more than just illustrative material; it can serve as the text itself. This presupposes an extremely practical application in the methodology of the instructor. It could also mean considerable digging since most Christian textbooks consider the Scriptures from the content-orientation instead of a methodological-orientation. Much work needs to be done to produce new Christian textbooks of this nature.

At the center of integration in communication studies is the problem of attitude or motivation. A few students may bring a positive orientation to their academic pursuits but most will not. Motivation or enthusiasm will probably require development. McKeachie has supported this by stating, "I presume that the teacher's own enthusiasm and values have much to do with his students' interest in the subject matter."[15] He further adds, "Probably non-verbal as well as verbal methods are used; i.e., facial expression, animation and vocal intensity may be as important as the words one uses."[16] In essence the total message communicated by the instructor's life will either encourage or discourage student involvement. A cooperative attitude between student and teacher will produce a higher degree of student integration in the learning situation.

Assignments can either assist or hamper the specific objectives of a given course. What freedom is the student given in the assignment? Is the assignment measurable? Is the assignment reflective of the truth taught? Does the assignment challenge but not overwhelm the student? Effective assignments serve not only as teaching devices, but also provide for student integration.

Activities used in class can be designed so as to enlist student participation. The whole concept of game theory is built upon integrating the student in the communication process.[17] The creative teacher could provide many in-class procedures which would make optimal involvement for the speech student.

Conclusion

Any understanding of communication begins by looking upward. Human communication depends upon divine communication. The self-revealing God has taken the initiative to disclose to His creatures who He is and what we are to be. In Psalm 19 we recognize the God who communicates through the natural world as well as the supernatural Word of the Lord.

Foundational in viewing communication is the concept of communication levels. Superficiality results when these communication levels are ignored. When different levels are comprehended, a greater degree of communicative effectiveness is achieved.

Mutual interaction in communication should be considered in defining the nature of communication. Transactions should be understood as an ongoing process, not just as single events. This multidirectional view of communication finds strong support in the interpersonal encounters of Jesus Christ (John 4).

A call for integration in Christian comunication has been sounded, To view the whole, multiple contexts and themes must be mastered. Increased Bible usage should be encouraged. Communicative transactions in Scripture need to be discovered, cataloged, and utilized in our speech classrooms. Assuming the validity of this approach, practical ways to implement these notions have filled the balance of this study.

We have journeyed on a route which has taken us from a justificatory beginning until we arrived at ways communication may be better implemented in our college classrooms. Along the way communication theory in harmony with a biblical philosophy has been suggested. We each can thank the God who communicates so well that we have a part in His communicative process.

Notes

1. Alvin Toffler, *The Third Wave* (New York: Morrow, 1980), p. 26.
2. Aubrey Fisher, *Perspectives on Human Communication* (New York: Macmillan, 1978), p. 91.
3. Frank Minirth, *Christian Psychiatry* (Old Tappan, N.J.: Revell, 1977), p. 21.
4. Cornelius Jaarsma, *Human Development, Learning and Teaching* (Grand Rapids: Eerdmans, 1961), pp. 169–70.
5. Isaiah 6, John 1, Colossians 1–4, Hebrews 1, and many other passages could be studied in this connection.
6. See such passages as Job 38–39; Isaiah 40:21–28.
7. Tulsi B. Saral, *Communication Yearbook 3* (New Brunswick, N.J.: Transaction Books, 1979), p. 398.
8. One needs only to note the current market which is flooded with "How to. . . " books.
9. Alan Monroe and Douglas Ehninger, *Principles of Speech Communication* (Glenview, Ill.: Scott, Foresman, 1975), p. 309.
10. William D. Brooks, *Speech Communication* (Dubuque, Iowa: Brown, 1974), p. 209.
11. See for example A.B. Bruce, *The Training of the Twelve* (Grand Rapids: Zondervan, 1961).
12. For further study note Matthew 14:22–33; 15:21–28; John 9:1–7; 21:1–6 and other related Scriptures.
13. William D. Brooks and Philip Emmert, *Interpersonal Communication* (Dubuque, Iowa: Brown, 1976), p. 235.
14. Such topics should include nonverbal communication, power in communication, bargaining, status, and other themes which genuinely cut through various communication contexts.
15. Wilbert J. McKeachie, *Teaching Tips* (Lexington, Mass.: Heath, 1969), p. 187.
16. Ibid.
17. See for example Brent D. Ruben and Richard W. Budd, *Human Communication Handbook* (Rochelle Park, N.J.: Hayden, 1975).

The Author

Pattie Linton specifically prepared herself to teach English and literature in a Bible college. She holds a B.A. from Houghton College, the M.S. from the State University of New York and an Ed.Spec. in English and literature from Florida Atlantic University. She became assistant professor of English and literature at Miami Christian College in 1972 after serving some fifteen years in public schools. Currently she teaches English at the Dade County (Florida) Public Schools.

The Subject

Over the past decade or so the Bible college movement has been made increasingly aware of the importance of the general education elements in its curriculum. Here the issue of integration of faith and learning is particularly significant for these departments often seen as service agencies, assisting in the broad preparation of those who major in one of the areas of professional education as well as Bible and theology. Beyond this students can learn to enjoy literature, using it to understand more of "the universality of the human condition" as well as for recreation.

11

ENGLISH AND LITERATURE

Pattie T. Linton

Since the inception of the Bible institute movement there have been polarized views regarding the worth of the English and literature department. At one extreme are those who view the language arts as extraneous, perhaps even dangerous; at the other are those who are adamant about its relevance and who demand excellence in performance. In between are faculties who view the department as a stepsister who must be tolerated and even treated kindly on occasion. Beyond making sure that students learn their grammar and how to write a term paper, however, the relationship becomes strained, especially if the English professor should want to attempt integration with the rest of the curriculum.

To be fair, there are Bible colleges which have effective English and literature departments within the general education division, or its equivalent. A few of the larger schools have majors in the field. The academic catalogs show a wide diversity of course offerings among AABC schools, with emphasis heavy on the freshman composition courses and literature survey courses.

Introduction

Explanation And Definition

"English" often is a catchall for that knowledge and those skills thought to be somehow related to language usage. The English and literature department is structured around the idea of separating the study of composition, vocabulary, and grammar from the reading of literary works in English or as translations from other languages. Sometimes speech courses fall under this department's purview.

Most freshman courses include study of vocabulary, grammar and usage, and writing techniques. Readings may be an integral part of the course in order that students have models to imitate. Incidental may be introductory units of structural-historical linguistics, brief glimpses into journalistic or creative writing, and analysis of the influences of the media. Thus, it can be rightly envisioned as that *final* preparatory class for producing correctly written college papers or as an introduction to the field of study. Schools with majors in the field offer further courses in language study and writing. The difficulty, of course, is that students with both terminal and preparatory goals study together in the same class.

Literature courses have traditionally been limited to survey courses, mostly of British writers and works. Some schools now offer several alternatives: American, Western, World, Christian. Colleges with English majors offer a broader course selection in both national and genre specialization.

The literature course is most commonly designed to acquaint the student with the most periods, writers, and works possible. Some professors select a few representative works to study in depth. Emphasis is placed upon sociohistorical perspective, writers' philosophies and artistry, literary techniques in general, or the content, according to the professor's preparation and inclination.

The student who chooses to major in this department has several career opportunities open to him, though most of them are contingent upon graduate study. He can write—as a free agent, as a staff member of a publication, as a script writer for radio or television; he can teach at the secondary or college level. He can remain in the Christian domain or move out into the secular world. For either sector, he is well grounded in his subject matter, and if his professors have properly handled the integration of this subject matter with the core of biblical studies, he is prepared for a life's ministry.

Rationale for Inclusion

With the broadening of the Bible college curriculum to include so many areas of ministry, the English and literature department must update its reason for existence to match the demands of an electronic age. Students *can* be taught to (1) formulate fresh expression in speaking or writing; (2) use a wide vocabulary for maximum effect; (3) operate within standard grammatical construction and accepted usage; (4) relate literary experience to the truth of Christianity as well as the everyday existence of humanity; and (5) prepare for a vocation within the domain of language, composition, or literature.

A practical benefit gained from the composition courses is the ability to write papers for current and future biblical studies. In addition, the student can apply his grammatical analysis to his exegesis or biblical language study. The benefits of literary study include the application of literary techniques—identifying genre, figurative language, and symbolism and interpreting content—to biblical studies. Furthermore, literature provides a broadened vision of man's search for truth, man's sin, and the results of human philosophy.

Finally, the student of English and literature is prepared to meet the challenge of the media bombardment with careful use of his language and with an understanding of the power of the media and the philosophies they may express. His ministry has the potential to exceed the influence of media in the lives of those to whom he ministers.

Biblical Foundations

The Written Record

An early mention of writing—in addition to the genealogies of Genesis—is found in Exodus 32:16. "The tables were the work of God, and the writing was the writing of God, graven upon the tables."[1]

Somewhat earlier, after the battle at Rephidim with the Amalekites, the Lord commanded Moses, "Write this as a memorial in the book, and rehearse it in the ears of Joshua, that I will utterly blot out the remembrance of Amalek from under the heavens" (Exod. 17:14).

Archaeological findings substantiate the possibility of a written code before Abram was called from Ur, but we find no biblical reference to writing until the Israelites left Egypt. Moses could have written in one of three languages. What is important is that God wanted a written record. We see this reemphasized when Moses was to view Canaan and Joshua was to lead the people in.

And on the day when you pass over the Jordan to the land which the Lord your God gives you, you shall set you up great stones, and cover them with plaster. And you shall write on them all the words of this law (Deut. 27:2–3).

And Moses wrote this law, and delivered it to the Levitical priests, who carried the ark of the covenant of the Lord, and to all the elders of Israel (Deut. 31:9).

And when Moses had finished writing the words of this law in a book to the very end, he commanded the Levites who carried the ark of the covenant of the Lord, Take this book of the law, and put it by the side of the ark of the covenant of the Lord your God, that it may be there for a witness against you (Deut. 31:24–26).

We can trace the advancement of the written process, the materials used, and God's desire for the written record as we move through the Old Testament. We see parchment and scrolls; we hear God's commands to prophets to write and to kings to study and administer the law; we rejoice with the rediscovery of and the delight in the law upon the return from captivity.

As we move through the New Testament we learn of the burden laid upon the writers to record Christ's life, teachings, and mission; to record the acts of the early church; to preserve the teaching of the apostles in their letters to the churches; to present the Christian with hope found in the revelation of future events.

It is clearly evident that God wanted written records kept because He knew that human nature would turn completely from Him were there no visible reminder. He wanted His hand in the affairs of man clearly seen. He also loved the tributes given to Him in the written songs of adoration.

And the Lord answered me and said, Write the vision, and engrave it so plainly upon tablets that *every one who* passes may *be able to* read [it easily and quickly] *as he* hastens by (Hab. 2:2). [This is an interesting call for legibility and clarity].

Let this be recorded for the generation yet unborn, and a people yet to be created shall praise the Lord (Ps. 102:18).

For whatever was written in former days was written for our instruction, that by endurance and the encouragement from the Scriptures we might hold fast *and* cherish hope (Rom. 15:4).

Write promptly what you see in a book and send it to the seven churches (Rev. 1:11).

The ultimate, eternal written record God has written and preserved for Himself:

> Thus shall he who conquers be clad in white garments, and I will not blot out his name from the Book of Life. . . (Rev. 3:5).

> . . . recorded from the foundation of the world in the Book of Life of the Lamb that was slain from the foundation of the world (Rev. 13:8).

Propositional Truth

Psalm 119 is the touchstone for truth in the Old Testament.

> Teach me good judgment, wise *and* right discernment and knowledge, for I have believed your commandments (v. 66).

> For ever, O Lord, Your Word is settled in Heaven (v. 89).

> You through Your commandments make me wiser than my enemies; for *Your words* are ever before me (v. 98).

> The sum of Your Word is truth and every one of Your righteous decrees endures for ever (v. 160).

Psalm 119 also reiterates the benefits of truth.

> I have better understanding *and* deeper insight than all my teachers, because Your testimonies are my meditation (v. 99).

> I understand more than the aged, because I keep Your precepts (v. 100).

Jesus advised those who had believed in Him concerning the source of truth: "If you abide in my Word, you are truly My disciples. And you will know the truth, and the truth will set you free" (John 8:31–32). Christ prayed that His disciples would be sanctified and protected from the evil one by the Word of Truth. "They are not of the world, as I am not of the world. Sanctify them by the Truth. Your Word is Truth" (John 17:16–17).

Paul and the other apostles wrote on numerous occasions that Christians should be discerning of the world around them, all the while firmly grounded in their faith. In Colossians 2:4–8, Paul wants to advise them in order that "no one may mislead *and* delude you by plausible *and* persuasive *and* attractive arguments *and* beguiling speech" (v. 4). He continues, "See to it that no one carries you off as spoil *or* makes you yourselves captive by his so-called philosophy *and* intellectualism, and vain deceit, following human tradition—men's ideas of the material world—just crude notions following the rudimentary *and* elemental teachings of the universe, and disregarding Christ, the Messiah" (v. 8).

Further biblical passages teach us concerning the source of man's "vain imaginings" and the results of man's own devisings. Matthew points to the *heart*:

> You offspring of vipers! How can you speak good things when you are evil? For out of the fullness of the heart the mouth speaks. The good man from his inner good treasure flings forth good things, and the evil man out of his inner evil storehouse flings forth evil things (12:34–35).

Proverbs 10:20 points to the *mind*: "The tongue of those who are upright *and* in right standing with God is as choice silver; the mind of those who are wicked *and* out of harmony with God is of little value." Isaiah says the wicked get their direction from the wrong source:

> And when the people shall say to you, Consult for direction mediums and wizards who chirp and mutter, should not a people seek *and* consult their God? Should they consult the dead on behalf of the living? Direct such people to the teaching and to the testimony; if their teachings are not in accord with this word, it is surely because there is no dawn *and* no morning for them (Isa. 8:19–20).

Add to this the declaration of Christ. "But I tell you, on the day of judgment men will have to give account for every idle word they speak. For by your words you will be justified *and* acquitted, and by your words you will be condemned *and* sentenced" (Matt. 12:36–37). The results of man's devisings are nought.

Our students must approach the study of literature with an insight into the end result of human philosophies and traditions. They recognize the truth of literature when it portrays the human condition and are better prepared to follow the admonition of Paul in Philippians 2:15–16:

> That you may show yourselves to be blameless *and* guileless, innocent *and* uncontaminated, children of God without blemish in the midst of a crooked *and* wicked generation. Among whom you are seen as bright lights—stars or beacons shining out clearly—in the world, holding out *and* offering the Word of Life, so that in the day of Christ I may have something of which exultantly to rejoice.

Toward A Theology of Language and Literature

Since all philosophy flows from theology, and since the evangelical Christian's theology is grounded in absolute revelation, several theological premises need to be synthesized at this point.

Theology Proper. Language is God-ordained. We believe Adam and Eve were created with the capacity for language. God has communicated through spoken and written language as well as more symbolical natural revelation. He spoke to men of Old Testament history directly and through visions. He spoke in New Testament history through visions and through His Son. He continues to speak through the canon of Scripture as the Holy Spirit interacts with the written Word.

Bibliology. The Bible is the only source of special revelation and therefore the basis for Christian philosophy. The study of man's literature by the Christian is always predicated on the belief that propositional truth is found only in the Scriptures and illumination by the Spirit in the mind of the believer. Man may express or reiterate truth in his various forms of literature, since man's search for verity is central to all great literature. The Christian, however, is given discernment to consistently weigh man's statements against those of the Bible—a process essential to the Christian teaching of literature.

Christology. Christ, His attributes and His earthly ministry are central to much of post-Incarnation Western literature. His birth, His teachings, His miracles, His crucifixion, His resurrection are recurrent themes, treated variously in beauty, in questioning and disputing, and (especially in contemporary literature) in derision. The Christian student reacts with affirmation of Christ's mission.

Pneumatology. The student of literature learns to recognize lofty expression, inspired by natural beauty, man's accomplishments, or life's exigencies. The Christian student recognizes the differences between the Spirit-inspired utterances of the Bible and those of merely human origin.

Anthropology. The Christian cannot read literature without having the doctrine of man's sinful nature confirmed. In ancient literature he sees the futile attempts of the Greeks and Romans to explain natural phenomena and their resultant effects on man; they could adequately explain neither the creation of man nor the source of his basic nature. In examining contemporary existential writing students see man without God futilely searching to explain himself, his society, and his universe.

Soteriology. Literature presents a panorama of human hopes, man's questions about life after death, man's search for meaning in this life. Man is pictured as restive, wandering, groping; his life is shown in various stages of meaninglessness. The Christian observes this confusion and contrasts it with the promised and fulfilled hopes in the atonement of Christ.

Ecclesiology. Literature adds to the sense of the church universal, as the influence of the church asserts itself in writings of all nationalities. Literature has attacked the church for her pomp, her inattention to the ills of society, her "pie in the sky" theology. The Christian student looks for the bases of these attacks, concedes that some are valid concerns, and replies from a firm biblical and historical base.

Eschatology. How comforting for the Christian to know, as he wades through the myriad of conjectures about the hereafter, that end things are, and have been, eternally settled. A favorite theme of literature has been that of proposing a utopian society. Science fiction is filled with imaginings, of the universe beyond, mostly without the possibility of a sovereign God. Against the backdrop of romantic and imaginary futility the Christian student is strengthened by the Bible's true projections of the future.

Philosophical Formulation

Since English courses tend to be more pragmatic than philosophical, this section will be limited to the philosophies basic to literature courses. In order that study in this area can be integrated with faith, the professor will have to bridge the gap between theological statement and classroom practice. This may be effected when the professor, and then the students, recognize points of application that are theologically, philosophically, and methodologically sound. Some philosophical areas with which they must grapple are metaphysics, epistemology, axiology, and objectives.

Metaphysics

The student cannot study literature without dealing with the supernatural and here the Christian student has the advantage of being grounded in the basis of ultimate reality: God. He recognizes errors in the speculation of writers of all periods as they have sought to define reality, explain supernatural phenomena, explore the extrasensory. The secular reading audience variously treats such discussion as artistic imagination, as an opiate dream, as a special gift, or as a serious philosophical probe. The reader may hallucinate with the writer while the selection lasts, then cast it aside; or he may dwell upon the questions raised and look further for explanations. The Bible college literature professor draws the student back to the Scriptures, showing parallels in the Bible where applicable (e. g., Macbeth's witches with Saul's witch of Endor).

Soon the student will begin drawing the parallels himself and garnering illustrations for future lessons and sermons. Reading Milton's *Paradise Lost* and *Paradise Regained* helps the student formulate, question, or confirm his angelology and demonology. When he understands the existentialism of Sartre or Camus, he can more clearly state the reality of life and the meaning of it from the biblical viewpoint.

Epistemology

The nature of literature has been defined broadly, narrowly, and as frequently as new writers have arisen. Classically, literature is that writing which has endured because it reflects the thought and times of the writer and because it deals with universal themes. The professor points again to biblical passages as illustrations for these qualities and points of comparison. He teaches his students to judge works for these qualities, and to be critical of works not measuring up to the criteria. Job has endured because it relates ancient wisdom; it deals with the everpresent themes of righteous suffering and the justice of God; and it evidences early scientific observation of the earth and universe.

Literature is also man's lofty, heightened expression of feeling, especially in poetry. The professor teaches his students to recognize the exultation and the exaltation in both Christian and secular works and to note the language and figures used. He may compare Psalm 24 with Tennyson's "Flower in the Crannied Wall" to see how God's truth finds expression in secular writings.

In the late twentieth century we have a vast body of works from which to draw for our study. The professor selects from particular cultures, time periods, genres, or themes to set up the reading for his course. The Bible college teacher selects carefully, deliberately, so that he can acquaint his students with the finest sampling, correlating his course with biblical studies when possible (e. g., the Greek epics with the Israelites' deliverance from Egypt and their wanderings and entrance into Canaan). He draws from Christian writers to form a separate course, or uses them when possible as representative works of a period, genre, or theme. He asks students to hold these Christian writers under the same scrutiny applied to their secular counterparts.

Axiology

Value choices are inherent in literary study, both for the teacher and the student. In selecting works for his class to study, the Bible college professor must often weigh the value of a particular work as a work of greatness against the values it expresses, implicitly or explicitly. If the professor is candid with his students about his choices, he then is teaching his students to think about their own reading choices. The professor certainly balances his own reading of pessimistic, degrading material with aesthetically and philosophically pleasing works.

After direct biblical, theological, and philosophical studies, no subject matter meets the problem of value choices more directly than literature. Students begin to recognize choices made and the resulting consequences. Getting inside a character (like Graham Greene's whiskey priest) and beginning to understand why he makes the choices he does can help the student better understand some of the real people in the world around him and why they choose as they do (e. g., How does one explain the values and choices in *Crime and Punishment*?).

Objectives

The objectives of literary study have been implied throughout this discussion. A foremost objective is to broaden one's world view through study that depicts eras of human thought and action and the universal human condition. The reading of great works verifies universal truths about the nature of man thereby contributing to one's understanding of secular philosophies. The Christian student learns to recognize the expression of biblical propositions as opposed to human suppositions. He also gains compassion for the misguided persons who have no Christian perspective.

A secondary objective is to acquire skills of literary interpretation which can be applied to Bible study and further reading of any type. The student gains confidence in observing the whole, breaking it into workable components for close study, then reuniting the parts into a whole that is both biblical and logical to him. He can make statements about its meaning or about the conclusions he has drawn from it.

Practical Application

To get to the heart of the matter: What are the implications for the professor and student of literature in the Bible college setting as to practical ways of harmonizing faith and practice and of harmonizing English and literature courses with the rest of the curriculum? Below are recommendations for curriculum as well as suggestions for dealing with both the positive and negative aspects of the integration.

Curriculum

That the study of literature is valid for the Bible college student has been established. The college needs to move away from adding literature courses merely to meet accrediting standards or present a window dressing for the general education division.

Further, consideration must be given to the literature courses offered. If the school is operating on minimum standards, or bare budgeting, it should offer Western literature and Christian literature, with two semesters scheduled for each. Most students should be encouraged to leave room for both in their course work. Western and Christian literature go far beyond the exposure of most high school students to British and American literature. The historical and philosophical frameworks are extended and Christian literature is an invaluable adjunct to the church history course.

Schools with majors in literature will offer the broadest exposure possible to the literatures of the world. Beyond this they should design courses that focus on a single genre or theme to provide depth to the student's interpretation skills. A very appropriate required course would be one designed specifically to show the serious literature student early on how he can correlate his major studies with the rest of his curriculum.

Positive Integration

Literature Study. Both Christian and non-Christian have expressed delight in God's world and His creatures through many heightened expressions. The main difference in expression between the Christian and secular poet or dramatist is that the Christian usually acknowledges the Source of the beauty as God. We are free, however, to unashamedly spend time with Bryant's "To a Waterfowl" or Holmes's "The Chambered Nautilus" and Anne Morrow Lindbergh's *Gift From the Sea*. The Christian reader has the greater capacity for sensitivity to beauty. He should, therefore, find more in whatever he reads.

The Christian is also more sensitive to the expression of truth. While the Bible is the only inerrant statement of truth, many writers have expressed the same truth in different figures, or in the actions of their characters. For example, Hawthorne parallels accusers of Hester Prynne with those of the woman taken in adultery (John 8).The Christian recognizes the universals of the condition of man, whether stated in the Bible, in literature, or in the lives of the people around him. He sees a Macbeth corrupted by the desire for power as he sees a president brought low by the same desire. He correlates a Babbitt with the hypocrisy of his fellow church members (and himself!) and the Pharisees of the Bible. He associates the deceit of an Odysseus with a modern union leader as well as with Jacob of the Patriarchs.

Of special advantage to the literature professor in integration is the fact that the Bible contains examples of so many forms of literature. We find poetry, biography, the epic, wisdom literature, didactic exposition, travel adventures, parables, and all the elements of fiction and drama. The student can quite readily identify parallels between such characters as Voltaire's Candide and the searcher in Ecclesiastes.

In addition to works which supply parallels to biblical literature, there is the constant and persistent use of biblical allusions in all of Western literature since the Christian era. The Christian need not read much of Shakespeare before he realizes that Shakespeare was a plagiarist of the highest order. Since much of the great verbiage ascribed to him came from the Bible, most secular texts are pressed to footnote these allusions with explanations. The Christian can enjoy such attempts to explicate, happy in his own firsthand knowledge of *The Book*.

Language Study. Linguists agree with the biblical records of earliest known civilizations and language in the Mesopotamian area. The earliest known form of written language is a close ancestor of the Semitic. Linguists also agree on the diversification of language as tribal movement began from the Fertile Crescent.

When we trace the history of the English language, we find our alphabet ultimately returning to the Hebrew. Much of the enrichment of our language, especially in synonyms, goes back to Latin and Greek origins, the influence having occurred through translations of the Bible more than through translations of Homer or Vergil.

The changes in English can be illustrated through pages of Bible translations and versions. Wycliffe was to Middle English what Luther was to German—the first to insist on the Scriptures in the language of the people. That the King James Version was written in the same language Shakespeare used may be of some comfort to an otherwise reluctant reader of Shakespeare. That the English language is now the *lingua franca* adds weight to the importance of the recent New International Version.

Negative Integration

Literature Study. Literature is not intrinsically antibiblical though the underlying philosophies of many writers from the ancients (pre-Christian) to the modern periods (fifteenth century humanists and forward) are definitely nonrevelational. Much has been written to propound their antibiblical philosophies: Homer's Ulysses wanders about without scruple; Boccaccio's young people in the Decameron take the way of expediency; Mailer's *Naked and the Dead* are ruled by their decadent values; Camus' Stranger finds no meaning for his life or any other. The Christian student can only approach such works with the intention of knowing the effects of the philosophy and counteracting with the truth.

The professor prepares Bible college students for reading antibiblical works by introducing the writer in his historical framework and noting the presence or absence of Christian influence at the time. Where appropriate, he notes the writer's movement away from Christian belief. He introduces the work with an overview of the content and warns, if necessary, of objectionable material. He gives questions or guidelines to aid students in their reading. The students then know what to expect and how they may deal with it.

The professor always keeps in mind the fact that philosophy is more subtly expressed and possibly more damaging than graphic descriptions or narrations. He is sure in his own mind that the reading of the work will have benefits that will make it more profitable than objectionable. This is the place for biblical discernment in not offending the weaker brother.

Language Study. The language teacher may find some available textbooks contain objectionable readings or writing samples. Usually there are choices of selections; the teacher will read and determine the best choices from the standpoints of content and appropriateness as examples.

If there is a chapter on the origins and development of language in the secular texts, theories that are antibiblical are presented as scientific assumptions. The biblical records of creation and the Tower of Babel may be mentioned and/or questioned. This is an opportunity to have students refute the suppositions from their solid base in biblical studies.

Conclusion

Using one's language correctly gives confidence to use it more effectively. The English class provides the opportunity for becoming more proficient in English usage. It lays the foundation for study of other languages or the field of linguistics. Composition practice adds to the confidence of facing other classes with assurance of success in fulfilling written assignments. Writing needs of the future will be tackled with more ease. No other course provides this base.

Literature provides vicarious experiences, transcending the limitations of the present to see the universality of the human condition. "Human nature doesn't change," is the comment most often heard as a result of reading from the classics in the Bible college setting. The imaginations and devisings of man are nowhere else in the fine arts so apparent; for while paintings are representational, they do not always explain themselves; for while music reflects cultures, conventions, and moods, it does not verbalize thought. May we be so bold to say that except for the Bible, nowhere else do we get the whole picture of man?

English and literature are at once foundational and enriching to the Bible college curriculum. As stated previously, the freshman English course is essential to progress toward the upper divisions. Literature adds to the understanding of biblical literature, history, and philosophy. Its movements parallel those of music and art; it balances the rationalism of mathematics and science; it adds to the world view of students contemplating any Christian vocation.

Future ministers find illustrative material. Prospective Christian educators round out their essential preparation. Communications majors have an essential base of verbalizing techniques. The missions student begins to wonder about the culture where he will one day minister. All have rubbed elbows with some of the culture that is common to most educated persons.

When integration has been mastered as a learning pattern, the Bible college graduate will not feel guilty about picking up a good book or poem and spending time with it, for he knows there are lessons to be learned and beauty to be enjoyed—and he is aware that God has ordained both. Whatever his area of ministry, he needs time apart from that ministry for enjoyment as well as for meditation. Such a student is the product of the holistic approach of his Bible college curriculum and its emphasis on the integration of faith and learning.

Notes

1. All Scripture quotations in this chapter are taken from The Amplified Bible.

The Author

Reinhard J. Buss has served on the faculty of Biola University for almost two decades. After undergraduate work at the University of Maryland (B.A.), he continued his education at UCLA earning both M.A. and Ph.D. degrees in Germanic languages. In addition to teaching duties in German and folklore, Dr. Buss serves as director of "Biola Abroad," the foreign studies program of the university. He was assisted in the preparation of this chapter by former student Samuel P. Scheibler.

The Subject

Though few Bible colleges offer full programs in modern language study, the renewed and increasingly technological efforts in world evangelization offer a theological as well as pragmatic reason for becoming more involved in language instruction. The concept of the world as global village intensifies the need for North Americans to learn foreign languages, as does the vastly increased number of Hispanics and other immigrants now living in North America.

12

MODERN LANGUAGES

Reinhard J. Buss

The intrinsic value of the study of modern language as part of the general curriculum in American institutions of higher learning was questioned emotionally by a generation of students in the late 1960's. With the utilitarian pressures of higher education during the 1970's and 1980's, the usefulness of modern language in the technically and vocationally oriented job market has once more come under scrutiny. The study of modern language has been relegated to a position of low priority during the past decade.

Introduction

Statistics indicate that foreign language enrollments in America's high schools have dropped from a high of 24 percent to 15 percent today.[1] Only an insignificant number of colleges and universities have retained a foreign language requirement for undergraduate admissions, and many collegiate institutions have diminished the foreign language requirement or abolished it altogether.

The consequences of this trend in education are now beginning to show up as symptoms of a national predicament. Foreign observers are commenting that "our language incompetence is beyond words."[2] An American foreign language specialist has pinpointed more specifically the dilemma America is facing:

> Never before in United States history has there been a time when foreign language education is needed as much as it is needed today. U.S. trade relations, political alliances, and national security may rely on our ability to communicate with our world neighbors. There is a large void which must be filled, if the U.S. is to maintain its current world leadership status.[3]

The President's Commission on Foreign Languages and International Studies has warned:

> Our gross national inadequacy in foreign language skills has become a serious and growing liability. It is going to be far more difficult for America to survive and compete in a world where nations are increasingly dependent on one another if we cannot communicate with our neighbors in their own languages and cultural contexts.[4]

Some 130 recommendations were submitted by the Commission to improve American language proficiency.[5]

As an example of the value to a nation's economy in learning a foreign language, consider that there are about ten thousand English-speaking Japanese business representatives assigned to the United States, while there are fewer than one tenth that number as counterparts in Japan. Of these, only a handful have a working knowledge of Japanese.[6] The consequences of this one-sided exchange can be disastrous in terms of initiative and results.

The tendencies of the 1960's and 1970's in the giant American state-supported educational system could not help but make an impact on the private sector of higher learning including Christian institutions. There has been a move to retrench in the humanities and cut back on the foreign language requirements in Christian liberal arts colleges during the past decade. In the Bible colleges the study of even the more prevalent modern languages, such as French, German, and Spanish has, by and large, not been encouraged. Such blurred vision seems incompatible with the strong emphasis given to foreign missions. Perhaps this is a good time to reevaluate our position and consider the teaching of modern languages in Bible colleges, especially in view of the weakening status of America on the international scene.

In stark contrast to post-World War II developments in the United States, there has been an insatiable desire on the part of the peoples around the world to learn English, the important but intensely difficult international tongue. There is also a persisting interest in other world languages including the central European tongues, Russian, and more recently, Chinese.

Bible schools in Europe, the Far East, and the developing nations have followed this mainstream and demonstrated a desire to cultivate the study of modern foreign languages. It is not uncommon to meet students from Bible schools outside of the United States who command two or three languages. Some European Bible schools as a matter of principle encourage prospective missionaries to have a working knowledge of English before striking out into distant lands and then learn an additional language. Perhaps we at Christian institutions in the United States can learn something here from our European counterparts. However, instead of merely emulating foreign sister institutions, we ought to search for fundamental reasons that are scripturally and educationally sound. We need to be able to relate learning to faith, if we are to validate our endeavors in the area of modern language study.

Biblical Foundation

A scriptural perspective on the evolving of languages leads us back to a time of linguistic unity, the pre-Babel era. The effect of man's fall on language up to this time appears to have been minimal, for we are told, "the whole earth used the same language and the same words."[7] This meant that there existed a free flow of information among all the inhabitants of the earth and along with it, a great potential for progress in the realm of intellectual pursuits and the possibility of an explosion of knowledge. The developing situation was playing into the hand of human pride, for we are informed that they wanted to make a name for themselves (Gen. 11:4).

Languages At Babel

The unity of an original language also demonstrates that people of like language tend to isolate themselves and become insular. God had commanded the people to disperse and fill the earth. Instead of obeying, they remained together and decided to engage in a giant project, the building of a city including a superstructure known as the Tower of Babel. No doubt this undertaking required extensive time for planning and construction, and it was during the stages of building that the diversification of language took effect. We read, "The Lord confused the language of the whole earth" (Gen. 11:9).

In our view the diversification of language need not have been an overnight development. Linguistic changes have continued to take place to this day inhibiting communication and separating people. Diversification of language was initiated by God to disperse people effectively and keep them separate by the formation of communication barriers. This method of dispersion was so effective that today there are over five thousand different languages and numerous additional dialects reaching to the remotest corners of the earth.

Languages at Pentecost

Only once does the Scripture record a major crossing of language barriers. This occurred thousands of years after the city and tower project on the plains of Shinar, and it took place at a strategic moment in history for a specific purpose. On the day of Pentecost, Jews of the Dispersion and proselytes speaking many different languages gathered together at Jerusalem in order to celebrate the feast. For the followers of Christ it was a time to acknowledge the power and works of God before launching on a worldwide proclamation of the gospel of Christ. There were gathered Parthians, Medes, Elamites, Mesopotamians, Cappadocians, people from Pontus, Asia, Phrygia, Pamphylia, Egypt, Libya, Rome, Crete, and the Arab lands (Acts 2:9–11). All these people heard the proclamations of Pentecost in their native languages without the aid of highly skilled simultaneous translators who had studied texts of the proceedings the night before. We are told: "The multitude came together, and were bewildered, because they were each one hearing them speak in his own language" (Acts 2:6). The crossing of language barriers at Pentecost was clearly a miracle that demonstrated the power of the Holy Spirit and pointed the way of the future.

The meaning of this miracle is as worthy of our consideration now as it was then (Acts 2:12). Why should all of the people receive the message of Pentecost in their own vernacular tongue when Aramaic, the trade language, Greek, the *lingua franca* of the day, or Latin, the politically important tongue, could have been used? I believe that the linguistic break between the Old Testament and New Testament is illustrated here by means of a miracle. In the Old Testament days

God had used the chosen people, the children of Israel, and their Hebrew tongue as the major channel of communication between God and man. Only in two books of the Old Testament is there a measured variation. Just as the veil of exclusivism was rent in two at the death of Christ, the linguistic exclusivism was similarly torn at the conclusion of the New Testament events when the Holy Spirit descended. From Pentecost diverse languages were to be used to proclaim God's redemptive work throughout the world. *Babel and Pentecost form opposite linguistic poles, the former leading to diversification and the latter illustrating unification and an overcoming of the consequences of Babel.*[8]

No doubt God had not intended the diversification of languages to inhibit communication between God and man, but only between man and man. The use of multiple languages at Pentecost seems to indicate God's concern to communicate His message into as many tongues as there are people who use them. It also illustrates the complete adequacy of any tongue to convey God's message to man. Diverse languages were to be used to spread the gospel of Christ even when a common trade language existed. And yet, the permanent record of Christ and the early church was not made in the lowly Aramaic dialect most frequently used by Christ and his disciples but rather in Greek, the cultural language of the day. It was preserved for posterity in the most highly developed linguistic vehicle available. This linguistic medium was Indo-European in character, unrelated to Hebrew or other Semitic languages, and points prophetically the way of the future torchbearers in the dissemination of the gospel.

Languages and New Testament Proclamation

The changeover in the linguistic medium of expression from the Old Testament Hebrew and its related Aramaic to the New Testament Greek took place almost imperceptibly and in the astonishingly short time span of one generation. When Jesus commanded His disciples to become witnesses and preach the gospel to all the world, this world was linguistically comprised of a multitude of different languages.

How was this commandment to be followed aside from the empowering of the Holy Spirit? The dynamics of a shift in the linguistic medium of communication were built right into the original church by Greek-speaking Jews of the Dispersion. Even so, the changeover in linguistic leadership during the first few decades in the history of Christianity is nothing short of miraculous. It represents a break with the esoteric Hebrew of one language family in favor of another that fed into an expanding network of related Indo-European languages and consequently facilitated the spread of the gospel. The chosen individual to help establish this new direction through disciple-making and writing was the apostle Paul, a multilinguist eminently qualified and carefully trained for the task.

We know of Paul that he was a Roman citizen who grew up speaking Aramaic. We also know that he spoke Greek and was a zealous Jew who had studied Hebrew at the feet of Gamaliel. When Jesus met Paul on the road to Damascus, there was thus a choice in language to be made in addressing him. Jesus chose Aramaic, the language of Paul's as well as His own upbringing. This made an enduring impression on Paul, for he still remembered this detail when he recounted the circumstances surrounding his conversion some twenty years later (Acts 26:14). Paul subsequently developed a particular burden to communicate the message of the gospel with clarity. He realized the power inherent in words and language and became a master at interpreting, synthesizing, and making a defense for the Judaeo-Christian faith in the context of European culture.

Languages and the Eschaton

Foreign languages have been and will continue to be an essential component of civilization until Christ's return. They are included in God's time table and are to serve at the consummation of time as an instrument of praise (Rev. 7:9). Judging from current events around the world, there is nothing to indicate that there will be a universal tongue. Languages have risen and fallen with nations, and the importance of the English tongue is not guaranteed for all time. The revival of nationalism in our day tends to suggest the reenforcement of diversification rather than unification of languages as a prospect of the future.

If foreign languages are indeed to play a major role on the human scene and we, in the United States, are losing a sense of their importance both from a secular and spiritual perspective, there is a need to reverse the trend. A summary of biblical observations both general and particular on the meaning, purpose, and challenge of foreign languages should focus our thinking and aid in formulating a philosophical bridge to implementation.

Some Summary Premises

1. The very existence of foreign languages is a result of man's sin nature.
2. As the intent of diversification of language was to confuse and disperse, it is easier to remain monolingual and become insular.
3. The bridging of language barriers runs counter to the intent of diversification and therefore cannot be accomplished without effort and some pain.
4. Language is the only way of communicating God's Word, and every language is adequate to convey His message.
5. God has commanded that the message of redemption be brought to all people and consequently be transmitted in all languages.
6. The scriptural pattern indicates approaching others with the gospel in their native tongue.
7. Not everyone is expected to be multilingual. Ability and background are two practical indicators.
8. Foreign languages are and will continue to be a major force in world civilization until the end of time.
9. By the end time God has willed that there be an open channel of communication for the gospel in all languages.
10. All peoples and languages are to be represented in ascribing ultimate praise and glory to God.

Philosophical Rationale

All Bible colleges have an educational philosophy that is expressed in part by their statements of objectives. Certainly subjects in the division of general education should also relate to the biblical core and in some way bring us closer to God. The American Association of Bible Colleges has suggested that its member schools include in their catalogs objectives expressed in terms of student behavior, e. g., the student graduating from a Bible college should be able:

To give evidence that he has acquired a deep appreciation of missionary service.
To give evidence of Christian culture in terms of refinement, appreciation, social attitudes, and skills.[9]

More individually tailored statements of objectives can be found in most Bible college catalogs, as for example:

> To guide the student into a deep sense of his mission in personal soul winning and world evangelism at home and abroad.[10]

Disseminating the Gospel

We believe that the basic strategy for disseminating the gospel has remained the same, i.e., from Judea to Samaria and to the uttermost parts of the world (Acts 1:8). Spiritual concern and missionary endeavors should begin at home, spread to the surrounding areas, and then reach out beyond. There is thus room for home as well as foreign missions. For those with a spiritual concern in foreign mission, learning a modern language becomes inevitable. This chore should not be deferred until such time when support has been raised and flight tickets are in hand. Bible colleges can meet the need for modern language instruction by offering at least one or two key modern languages as a bridge to further language learning. An exposure to at least one European tongue at the college level will be invaluable as a head start, no matter what other languages are later learned.

The study of modern languages at Bible colleges can and should also be viewed as a means for cross-cultural experience. However, classes in linguistics and intercultural studies should not be allowed to become substitutes for the study of language. Classes in linguistics are excellent as an analytical exercise to facilitate language learning, but they do not necessarily contribute to the understanding of another culture. The basic tool whereby a culture structures the conceptual world around it is its individual language.[11] Thus, if we want to strengthen cross-cultural understanding, we should begin with foreign language study. We can then expand to include other aspects of culture and add courses in intercultural studies. However, cross-cultural exposure without a study of foreign language undermines the foundations of the bridge we are trying to build.

There are some missionary-minded evangelicals who entertain the commendable vision of reaching out to this country's internationals, especially those in institutions of higher learning. This is a strategic work that demands our wholehearted support, but this endeavor must not become exclusive. During the current decade there will be several thousand evangelical missionaries, the postwar generation, who will be retiring. Missionary activity with internationals in this country does not diminish the urgency of the Great Commission. World events of recent years have increased that sense of urgency. At the same time modern technology has vastly multiplied the capacity to reach people. Bible college students need to be able to sense these needs as well as opportunities.

Reversing Babel

The natural flow of language acquisition is from the languages most closely related to one's own, to the more distant. The move from Judea to Samaria should follow the deductive pattern of progression from the simple to the more complex. For practical pedagogic reasons, French, German, and Spanish are logical first steps in the effort to overcome Babel, not only because of their influence on and relationship to English, but also as stepping stones to the "Samaritan languages" of Europe, Asia, and Africa.

English is the meeting ground of the Romance and German language families. From that starting point both French and German are bridge languages, for both will help the student understand his own language in a deeper way while moving him toward more complex relatives in the Indo-European language family. *French* cognates make up over 60 percent of the English vocabulary making it a logical first step in foreign language study. As a bridge language, French is the key to proficiency in many languages which have modeled themselves after French, such as modern Turkish and the trade languages of West Africa. As a vehicle of cross-cultural and missionary endeavors, French opens the doors of communication with over fifty nations in Europe, Africa, Asia, the Middle East, and the South Pacific.

German is the leading language of Europe—the language of art and science, of theology and philosophy, as well as trade and technology. Its 100 million speakers not only embrace the peoples of East and West Germany and Austria, but also three-fourths of Switzerland. Among nations speaking German as a second language are Holland, Denmark, Sweden, Poland, Czechoslovakia, Hungary, Yugoslavia, northern Italy, and eastern France. In addition, the study of German as a second language is popular in such widely separated areas as Japan, Russia, Chile, Egypt, and Turkey.

Ethnic background and cultural heritage should be a definite consideration in choosing a foreign language. For example, apart from the countries in which *Spanish* is spoken, the Spanish-speaking population of the United States is currently approaching 20 million in the border states of the Southwest and Florida alone. Demographers suggest that by the year 2000 Hispanics will be America's largest minority group. As these areas become both legally and practically bilingual, Spanish language education is becoming fundamental to the public school curriculum. More importantly, Los Angeles, whose suburbs spread to within 100 miles of the Mexican border, is the home of some 3 million Hispanics of whom only 1 percent profess a personal faith in Jesus Christ.[12] The scriptural question "how shall they believe unless they hear" seems soundly promotional of a strong Spanish language department in those Bible schools whose "Judea" is highly Hispanic. A similar argument can be made for the French in the border areas of the Northeast and the Germanic languages in the Midwest.

The need for cultural awareness and understanding runs parallel to that of learning foreign languages, for the diversification of culture is a corollary to the diversification of language. One needs to be reminded here that the diversification of language came first and resulted in the inhibiting of cultural achievement, namely the building of a great city with a tower that would touch heaven itself.

Cultural Awareness

Since the advent of Christ the need for cultural appreciation has grown in importance. Christ, the pivot and focal point of history, has exerted an unparalleled influence on the creative endowments of man. All forms of creative expression in Western culture including art, literature, and music have drawn heavily for inspiration on the Christian faith. There is a stream of individuals who have used their God-given talents with integrity. The impact of Christ on the attitudes and activities of Western man has been so great that Western civilization could not be comprehended apart from its Christian influence. Even the evolution of thought and language are closely intertwined with the Christian faith.

It is one of the objectives of Bible colleges to instill growing cultural awareness and understanding in their graduates, enabling them to integrate a total theological education with real world experiences. During the last decade there has been a growing interest in the study of one's roots, and we believe that the study of any modern language forming a major element in American ethnic composition will provide a secure anchor for cultural studies. Only when we have a good grasp on our own cultural heritage, will we be able to expand our horizons to understand other cultures. Modern languages are the key in the instilling of cultural awareness; they form the bridge to the study of culture other than one's own.

Social Involvement

Expression of social concern commonly found in the pages of daily newspapers should speak pointedly to the heart of the believer. Jesus had compassion for the bereaved, the poor, the social outcasts. He healed the sick and fed the hungry and was interested in the physical and material well-being of man in addition to being concerned about his spiritual welfare. Jesus specifically sought out those who were in need, always working in the framework of culture.

The need for social involvement exists now as it did then. A shrinking globe has brought the suffering of man closer to our doorstep than ever before, and the hungerbelt runs through lands in which foreign tongues are spoken. However, one need not even leave the shores of North America for social involvement. There is a need for bilingual nurses and social workers in many cities of our own land. Service in the area of social involvement has opened opportunities here and abroad to express spiritual concern as well. Some of the doors of spiritual opportunity can, as a matter of fact, only be entered by means of social involvement. Facility in a modern language and an appreciation of culture usually go hand in hand in meeting the prerequisites for such assignments.

The three areas of educational interest specifically spelled out in most of the catalogs of Bible colleges, namely spiritual concern, cultural awareness, and social involvement are absolutely valid. We believe they can best be satisfied by allowing students to gain solid exposure to one of the common modern languages as a basis for further study of the same language, as a bridge to another tongue, or as basic support in general education and other departments of the divisions of biblical or professional education. The consistent effort required for language study will also be an exercise in patience and discipline that will profit the student in a personal way throughout his college career.

Practical Application

The integration of faith and learning in the foreign language departments of North American Bible colleges involves the implementation of the school's spiritual, cultural, and social goals within a strongly practical framework. Because the Christian is commanded to communicate to all the world, the basic rationale for foreign language education rests on biblical principles. The realization of those principles cannot be achieved, however, without pragmatic planning and efficient performance in the classroom.

Curriculum Design

A realistic appraisal of curriculum flexibility and the availability of faculty must always include cost efficiency. Curriculum development in the field of foreign language should be approached as a service function designed to support and complement biblical studies and professional studies as a strategic part of general education. An individual trained to teach a modern foreign language should have had firsthand exposure to the living language and culture, and possess a love for students as well as his subject. As in the case of all general education faculty, biblical and theological training is essential. Such teachers are cultural generalists, Renaissance people with a broad background in art, history, literature, music, and philosophy.

If small class size makes for inefficient operations, language sequences can by cycled to be offered alternate years, and instructors can be readily utilized in another department. Securing a quality teacher is the crucial first step. Curriculum development should then revolve around the competencies and interests of the instructor and match the needs of the college as closely as possible.

An important next step is establishing the cultural relevance of a language. Toward this end, an appreciation of the geographical location and ethnic demographics of the area can be invaluable. Areas with large minorities can provide great support to a language program. Ethnic communities serve as a ready source for field trips, guest lectures, practical conversational experiences, and cultural activities that provide welcome stimulus to learning a second language. Most importantly, the exploitation of available resources in the community gives foreign language education an edge of living dynamism and a sense of relevance. Just as language is the product of cultural, social, historical, and religious factors within a society, so the study of language should be a vehicle to open student awareness to the forces which shape a culture. Building cultural awareness and practical application into the curriculum are primary steps in combating the tendency towards insularity and entrenched monolingualism.

Classroom Methodology

Integration of the foreign language into a student's life necessitates some mastery of the language, not just an introduction to it. If a student cannot speak the language after fulfilling his academic requirements, then relevance and applicability are compromised. Three semesters emphasizing vocabulary, grammar, reading, and conversational skills should provide a solid foundation for proficiency. A fourth semester of specialization in culture and conversation can sharpen and focus student skills and provide a basis for advanced study.

Comparative studies utilizing language provide a stimulus for student interest and build a bridge between language study and the fields of history and literature. Guided studies in folklore and mythology as an integral part of the language program, for example, broaden appreciation for universal motifs and establish the inherent unity of the race in Adam. A student of German studying the legend of the dragon slayer will find a similar story in Dutch, French, Spanish, Russian, and dozens of other languages.[13] This pervasive legend, like the omnipresent Deluge accounts, can be associated with fragments of it in the biblical record as found in the books of Job, Psalms, and Revelation, thus bringing the language student through literature and comparative studies back to the threshold of Babel. Similar comparative studies can be undertaken in historical linguistics. The close intertwining of the Judaeo-Christian faith and Western culture can also be unraveled through comparative studies.

Just as God sought to communicate the gospel to each hearer in his own tongue at Pentecost, so each language seeks to acknowledge God's presence and communicate with Him in a unique way. The English term "Savior" is expressed in German as *Heiland*, or healer. This idea is consistent with the German interpretation of a man as a critically ill creature in need of Christ's healing touch. To the French, Christ is *Seigneur*, the great Lord, who saves through omnipotence. Each term is an expression in language of a mindset

and conception of God and man's relationship to Him. The apprehension of such concepts can not only make the student more
capable in reaching these peoples with the gospel, but if internalized, can serve to broaden and strengthen the individual's understanding of and relationship to God. In this way the foreign language
classroom brings faith alive by showing how God communicates
within culture and by providing a new perspective on God's
relationship to man.

Language is a vehicle of communication and should always be
taught with this fundamental thought in mind. As an attempt to
improve the communication between God and men, between the
creature and the Creator, language education should strive to follow
natural language acquisition patterns. As an infant learns through his
senses and by experience to communicate first primary then abstract ideas and needs, so the foreign language classroom should be
a laboratory building systematically and utilizing all means that
stimulate language acquisition.[14]

Interdisciplinary Potential

In creating a relevant, culturally alive environment, foreign language can support missions and biblical studies through direct
application. Use of foreign language Bibles (particularly modern
translations) as readers in the classroom synthesizes the grammar
and vocabulary of the language with Scripture. Translating familiar
Bible stories not only facilitates proficiency but also lays the
foundation for outreach and evangelism.

Integration can demonstrate the common bond of Christianity as
hymns and gospel choruses make a solid addition to foreign
language study. Pedagogically, singing is a pleasant and efficient
way to improve pronunciation and is usually welcomed with
enthusiasm by students. Introducing such choruses as "God Is So
Good" from Africa and hymns as "Fairest Lord Jesus" from
Germany not only gives the student a headstart in cross-cultural
ministry, but also points out that believers share in a common
musical heritage that transcends the limitations of Babel.

A cultural approach to language fits the spirit and goals of the
Bible college. A student should learn to speak as the language is
spoken naturally, within its cultural milieu. In addition to the use of a
good basic textbook stressing culture, this can be accomplished
through the use of films, slides, multimedia presentations, records,

and tapes. Generous time must be allowed to insert historical, social, and traditional folkloric material into the curriculum. Personal interaction and response is essential. Mechanical aids such as electronic equipment should be used only for reenforcement and not as a substitute for personalized instruction.

Opportunities to express social concern while establishing oneself in a foreign language can be found almost anywhere on this continent, if such opportunities are seriously sought. The Christian service office might be of help in locating minority churches, and those of various ethnic backgrounds living in rest homes, hospitals, or isolation who have particular needs. Special seasons, such as Thanksgiving and Christmas, provide natural occasions for caring and sharing.

Conclusion

After suffering from decades of neglect and deterioration, foreign language education in America is again gaining credibility. The decline of American influence and power overseas and the rising tide of nationalism around the globe are contributing to a communication crisis among monolingual businessmen, diplomats, and professionals. The intrinsic value of modern language study and the steady growth of non-English speaking minorities in the United States in the last twenty years makes proficiency in a second tongue desirable even for those who never cross an international border. There exists today an opportunity in leadership for evangelicals with a vision.

As institutions of higher learning, Bible colleges have a shared and common responsibility to respond to these and the additional spiritual challenge. Since Babel, the diversification of languages, and through language, cultures, has built seemingly impregnable walls between peoples. In the midst of this chaos, Jesus Christ became man and declared that His gospel was to be preached to all men in all places. Ultimately, foreign language education brings the student back to God. To a people called to spread the gospel, modern language education is an imperative.

The validity of the Christian faith depends on the statement "Thus saith the Lord." It is a relationship of language. God speaks and His people listen and respond. The Bible clearly teaches that God seeks to communicate to man and that His communication must be comprehensible. Modern language education is an important part of establishing a bridge between peoples and cultures. It is an essential prerequisite for the spreading of the gospel and will continue to be until the day when every knee shall bow and every tongue confess that Jesus Christ is Lord.[15] Babel cannot be undone, but it can be overcome.

Notes

1. *Higher Education and National Affairs,* 28 (9 Nov. 1979): 3.
2. Lynn Sanborne, "Our Language Incompetence Is Beyond Words," *Los Angeles Times,* 24 April 1980, p. 13.
3. *Educational Media News* (Spring 1980), p. 6. For another article on the same subject see Ronald W. Rosken's "Legacies of the Tower of Babel," *The Modern Language Journal,* 64 (Summer 1980): 173–78.
4. Ibid., p. 7. For a more complete discussion of the President's Commission on Foreign Languages and International Studies see *The Modern Language Journal,* 64 (Spring 1980).
5. Malcolm G. Scully, "Require Foreign Language Studies, Presidential Panel Urges Colleges," *The Chronicle of Higher Education,* 19 (13 Nov. 1979): 10–12.
6. *Higher Education and National Affairs,* p. 3.
7. Genesis 11:1. Quotations from the Scriptures are taken from the New American Standard Bible.
8. George M. Cowan, "Overcoming Babel," *Christianity Today,* 16 July 1971, pp. 8–10.
9. John Mostert, *Bible College Objectives* (Wheaton: AABC, 1973), p. 20.
10. *Briercrest Bible Institute Catalog 1979–81,* Caronport, Sask., p. 10.
11. For insight into the centrality and tenacity of language in the ethnic community see the work of Joshua A. Fishman, *Language Loyalty in the United States* (The Hague, 1966), and his selected essays *Language in Sociocultural Change* (Stanford: Stanford University Press, 1972).
12. John Maust, "The Exploding Hispanic Minority: A Field in Our Back Yard," *Christianity Today,* 8 Aug. 1980, pp. 12–13.
13. Antti Aarne and Stith Thompson, *The Types of the Folktale* (Helsinki, 1964), pp. 88–92.
14. A sound book on this subject is Thomas and Elisabeth Brewster's *Language Acquisition Made Practical* (Colorado Springs: Lingua House, 1976).
15. Compare Isaiah 45:23, Romans 14:4, and Philippians 2:10–11.

The Author

The combination of excellent credentials and solid experience makes Robert O. Woodburn one of the outstanding academic leaders of the Bible college movement today. Presently vice president for academic affairs at William Tyndale College, Woodburn is a graduate of Dickinson College (B.A.), Dallas Theological Seminary (Th.M.), and Washington's American University (M.A.; Ph.D.). He has held faculty positions at Shelton College, Charlotte Christian School, and Washington Bible College where he served as academic dean before joining the Tyndale team in 1979.

The Subject

The study of the humanities is central to a well-rounded Bible college education. According to Woodburn, "the humanities are essentially those areas of human and cultural thought and expression reflected in man's literature, language, art, philosophy, religion, and history." It is obviously necessary to use one specific discipline as a representative model, and Dr. Woodburn has chosen history, pointing out that much of the Bible is history and that the study of any history leads to significant philosophical insights.

13

HUMANITIES

Robert O. Woodburn

The propriety of including the humanities in the Bible college curriculum would seem to be easily justified. Grappling with human values, ideals, and aspirations and evaluating these in the light of Scripture should be a natural exercise for the thoughtful student. Becoming conversant with the great literary, artistic, and philosophical expressions of man would seem to be a part of the student's educational legacy. Gaining a sense of history and historical processes should provide an indispensable perspective from which to view life and ministry.

Although the humanities furnish a bountiful reservoir of information and experience, educators within the Bible college have often felt uncomfortable with the inclusion of these studies in the curriculum. Perhaps to gain a degree of legitimacy or acceptability in *academia*, the humanities have been reluctantly introduced with insufficient rationale. The specter of secular courses within the biblical framework creates for some an uneasy, if not unholy, alliance.

Surely, there must be a coherent theory or approach to Christian education that can provide a philosophical foundation compatible with an academic superstructure fashioned in part from the humanities.

Introduction

Explanation and Definition

If any broad subject field falls under the purview of the Bible college curriculum, it is the humanities. It is here that God is revealed at work within the varied expressions and experiences of man throughout history.

The humanities are essentially those areas of human and cultural thought and expression reflected in man's literature, language, art, philosophy, religion, and history. It was during the Renaissance that the humanities became a discrete area of consideration and study. This came about with the rediscovery of the classical past and the designated "more humane letters"—*litterae humaniores*—of revived Greek and Latin writers in contrast to the theological letters of the medieval schoolmen. A further refinement of this interest arose in northern Europe with the emergence of a "Christian humanism" which was more religious in character.

More recently, the term "secular humanism" has been added to the educational glossary. This is, however, a philosophical term, not a technical or academic term. *Secular humanism is a philosophy that rejects supernaturalism and asserts the inherent worth of man and his ability to achieve self-realization through his natural capacities and unaided reason.* This theological deviation should neither cloud nor confuse the legitimate study of philosophy, literature, or history.

Rationale for Inclusion

The humanities are of special interest to the Christian student. They provide a framework within which the student can systematically explore and investigate certain ideas, trends, and concepts which have characterized the collective experience and expression of man. To be sure, the Bible remains the ultimate authority and standard by which we judge all things; however, to disregard what man has done, whether negative or positive, is to obviate life itself and to ignore the importance of the human marketplace within which the Holy Spirit must ultimately work through us.

Man's *literary* expressions, for example, can not only provide working models for all kinds of communication and expression, but, more importantly, open up to us artistic insights into the world around us, provoke thought, and challenge our capacities for evaluation and aesthetic appreciation. The writings of Milton, Tennyson, or Robert Frost provide such experience. Negatively, literature can dramatize in such a poignant way the alienation and frustration of man as he wrestles with the eternal verities of life apart from God. Hemingway and Faulkner are illustrative of this struggle. This provides opportunity to exercise and develop our skills as we "test the spirits. . . ." If the Christian is to remain in touch with the world in which he lives and somehow effect change within it, he must be aware of the literary expressions of his day.

History, too, as a part of the humanities, provides the framework and the ordered sequence of events to aid our understanding of the past, present, and even future. The Christian student cannot be a-historical because God Himself has chosen to work within history both to reveal Himself and to implement His redemptive plan. History provides perspective and the accumulated experience of the past so essential to one's personal enrichment and sense of balance. The amnesiac can readily testify to the hopeless dislocation from those things which are and were known.

The humanities also encompass the academic study of man's *religion* and *philosophy*. Some would question their legitimacy within the Bible college curriculum. The value here, though, is to see the failure of man to fashion systems of thought which ignore or exclude the revelation of God in the Scriptures. The comparative and historical study of religion and philosophy can enliven and open up one's understanding of a given period of time. Positively, it can challenge the student to develop his own world view and use the categories which philosophy provides in that development. At many points, theology and philosophy coincide and address, though perhaps from different vantage points, the same questions and concerns.

Biblical Foundation

Using *history* as a representative model for the humanities, one is immediately struck by the fact that the historian is especially at home in the Scriptures. The Bible itself is history. The Egyptian sojourn and wanderings of Israel in the wilderness are clearly historical. David, Solomon, Daniel, and Jeremiah were figures who left an indelible mark upon the narrative of history. The birth, ministry, death, and resurrection of Jesus took place during a specific time period.

Identification and Explanation of Passages

The Bible provides the philosophical framework within which the historian labors. Furthermore, the Bible specifically identifies the "signal events" of history—past, present, and future.

The great historical watersheds set forth in the Bible center around three events: the creation of man, the incarnation of Christ, and the consummation of this age. Within these time periods, the student sees the hand of God at work through His sovereignty, His grace, and His judgment.

Creation. The Book of Genesis sets the historical stage for all that is to follow. The keynote is given in Genesis 1:1: "In the beginning God created the heavens and the earth." This is a fundamental historical assumption that God exists and that He has actively and creatively involved Himself in time and space. Any adequate interpretation about history must flow from this divine act.

Subsequently, "God created man in His own image" (Gen. 1:27). Man became an integral part of the historical process and since he was created in God's image, he was active in the historical process as a moral, intelligent, reasoning, and responsible being. He was not the by-product of an impersonal evolutionary process. Yet, man was to alter the intended course of history by his willful disobedience: " . . . and [she] did eat, and gave also unto her husband with her; and he did eat" (Gen. 3:6). This incident laid the groundwork for a continuing historical struggle in which the standards of God are pitted against those of Satan. Man is at odds with himself, his neighbor, and society; and history is shaped in part by these tensions between good and evil.

There is also anticipation in the historical record at this point. God curses the serpent for his role in man's fall and then declares: "And I will put enmity between you and the woman, and between your seed and her seed; he shall bruise you on the head, and you shall bruise him on the heel" (Gen. 3:15, NASB). This anticipates not only the coming of Christ to die on a cross but also His eventual historical triumph over Satan at the end of time and as a prelude to eternity.

Incarnation. The next great historical watershed is the embodiment of God on earth in the person of Jesus Christ.

Jesus came physically, He came historically. Paul spoke of this event in Galatians 4:4–5: "But when the fulness of the time came, God sent forth His Son, born of a woman, born under the Law, in order that He might redeem those who were under the Law, that we might receive the adoption as sons" (NASB). Paul sets forth here the pivotal event of human history. God again dramatically intervenes at the appropriate time within the flow of human events to provide hope and redemption for humankind through His son. The historical events surrounding the appropriateness of this special point in history together with the events flowing from it come under the purview of the Christian historian.

Peter in his second sermon, following Pentecost, sets forth the comprehensive historical force of the Incarnation by reaching back to the "holy prophets" and reaching forward to the "period of restoration." Peter commented: "And that He may send Jesus, the Christ appointed for you, whom heaven must receive until the period of restoration of all things, about which God spoke by the mouth of His holy prophets from ancient time" (Acts 3:20–21, NASB).

Consummation. Even for the student of Scripture, prognostication about the future has its difficulties. However, the Bible is clear that there will be a God-initiated resolution to the perplexities and problems of human history. When the disciples came to Jesus inquiring about the "end of the age," He spoke in historical terms when He said "you shall hear of wars and rumours of wars. . . . nation shall rise against nation and kingdom against kingdom" (Matt. 24:6-7). Then Jesus noted that the "Son of man shall come in His glory . . ." (Matt. 25:31) and will judge the nations.

Furthermore, John stated in Revelation 21:1: "And I saw a new heaven and a new earth: for the first heaven and the first earth were passed away . . . ." This apocalyptical observation moves the student in his thinking from time and history into the eternal state. Historical trends and institutions as they are known today will cease, and a new order will begin.

These events, though anticipated and still future, are also the stuff of history and must be included in the purview of the Christian teacher-historian.

In addition to these three signal events, it must be remembered that God not only intervenes in history but *superintends* the entire flow of history and that He elects to work through men, nations, and governments to accomplish His purposes. God is not passive but active in history.

Nations which have been responsive to the principles of Scripture have been blessed of God. Solomon, a national leader in his own right, wrote: "Righteousness exalts a nation; but sin is a reproach to any people" (Prov. 14:34). There does seem to be an inexorable historical relationship between man's obedience to God and God's willingness to bless and prosper that nation (cf. 2 Chron. 7:14).

Furthermore, *man* owes his eternal allegiance to God while at the same time being responsive to his temporal obligations on earth. Jesus set forth this principle in Matthew 22:21: Give to Caesar what is Caesar's and to God what is God's. This twofold citizenship underscores the importance of understanding the interrelatedness between the principles of the Bible and our temporal interaction and conduct within society.

God has also ordained human *government* as a vehicle to provide protection of the citizenry and to act as an agent for the administration of justice. The Christian can hardly remain ambivalent to these issues. In Romans 13:1-7, Paul outlines the mutual responsibilities of government and the governed.

Systematization of Passages

Following this brief review of some essential passages relating to historical processes, certain theological statements can be made which provide a transition from exposition to philosophy.

Theology Proper. God initiates, superintends, and brings to consummation the flow of historical events. He stands outside history yet has become involved in history as Creator and Savior. God is sovereign as He directs and moves within history through nations, individuals, and institutions.

Bibliology. The Bible itself is an inerrant historical record of God's gracious dealings with humankind from the beginning. The Bible is essential to any correct interpretation of history whether through specific recorded events or through broad principles which apply to all times and places. Historiography and bibliology can hardly be separated.

Christology. Christ through the incarnation entered time and affected all subsequent human events. He lived and labored within the historical timeframe. He died on a cross, arose from the dead, and ascended into heaven—all historical and far-reaching events. History must be calculated and interpreted christologically.

Anthropology. History only reaffirms and illustrates what Scripture has already declared about the nature and activity of man.

Although man was created (not evolved) in the image and likeness of God (*imago Dei*), he fell from his lofty estate through an act of disobedience. Though man is inherently evil (the Neronian persecutions or the Holocaust), he is capable of doing good things (charitable work or prolonging life through scientific advances). History eloquently demonstrates these tensions. By means of Christ's atonement for sin, man has become the object of Christ's redemption and the restorative work of the Holy Spirit.

Soteriology. God has always acted redemptively in history. The Bible itself is a divine record of God's redemptive work. Broadly speaking, history illustrates how God has reached out through His eternal law and requirements of religious ceremony. His ultimate provision is seen in the death of Christ. The ebb and flow of man's response to God's redemptive work throughout time provides significant insight into the patience and longsuffering of God and the pernicious and corrupt nature of man.

Ecclesiology. The church is an historical institution among other things. Jesus had predicted its emergence. At Pentecost it became reality. The Book of Acts traces its early history. John issues warnings and commendations to seven local churches in Asia.

The extrabiblical historical record traces the growth and development of the church from that point to the present. History has revealed significant insight into the strength and durability of the church through periods of persecution, theological controversy, and schism. Without the historical record, the enduring heritage and imposing record of the church would be impoverished.

Eschatology. The biblical record clearly indicates that history is moving toward a period of climactic events in which there will be political, social, and spiritual revolution arising out of the increasing tensions and troubles of the world. The careful study of the historical record provides a background for cautious prognostication and, perhaps, an "early warning system." Even though the "day (or) the hour" are eternally sealed in the mind of God, to ignore "the signs of the times" is historical folly.

Philosophical Formulation

A critical phase in the move toward effective integration in the classroom occurs at this point. Theological statements must be translated into philosophical categories so that methodology for positive integration can be generated. Since "Philosophy," according to Matthew Arnold, "is the attempt to see life steadily and to see it whole," it would seem consistent to move into this phase in an effort to see the interrelatedness between Christian faith and various areas of learning—in this case, history.

Metaphysics. The Christian historian need not be tentative when it comes to the issues of ultimate reality or supernaturalism. God is alive, real, transcendent, active, and personal. "For in him we live, and move, and have our being . . ." (Acts 17:28). Ultimate reality originates in the person of God who initiates, superintends, and sustains all human activity and the flow of historical events. History is not accident, coincidence, or calamity but an ordered framework within which man functions. Biologism and social evolution are not satisfactory responses to the questions of the past, much less the present.

Likewise the Christian historian is able to respond to the issue of causation in history by postulating the presence of a sovereign, not capricious, God who acts justly and mercifully and " . . . who works all things after the counsel of His will" (Eph. 1:11, NASB). His Providence moves all events toward a predetermined end that will eventuate in His ultimate glory. This should not be confused with the mechanistic and impersonal interpretations of Hegel, Spengler, or Marx.

God is also active in history in very specific, personal ways. He is not the absentee god of the Deist. God acted decisively in Creation and He worked through the nation of Israel. He incarnated Himself historically in Jesus Christ and made provision for the work of the Holy Spirit through the church. He will bring to fruition the whole of human history by means of judgment and divine resolution, and provide a new heaven and a new earth.

These things constitute, in part, the metaphysical realities of the Christian historian and teacher which in turn must be carefully woven into lesson preparation and classroom presentation.

Epistemology

Determining the nature, source, and validity of historical knowledge is a part of the historian's craft. Napoleon's statement notwithstanding, that "History is but a fiction agreed upon," the historian's burden is to accurately reconstruct the past and then to bring some degree of meaning to it. This is the technical function of historiography.

For the Christian historian and teacher, the facts are drawn primarily from two sources: special revelation (the Bible) and general revelation (the human record of past events). This categorization is not intended to deny natural revelation (the hand of God in creation and sustenance of His universe), which is more the prerogative of the Christian biologist and physicist. Special revelation gives an inerrant record of God's dealings with man throughout time. It is not only special revelation but special history dealing with particular people, issues, and institutions. The Christian historian and teacher must be conscious of the relationships between these two forms of revelation and feel intellectually, spiritually, as well as professionally comfortable and conversant with both.

Although the Christian historian would not question the validity of the biblical record, he must have a sufficient grounding in hermeneutics as well as the narrative of Scripture in order to feel confident in this foundation document. Furthermore, he must have a grounding in historiography in order to bring the skills and techniques of historical selection, evaluation, and interpretation to the extrabiblical record.

Also, the Christian historian must be especially sensitive to the problem of drawing unwarranted inferences from the record of history and attempting to justify a pet notion or doctrine. Though bias will always creep into the interpretation of the facts, radical assumptions and even propaganda will disrupt learning and mislead the student. We still "see through a glass darkly."

Anthropology

In an effort to arrive at certain philosophical assumptions about the nature of man, his freedom to act, or even his moral status, it seems clear that the historical record provides many valuable insights that coincide perfectly with the teaching of Scripture about man himself.

The popular notion that man is inherently good and subject to improvement through environmental engineering (or even biological engineering) not only opposes biblical teaching but is controverted in the historical record. Although man has, in many cases, mastered his surroundings, he has yet to master his own passions and pernicious ways. He continues to act autonomously and selfishly. The military despotism of Diocletian, the personal excesses and de-

bauchery of King Henry VIII, the "final solution" of the Nazi regime
are all symptomatic of the troubled spirit of humankind. The Bible
declares how man should live; history demonstrates how man does
live.

In spite of man's poor record as a citizen of earth, man does retain
a certain freedom of choice and the capacity to act constructively
and benevolently on behalf of others. This is borne out in the
historical record. These positive attributes are a clear reflection of
the universal *imago Dei*. Apart from this divine influence and the
continued restraint of God in the world, man would have been the
subject of his own annihilation. This is, in part, the rationale for the
establishment of human government.

Axiology

The search by man for the "highest good" is a significant thread of
the historical record. The value that man has placed on human life,
home, community, government, and natural resources has been
checkered. Man has often put the value of others before himself.
The brave stand of a small Spartan force against a superior Persian
army at Thermopylae would be considered by some as an admi-
rable effort and worthy of praise. The self-aggrandizement of Louis
XIV of France at the expense of others is considered reprehensible
behavior.

Man's conduct and the things he has valued most throughout
history have fluctuated dramatically. He has generally acted in his
own self-interest. Such conduct must always be measured against
the absolute standards set forth in Scripture. Ultimately, all things
are to be done "to the glory of God." This is the *summum bonum*.

Objectives

The objective of historical study is to insure the honest and un-
prejudiced reporting of the past through a careful analysis of the
evidence that remains. This is followed by a more difficult and
hazardous task. It concerns the interpretation of the events. What
does history mean and what answers does it bring to the questions
raised by contemporary man? The interpretative task of the
Christian teacher-historian naturally follows. Meaning and understanding of past and present events and inferences about the future
can provide insights for all to see. Above all, the historian should
endeavor to avoid parochialism and "single issue" historicism. The

complexities of each age are so great that a single focus approach will inevitably create distortion.

Practical Application

Because of the invaluable contribution of historical studies to the thinking and maturing of the Christian student, it is incumbent upon the college administration and faculty to provide sufficient exposure and experience in this area. The theological and philosophical assumptions which have been generated would seem to make this clear. The Bible college is in a good position not only to provide sufficient history curriculum but also to insure cross-pollination between historical studies and the courses in Bible and theology. It is at this point that the integration of faith and learning can become a practical reality.

Integration

The process of identifying historical issues or concepts which correlate in a positive way with Scripture is far from a troublesome task. In fact, the student or teacher of history may unwittingly overlook many obvious correlations. However, a word of caution. Careless and artificial correlations between the two are dangerous and dishonest. A thorough grounding in the Bible and history helps to prevent artificial linkage.

Both Scripture and the historical record *deal with similar and even the same time sequences* and, more importantly, *deal with much of the same subject matter*. The Bible is specialized history and the record is inerrant. History is a more generalized narrative and is flawed. However, there are many things common to both.

Sovereignty, providence, grace, and judgment are common themes in both general and special history. The tenuous and uncertain days of Israel's wanderings in the Sinai and the nation's remarkable survival point up the providence and care of a loving God. Growing out of similar circumstances, seventeenth century Separatists made an uncertain journey to the New World and barely survived their first New England winter. Yet, it can be safely concluded that through a remarkable set of circumstances, or providence, the Separatists were spared and eventually flourished as a society.

Insofar as it can be reckoned by the perceptive student, judgment is a recurring historical theme. God's declaration to Abraham that He would bless those who blessed him and curse those who cursed him was borne out historically in the Bible. The gradual decline of Egyptian power following Amenhotep II was evidently precipitated by the enslavement of the Israelites. More recently, the so-called "final solution" of the Jewish problem spelled eventual defeat for the Third Reich. In spite of its military superiority, Nazi Germany's obsession with Abraham's descendants led from the Warsaw ghetto to Auschwitz, Buchenwald, and the eventual collapse of Germany.

One problem area in integration is that, while the historical record is not intrinsically antibiblical, the way history is recorded or written down can be clearly antibiblical. The honest historian endeavors to maintain some semblance of objectivity and avoid extreme forms of bias (complete objectivity is an impossibility). Yet, there are those who deliberately bend the facts of history to suit their own prejudices or points of view. The Marxist historian will bend if not distort the facts surrounding the Russian Revolution of 1917. In Russia, textbooks were rewritten and edited so that the official point of view became the only point of view.

Another problem area is that interpretations of history are many and varied. Some interpretations are clearly antibiblical. Others are simply troublesome. Karl Marx's economic determinism deliberately excludes the supernatural. Oswald Spengler's cyclical interpretation is entirely too pessimistic. Admittedly, the historian is more than a reporter of facts. Rather, it is the business of the historian to make valid judgments and establish causal relationships between facts. The Christian approaches this task with a unique point of view and, thus, should not hesitate to alert others to the problems and dangers of history.

Curriculum

Sensitizing the student to the importance of the integration process must be planned—*it will not happen automatically*. There must be a fundamental agreement among all members of the faculty that such an effort is worthwhile. Integration must be a cross-pollination endeavor involving an interdepartmental thrust. Liberal discussion and an overall strategy by the faculty are essential.

In addition to the biblical core to which all students are exposed, the administration and faculty (and history department, if there is one) must insure sufficient exposure to the historical field itself. The history curriculum should expose the student to the broad flow of historical events (including the traditional survey of the history of civilization) as well as some specialization in those areas which have a bearing upon student interest or need (church history, Latin American and Asian history). Exposure to cognate fields such as political science and sociology may be helpful. Ideally, a student should have one course that covers the main currents of world history with sufficient modern emphasis on Third World nations, the Middle East, and the Orient. A course in the history of religion is a natural for the Bible college student. Most of all, the student should be exposed to the basic methodology of the historian. The elements of historiography are easily grasped and provide a natural sphere in which the integration process can unfold.

Conclusion

The study of history can be a dreary and tedious exercise which often leaves the average student in a state of indifference and apathy. Students view history as did Carlyle—"a great dust heap." Yet, if the student is to understand life and see it whole, he must have a sense of history, the flow of human events, and the inexorable involvement of a sovereign God in the whole process. The issues of grace, judgment, and providence examined within the historical matrix are drawn out of the abstract and given a special animation.

A deliberate and creative study of history can also give the individual a spiritual and intellectual perspective not otherwise acquired. The teacher and student can look back to Creation for a sense of initiation, orientation, and direction, to the Incarnation for redemption and hope, and to the future for a sense of expectation and cosmic resolution to the problems and perplexities created by man himself.

Furthermore, history can be a corrective to provincialism, over-indulgence, and lawlessness. Extremes have always foreshadowed the eventual decline and fall of nations and movements. Surely "these things happened as examples . . . that we should not crave evil things" (1 Cor. 10:6, NASB).

History, by its very nature, is a catalytic field for many disciplines within the Bible college. Bible, theology, the arts, and the professions all have an historical framework and the potential linkage is plain. In fact, history has an integrative quality of its own.

Also, history is an actual part of most fields of study and establishes a singular context and set of events within which those fields of study unfold. The case has already been made for the relationship of Bible and history. Closely related would be historical theology and the study of the progress of Christian doctrine. The arts and sciences, the professional study of music, education, or missions all carry an historical treasury of facts, concepts, and presuppositions.

Earlier I spoke of using history as a representative model for the humanities. Of course this is not to suggest for one moment that religion, philosophy, language and other aspects which rest under the broad umbrella of "humanities" are less important. In a monograph of this length one must significantly delimit in order to make any contribution at all. Indeed, all of the humanities stand under the threat of minimal attention by both Christian and secular educators. Kenneth Woodward and Eric Gelman report on "The Humanities Crisis":

> For most of Western history the study of the humanities needed no defense. To know the best of what had been thought and written, to be able to think critically, to be morally discerning and aesthetically discriminating were the marks of an educated person and leader of the *civitas*. Today, however, American universities teach whatever students want to learn and confer degrees in almost any "discipline." In 1978, for example, less than 20 percent of all undergraduate degrees were awarded in the humanities—literature, language, philosophy and other liberal studies. Education, in short, is a buyer's market, and what most students want is not a philosophy of life but a salable skill.[1]

The whole task of mobilization and integration of one's faith and learning into a cohesive and harmonious whole is *not instinctive but rather deliberate*. Simply being a Bible college does not automatically insure an institution's success in this endeavor. There must be a corporate sense of will and desire to bring new dimension to education. We must proceed reverently, critically, thoughtfully, expectantly, and even optimistically.

Notes

1. Kenneth Woodward and Eric Gelman, "The Humanities Crisis," *Newsweek*, 13 Oct. 1980, p. 113.

The Author

Harlan W. Wyborny brings to this chapter the rare combination of scientist and theologian. He holds the B.S., M.S., and Ph.D. degrees from the University of Iowa and an M.A.B.S. from Dallas Theological Seminary. After serving five years at Sterling College in Kansas, in 1976 Dr. Wyborny joined the faculty of Miami Christian College where he now serves as academic dean. Dr. Wyborny not only understands the process of integration of Scripture and science, but practices it in his classroom as a physicist and on the lecture circuit when he speaks on biblical creationism.

The Subject

The crucial issues in natural science and the Bible do not focus only on the timeless evolution debate. Genetic engineering and a host of other modern technological advances have made this fascinating field one of great concern for the Christian who would live biblically in the late twentieth century. Dr. Wyborny communicates his concern that all Christian leaders thoroughly grasp the harmony of God's truth in both natural and special revelation. He recommends that attention be paid to scientific principles and facts included in the Bible and that an apologetic approach to the teaching of science is often very effective.

14

NATURAL SCIENCES

Harlan W. Wyborny

Meltdown. Ozone depletion. Cloning. These and numerous other popular terms are a product of the unprecedented scientific research and technological development of recent generations. For decades the natural sciences have enjoyed a supremacy among academic and applied disciplines of study, having reached the apex of their glory when man landed on the moon. The past decade, however, has witnessed the emergence of an ever-darkening veil over that glory. In spite of tremendous progress in communications, computer technology, weather prediction, medicine, etc., and in spite of the hundreds of efficiency-increasing devices provided for home, factory, hospital, and farm, science and technology of late have been viewed with growing suspicion—and sometimes even fear.

It seems that science has always been able to solve any problem to which it has given first priority. But why has science not produced a cure for cancer? (What is the truth regarding Laetrile?) Why does science not suggest some acceptable ways of eliminating the energy crisis (in a manner that will not impose restraints on the American lifestyle)? Are these scientific issues or political problems? Obviously such questions will not be addressed in this chapter. But the expectation is that the Bible college graduate who has been instructed in accord with the principles herein will have a basis for approaching such questions in a sound biblical and scientific manner.

Introduction

Generally the disciplines of study included in the broad category of natural science are understood clearly. Webster offers as a definition for natural science the following: "The systematized knowledge of nature and the physical world, including zoology, botany, chemistry, physics, geology, etc."[1] In addition to *knowledge*, science is considered to be a *process*—usually the scientific method of investigation. The methodology is not fixed but may take several forms since some disciplines, such as historical geology and astronomy, do not lend themselves well to objective experimentation in a normal sense. Henry Morris offers this definition: "Science seeks to understand and describe the nature of the universe and all its components, the processes that take place therein, the nature of life and all living creatures. . . ."[2]

Few Bible colleges will have well-equipped laboratory facilities. And few of their science professors will have the opportunity to teach science at a level of sophistication beyond what they studied in their freshman year of undergraduate education. Furthermore, few Bible college graduates will seek employment in a vocation which requires a significant knowledge of science. So why should a Bible college offer any courses in natural science?

Although most Christians can quote Psalm 19:1, few know even the most elementary facts about the stars and solar system. And it is likely that those "facts" are conclusions drawn from an atheistic, evolutionary model of the universe. Unfortunately, Christians often know far less about the natural environment and demonstrate far less concern for God's creation than do unbelievers.[3] Consequently many Christians are incapable of intelligently utilizing God's natural revelation as a point of common interest in directing unbelievers to a saving knowledge of the Creator.

It is expected from his studies of science that the student will gain a deeper understanding of God's creation. But, in addition, he should have learned to discern when teachings of modern science are in conflict with statements and principles of Scripture. His science courses should provide him with a more complete theological education, a more biblical world view.

The Christian worker has additional responsibility for being articulate in science-related matters. As the realization that we are living in a post-Christian era becomes more evident, greater will become the number of potential applications of science which were once considered morally and socially unacceptable. If Bible college graduates are unable to address such issues, to whom will the church look for direction?

Either of the above objectives—learning more of the Creator through study of natural revelation and being prepared to cope with controversial scientific applications—provides sufficient justification for including this subject area in the curriculum of a progressive Bible college. However, at this point in history, the greatest service that can be rendered by a professional who is competent in both natural science and theology is in the area of apologetics. Such a person can lend credibility to standard refutations of alleged contradictions between scientific statements in the Bible and modern science. In addition, he can share numerous personal insights to aid in solving other such "problems." But the main contribution he can make will be to provide a Christian defense of the Bible by exposing the atheistic, naturalistic, evolutionary teachings of secular science.

Biblical Foundation

Scripture Passages

Scripture passages relating to natural science will be presented in five categories: (1) teaching on creation; (2) speaking of God's glory; (3) presenting a biblical cosmology; (4) relating nature to eschatology; and (5) anticipating principles of modern science.

Creation. An investigation of all biblical references to nature reveals creation as the dominant theme. There are over seventy references to creation. Chapter 1 of Genesis is the only accurate record of the origin of the universe and its components. Francis Schaeffer writes, " . . . what is given in Genesis 1:1 has no relationship with the Big Bang theory because from the scriptural viewpoint, the primal creation goes back beyond the basic material or energy."[4] This supernatural action is attributed directly to the wise and omnipotent God, *Elohim.*

Chapter 2 records additional details of the sixth day of creation, revealing God's ordained relationships between man and woman. This chapter also contains God's pattern for man to reserve one day each week for worship and rest. Throughout the Bible are passages which yield additional information about creation: matter was created out of nothing (*ex nihilo*, Heb. 11:3); the creative acts were essentially instantaneous (Ps. 33:6, 9); the fact and method of creation must be accepted by faith (Heb. 11:3); the Son of God, before becoming the Redeemer, was the Creator (John 1:1–3, 14).

Nature and God's Glory. God is pleased when man recognizes and testifies of His magnificent attributes. As man "creates" and builds, possibly even with the purpose of glorification of God, too often man himself receives much of the credit, robbing God. But nature belongs uniquely to God! Man has defiled nature; he has tainted its perfect expression of God's glory (Gen. 3:17–18; Rom. 8:19–22). But man cannot usurp the glory that God has displayed in His creation (Rom. 1:20; Ps. 19:1).

Biblical Cosmology and Natural History. Two cataclysmic, supernatural events were prominent in the earth's history (2 Peter 3:3–6). The first of these two revealed events was creation by the Word of God as discussed above. From Genesis and other Old Testament writings, a physical model of the primeval earth and atmosphere can be constructed. That early earth was destroyed by the second cataclysmic event, the Flood. The tremendous earth-shaping forces associated with this hydrologic and tectonic upheaval have been described by Whitcomb and Morris.[5] The physical principles relative to a water-vapor canopy which may have encompassed the early earth (Gen. 1:6–7) have been discussed by Joseph Dillow.[6] Psalm 104 indicates that mountains were formed at the end of the Flood. Obviously the biblical flood must have an integral, if not central, role in any legitimate model of geologic history.

Nature and Eschatology. Spiritually redeemed humankind awaits the redemption of the physical body. And all of nature awaits the removal of the consequences of man's sin that it has had to suffer (Rom. 8:19–22). The present earth will be destroyed, and God will create a new heaven and a new earth (2 Peter 3:10; Rev. 21:1). There will be no further need for the sun or moon since illumination will be provided by the glory of Christ (Rev. 21:23). Just as man and the animal kingdom lived in harmony before the fall of the first Adam, a peaceful coexistence will return with the Second Advent of the last

Adam. Again "the wolf will dwell with the lamb, and the leopard will lie down with the kid . . ." (Isa. 11:6).

The Bible and Anticipation of Modern Science. Several books have been written in this century to demonstrate a harmony between statements of Scripture and concepts of modern science.[7] Many scientific principles are unmistakably present in Scripture. For example, the statement of the inviolability of natural law is found in Jeremiah 31:35-36. The thermodynamic law of entropy, or deterioration, is stated several times including Isaiah 51:6. Other concepts are stated, and still others are implied throughout the pages of Scripture.

The question is raised whether Hebrew expressions written 3500 years ago to communicate theological truth should be expected to withstand the scientific scrutiny of today. Unfortunately, there is sharp disagreement among Evangelicals over this question. The reader is asked to read the representative Scriptures below in their contexts and decide for himself whether the evidence warrants the suggested scientific concepts.[8]

Scientific Concept	*Reference*
Hydrologic Cycle	Ecclesiastes 1:7
	Isaiah 55:10
Shape of the Earth	Isaiah 40:22
Rotation of the Earth	Job 38:12, 14
Earth in Space	Job 26:7
Uniformity of Natural Law	Jeremiah 31:35-36
Vastness of Space	Jeremiah 31:37
Inaccessibility of Center of Earth	Jeremiah 31:37
Number of Stars	Jeremiah 33:22
Variety of Stars	1 Corinthians 15:41
Relation of Rain to Lightning	Jeremiah 10:13

Theological Premises

Because of the special concerns in the teaching of natural science, no attempt is made to reclassify all scriptural passages listed above into theological categories.

Theology Proper. God's creation provides a natural revelation of His eternal power and divine nature. It also furnishes a glimpse of God's impending judgment upon man for his sin.

Christology. Christ's first contact with the physical universe was not as a developing embryo in the womb of His mother, Mary. Rather, the One born to redeem sinful humankind was the One who a few thousand years earlier brought man and his world into existence from nothing. The physical redemption for which man waits at Christ's return will also include the natural world—all of creation. In the meantime, the very sustenance of natural law, the ultimate source of every natural force, is the power of Christ (Col. 1:17; Heb. 1:3).

Pneumatology. Jesus Christ, the second person of the triune Godhead, had the primary responsibility for executing the act of creation. But this did not occur, of course, apart from the Father or the Holy Spirit. The Holy Spirit seems to have been the superintendent over the activities of the creation week (Gen. 1:2). It is likely that the Holy Spirit, who regenerates man with "new life" in Christ, is the One who first gave life to Adam (Gen. 2:7).

Bibliology. This is undoubtedly the most controversial area in the integration of Bible and science. It was not God's intention to provide through writers of the Bible a complete handbook for the natural sciences. But a multitude of verses speak directly of, or have inferences of, principles of natural science. Apart from the desire to maintain consistent hermeneutical principles, the numerous scientific concepts which are manifest by employing the normal, literal method of interpretation of Scripture warrant this approach.

The topic of science and the Bible, the natural versus the supernatural, has played a critical role in local churches, particularly in America. Individual congregations have split over science-related issues. Even denominational splits have occurred over disagreement as to whether the Genesis record of creation and the worldwide flood should be interpreted literally.[9] In the 1970's, conflict within the Lutheran Church (Missouri Synod) was a demonstration of this point.

Anthropology. Man's creation was the climax of God's creative activity. Contrary to contemporary secular opinion, the world was created for man who was placed in dominion over the rest of creation. Made in the image of God, man was compared by Scripture writers, not to animals, but to God Himself and to the angels (Ps. 8:4–5; Heb. 2:6–7).

Soteriology. The existence of the Creator, His power, and His wisdom are evident to all through nature, God's natural revelation of Himself. But presently no one can be regenerated apart from a knowledge of the person and work of the Lord Jesus Christ. Salvation is possible only through the special revelation of the written Word of God. It seems consistent with the character of God and the Bible that if one would accept God's natural revelation of Himself, God would, in His sovereignty, direct that one to a place of hearing the gospel of Christ.

Eschatology. The Second Advent of Jesus Christ will herald the termination of the suffering of nature. Redeemed man has the hope of receiving a new (resurrection) body. With that new body he will dwell in a new heaven and a new earth which will have been restored to the state of perfection in which they were created originally. Many signs in nature will precede and accompany Christ's return in judgment.

Philosophical Formulation

According to Bernard Ramm, "The battle to keep the Bible as a respected book among the learned scholars and the academic world was fought and lost in the nineteenth century."[10] Dr. Ramm laments this fact, attributing the blame for the cleavage between Bible and natural science to both secular scientists and evangelical Christians. He contends that evangelical Christianity defaulted by taking a much-too-narrow stance on the interpretation of Scripture.

The critical question which must be answered is this: What degree of credibilty and priority should be given to concepts of modern science when interpreting Bible passages? This is particularly relevant when there is an apparent contradiction between the traditional interpretation of Scripture and a widely accepted view of modern science. One answer to the above question, termed the "double revelation theory," was suggested by a liberal preacher approximately one hundred years ago.

> It is frequently said that science and the Bible are complementary revelations of God and that therefore there can be no conflict between them. It is maintained that since the Bible is not a textbook of science, the scientists should be taken as authorities in matters relating to science, and the Bible should be the authority in matters of a spiritual nature.[11]

Natural Science and a Literal Hermeneutic

Admittedly, tensions are created when the Bible student holds to a normal, literal interpretation of such passages. However, consistent hermeneutics require such an interpretation unless the context or other biblical statements suggest otherwise. Often the conflict arises, not between the Bible and objective facts of science, but between the Bible and untestable theories of science. When one recognizes the ephemeral nature of most scientific theories, particularly in the area of cosmogony, there is far less motivation for reconciling biblical statements with modern science. Just as objective archaeological research has continued to justify a biblical priority in studies of ancient history, objective scientific research will continue to vindicate a literal view of science in the Bible.

Such a God-honoring approach will not result in contradiction between the Bible and objective data or proven laws of modern science. If the Bible cannot be trusted to mean what it appears to state in an area subject to empirical investigation, how can it be trusted in areas which do not lend themselves to objective verification or falsification? Concerning the interpretation of the creation account, Francis Schaeffer writes,

> What the Bible tells us is propositional, factual and true truth . . . It *is* a scientific textbook in the sense that where it touches the cosmos it is true, propositionally true. When we get to heaven, what we learn further will no more contradict the facts the Bible now gives us than the New Testament contradicts the Old. The Bible is *not* a scientific textbook if by that one means that its purpose is to give us exhaustive truth or that scientific fact is its central theme and purpose.[12]

Although the Bible is not a complete textbook of natural science, biblical statements touching areas of science must be regarded as literal, factual, scientific truth. To reinterpret the Bible to conform to modern science may be the ultimate in hermeneutical folly.

Metaphysics and Empiricism

Both Paul and Peter give us clues that the rift between clear statements of the Bible and modern scholarship is rooted in moral and spiritual problems, rather than intellectual (1 Cor. 1; 2 Peter 3). Christians sometimes forget this and consequently expend much energy gathering support from secular science for biblical concepts to "show the world that the Bible is true." In addition to the problem of unregenerate man's spiritual blindness (1 Cor. 2:14, 2 Cor. 4:4), there are some inherent weaknesses in the scientific method as well. How can scientists arrive at *absolute* understandings by *relative* methods using *arbitrary* standards of reference? It is not only vain, but unscriptural to use science to authenticate biblical revelation for unbelievers. The Scriptures are self-authenticating.

Christians considering these areas have often failed to make some important metaphysical distinctions. Scientific laws and natural laws are not the same. Natural laws were ordained, and are maintained, by God. Apart from supernatural intervention, they are immutable. Obviously man's comprehension of these, expressed as "scientific laws," varies. Now the scientist's first step in understanding the concepts relative to a natural law is to construct a model he thinks could represent that law. Usually this model is oversimplified, representing something under rather idealized, unnatural conditions (e.g., the liquid-drop model of the atomic nucleus). Scientific laws are by necessity formulated from limited data and often by unreal models.

The history of science has demonstrated repeatedly that as research continues, more sophisticated models emerge; and subsequently more precise laws are stated. (Occasionally concepts which are called "laws" are later rejected completely.)[13] But the important distinction between model and reality is emphasized far too seldom. The lay public believes as established fact ideas which research scientists regard only as crude approximations to reality. Consequently Christian communicators must exercise caution when quoting findings of modern science to illustrate attributes of the Creator. From astronomy many speakers recite the alleged age of the universe and size of the Milky Way galaxy to illustrate the omnipotence of God. Seldom do these speakers know whether such astronomical concepts are based upon well-verified observations and direct measurements or upon weakly supported hypotheses and evolutionary presuppositions.

The Cosmic Center

Secular science is constrained to remove man as far as possible from the center of the universe, both geographically and philosophically. Man is presented simply as the latest link in an all-inclusive evolutionary chain, no more than the product of chance and natural law operating over billions of years of time. He is told to view himself as a rather insignificant creature on a rather common planet which orbits a typical star in an average galaxy. Interestingly, nearly 3000 years ago a Hebrew philosopher raised and answered the following rhetorical question which should have obviated such thinking: "What is man . . . ?" In Psalm 8, David recognized that God made the world for man. He did not view man as a mere idiosyncrasy of the natural operation of physiochemical laws in the cosmos. Man was placed above the animals by God for His glory.

Concomitant with its judgment on man's value in the universe, relegating him to the level of an animal, science paradoxically claims no right to pass judgment on the merits or values relative to the moral dilemmas which science and technology have created. The assertion is that social scientists, politicians, and theologians—not natural scientists—must make the moral and ethical decisions. The natural sciences are limited, it is said, to the objective reduction of data. But the presentation of natural science as an impersonal, objective, and trustworthy statistical process of gathering, sifting, and correlating data is too often a misrepresentation of science. As with any other discipline, it is comprised of people with normal, sinful prejudices and desires for personal recognition and advancement. Such self-centeredness can result not only in less-than-objective presentations of data, but even in their falsification. The temptation is great to misrepresent models as "good data fit" in order to justify and/or increase the level of research funding.

Science and Values

Unconscious presuppositions and prejudices of scientists may result in a biased presentation of a problem and its associated data to the public. In addition, special interest groups often present scientific propaganda to gain support for or against a particular technological development. When this occurs, Christians too often lack sufficient information to avoid falling prey to such manipulation. Not that such information is unavailable, but the average Christian lacks the background to read relevant articles with the confidence that he can comprehend their content. There are Christians who do have the background to understand, from a technical point of view, the issues of a technologically related social problem. But rare are those whose understanding goes further to discern the spiritual causes of the problem, who are able to suggest how believers should react to the situation.

When the population biologist recommends the control of the human birth rate, he *has* made a moral decision. The "lifeboat" analogy of human survival may have been articulated first by social scientists, but it has been promoted in classrooms and textbooks by like-minded natural scientists.[14] When Lynn White, Jr., a historian, attributed the current ecological crisis to the basic "Judaeo-Christian attitude which is rooted in Genesis 1:28," non-Christian ecological publications and biology teachers around the United States raised a choral "Amen." The values of our secular, humanistic scientists are being manifested. Through the classroom and popular media, their philosophies are being imprinted upon our society. Relying totally upon the secular media for information, the Christian is receiving counsel from the ungodly (Psalm 1). Without a proper biblical perspective, the contemporary believer has the task of making moral and spiritual judgments on issues about which he is inadequately informed.

Such must not be the case with the Bible college graduate! But he will be adequately prepared only if the following four goals are met. (1) He must be familiar with the standard Bible-science "problems" which critics continue to raise but which for years have had plausible, conservative solutions. (2) He must have an adequate vocabulary and conceptual knowledge in the physical and biological sciences to understand these "problems." (3) He should have been taught to read widely enough to gain a balanced view of technologically based social issues from secular sources. (4) He should have been placed in touch with *several* sources of current evangelical, Bible-science information. In the latter should be found summaries of recent research which may be too technical for the layman but from which come important implications for the Bible-believing Christian.

Practical Application

Positive Integration

Slowly, science curricula reflecting an evangelical Christian perspective are being written. These are being prepared almost exclusively for elementary and secondary Christian schools. Some of them present an excellent integration of biblical and natural truth. Measured from an educational, pedagogical point of view, the quality of these books varies widely. (These can be helpful to the new Bible college professor who needs resources for ideas in developing his own courses.)

Science classes at the Bible college should never be mere lessons in secular science preceded simply by a devotional and prayer. There are few scientific concepts, if any, which cannot in some way be related to spiritual truth. For example, what spiritual truths might be brought to bear on the topic of nonrenewable minerals? This author integrated that subject by relating it to Christian stewardship. Following are some of the principles which one class suggested for Christians in slowing the overuse of nonrenewable mineral resources: (1) Demonstrate the fruit of the spirit of self-control; (2) Limit exposure to the worldly philosophy of materialism; (3) Refuse to buy depreciating items on credit; (4) Buy nothing which will not enhance one's ministry; and (5) Depend more on sharing.

A Christian perspective needs to be delineated in each subject area of the natural sciences. Francis Schaeffer has attempted to articulate the Christian view of the interdisciplinary topic of ecology.[15] The classic work of Seiss on constellations correlated astronomical names and figures with scriptural concepts.[16] A recent book by Steidl, which more closely resembles an astronomy textbook, is a significant contribution to the area of astronomy and the Bible.[17] DeYoung and Whitcomb's book, *The Moon*, is also a welcome recent addition to the field.[18]

The Creation Research Society's publication in biology, *A Search For Order in Complexity*, presents an antievolutionary, creationist view; but it does not incorporate other biblical truths and principles into its pages.[19] Although not comprehensive, the best source for help in approaching modern geology is the classic, *The Genesis Flood*.[20] The physical science textbook by Mulfinger and Williams demonstrates how seemingly secular subjects can be related to spiritual truths.[21] Ramm's offering of Christian perspectives in astronomy, biology, and geology is generally unacceptable.[22]

Science has a significant contribution to make in the area of Christian evidences. Scholars are aware of scores of scientific facts which are presented in the Bible.[23] As with any set of Christian evidences, their utility lies in their inherent ability to intrigue man's rational mind. The demonstration of the presence of modern scientific concepts in the Bible satisfies that criterion for some people. Hence they can be used as a conversational starting point, a basis of common interest for sharing the gospel of Christ.

Negative Integration

The Bible college science professor could spend a fruitful lifetime working exclusively in the areas of positive integration alluded to above. The work that could be accomplished, and the satisfaction derived therefrom, are unlimited. But unfortunately, he may deem it necessary to devote most of his time in refuting and preparing his students to discern the errors of unbiblical theories of modern science. As indicated above, great tension exists between a normal, literal interpretation of the Bible and secular teachings of natural history. Although the degree varies, all disciplines of natural science are implicated. The scenario of mechanistic evolution is well established from cosmic beginnings through the spontaneous formation of the first living cells to the development of sophisticated man.

The necessity for every Bible college student to study the subject of origins from an apologetic approach can hardly be questioned. The science teacher must be more than casually familar with the key issues in this vast, multidisciplinary subject (biology, geology, astronomy, nuclear physics, thermodynamics, chemistry, meteorology, etc.). Teaching it is a formidable task since many students have "never been interested in science." But when students and graduates begin to utilize this information in providing biblically sound answers to sincere inquirers, the effort is justified.

Student Integration

Science is difficult for many students. Typically they are required to take only one or two classes in natural science. To bring students to even a minimal level of competency, as measured by standard objectives, is probably hopeless. Is it not futile then to attempt to teach science in the Bible college from *any* perspective, secular or Christian? If Bible college science classes differ little in content and format from those taught at secular institutions, the natural sciences may as well be removed from the curriculum. But if the courses are uniquely designed to meet the needs of the ministry-oriented student, the investment can be invaluable.

The typical lay response to the presentation of scientific information is, "I have neither the ability nor the time to research the issues. I will just have to take the experts' word for it." Outside of satanic delusion, which dare not be minimized, the main reason people end up accepting unbiblical speculations of science as true is simply laziness. It *does* take an effort to think issues through for oneself. If the science professor does nothing more than cause his students to begin to challenge what they have been taught in their previous years of education, he will have attained a measure of success.

At nearly every point of the teaching of a concept, the student must be taught to ask, "What are the assumptions? Are they reasonable? Has anything been overlooked? Are there other possible explanations of the data? Do any data fail to fit the model? If so, why?" Here is where the experience of the professor is invaluable. He can challenge students with models which they may not be able to disprove (even though he may know of flaws in those models). In astronomy, for example, he could challenge the popular heliocentric model of the solar system with Tycho Brahe's compromise model.

Bible college students will normally adopt the philosophy of Bible and science held by their professor. The development of that aspect of the student's world view will determine his ability to discern whether or not scientific models and applications of technology are compatible with biblical Christianity. Much is dependent upon the instruction he receives in science.

Conclusion

Contemporary society no longer accepts the Bible as a trustworthy book from God. This results in part from the prevailing opinion that modern science has disproven the Mosaic record of creation and the early development of human civilizations. In the nineteenth century many Evangelicals yielded to the secular geologists' insistence of a billion-year-old earth. Some theologians accommodate the aeons of time with the gap theory of Genesis 1:1–2.[24] Christian biologists went further and accepted the concept of organic evolution as God's method of creation, with a forced spiritualizing interpretation of the creation account.[25] A remnant of Bible-science scholars has always resisted the pressure of secular science and compromising theology, but making themselves heard has been extremely difficult.[26]

Led by Dr. Henry Morris, a recent awakening has taken hold among committed Christian scientists. Over five hundred scientists, each holding at least a master's degree, belong to the Creation Research Society.[27] Its members hold to a normal, literal interpretation of Scripture, believing that no facts of science controvert the Bible. Supporting a *fiat* creation of distinct biological kinds, these scientists also affirm the compelling support from natural phenomena for the earth's age to be set at under ten thousand years.

Our young people are continually being bombarded with antibiblical teachings in science. And since Christian pastors, youth leaders, and Sunday school teachers are expected to be repositories of wisdom and information on every subject, each must be able to provide these young people with a satisfactory biblical and scientific apologetic. Even if a leader does not have the answer, he must be able to demonstrate the confidence of one who knows answers do exist and who knows how to find them.

Here is where the Bible college can make the difference! Few Christian liberal arts colleges prepare their students to give an answer for the hope that is in them. And far too few seminaries deal adequately with these issues. If nothing else is provided, a natural science program requiring a one semester course in a biblical and scientific study of origins is a must for every Bible college.

Other elective courses in natural science can provide insights for contemporary issues and focus on seeing God's glory in nature. From the natural sciences can come sermon illustrations to which everyone can relate. Since many non-Christians are interested in science, such discussions at the layman's level can provide a context for sharing the gospel of grace.

The Bible college graduate who has not studied the revelation of God in nature has an incomplete theological education. By coming to a biblical understanding of God's purposes, organization, and wisdom in nature, the believer is brought to a fuller comprehension of God's attributes. In the scientific enterprise, many questions will be raised. Many will be answered; some will have to await further research, possibly going unanswered in this life. Although man is limited, God is infinite. His hidden mysteries are only partly unraveled in nature. "Oh LORD, our Lord. How majestic is thy name in all the earth."

Notes

1. *Webster's New World Dictionary*, 2nd college ed. (Cleveland: Collins-World, 1976).
2. Henry M. Morris, *Many Infallible Proofs* (San Diego: Creation-Life Publishers, 1974), p. 229.
3. Francis Schaeffer, *Pollution and the Death of Man* (Wheaton: Tyndale, 1970).
4. Francis Schaeffer, *Genesis in Space and Time* (Downers Grove, Ill.: Inter-Varsity, 1972), p. 28.
5. John C. Whitcomb and Henry M. Morris, *The Genesis Flood* (Nutley, N.J.: Presbyterian and Reformed, 1961).
6. Joseph Dillow, "Mechanics and Thermodynamics of the Pre-Flood Canopy," *Creation Research Society Quarterly*, 15 (December 1978): 148.
7. For extensive pre-1968 bibliographies see Henry Morris, *The Bible and Modern Science*, 2nd ed. (Chicago: Moody, 1968) pp. 124–28, and Bernard Ramm, *The Christian View of Science and Scripture* (Grand Rapids: Eerdmans, 1954), pp. 246–50. The organization of the latter bibliography reflects a bias against a universal flood and a recent creation. The arguments of Ramm against a universal flood have been skillfully refuted by Whitcomb and Morris in *The Genesis Flood*.
8. Adapted from Morris, *Many Infallible Proofs*, p. 240.
9. John Hannah, Dallas Theological Seminary classnotes.
10. Ramm, p. 15.
11. Bolton Davidheiser, *Evolution and Christian Faith* (Nutley, N.J.: Presbyterian and Reformed, 1969), pp. 140–41.
12. Schaeffer, *Genesis*, pp. 35–36.
13. Such an example was the "fundamental biogenetic law." Cf. Davidheiser, p. 241.
14. Robert C. Belloli, *Contemporary Physical Science* (New York: Macmillan, 1978), pp. 4–5.
15. Francis Schaeffer, *Pollution*.
16. Joseph Seiss, *The Gospel in the Stars* (Philadelphia: Philadelphia School of the Bible, 1884).
17. Paul M. Steidl, *The Earth, the Stars and the Bible* (Phillipsburg, N.J.: Presbyterian and Reformed, 1979).
18. John C. Whitcomb and Donald B. DeYoung, *The Moon* (Winona Lake, Ind.: BMH Books, 1978).
19. John N. Moore and Harold Slusher, eds., *A Search for Order in Complexity*, 2nd ed. (Grand Rapids: Zondervan, 1974).
20. Whitcomb and Morris, *The Genesis Flood*.
21. Emmett L. Williams and George Mulfinger, *Physical Science for Christian Schools* (Greenville, S.C.: Bob Jones University Press, 1974).
22. Ramm, *Christian View*.
23. Morris, *Bible and Modern Science*; A. O. Schnabel, *Has God Spoken?* (San Diego: Creation-Life Publishers, 1974).
24. G. H. Pember, *Earth's Earliest Ages* (Grand Rapids: Kregel, 1942), p. 31.
25. See discussion of the American Scientific Affiliation by Davidheiser, *Evolution and Christian Faith*, p. 114.
26. George McCready Price, *The Phantom of Organic Evolution* (New York: Revell, 1924), p. 8.
27. Creation Research Society, 2717 Cranbrook Road, Ann Arbor, MI 48104.

The Author

Dr. Roger G. Soule is professor and chairman of the department of physical education at Biola University, having also taught at Liberty Baptist College, Boston University, and Washington State University. For some six years he served as a research physiologist with the U.S. Army Institute of Environmental Medicine and has authored a number of articles in such journals as *Scholastic Coach*, *American Journal of Physiology*, and *Medicine and Science in Sports*. His academic credentials include a B.A. from the State University of New York at Cortland, an M.S. from the University of Illinois, and a Ph.D. from Washington State University.

The Subject

Dr. Soule considers his subject from the general viewpoint of physical activity, narrowing to specialization in athletics and physical education. He emphasizes the importance of physical well-being and recreational values for the Christian and treats the matter of leisure time activity for the Christian worker. Carefully he builds a case for the importance of physical education in the Bible college framework and in line with its distinctive philosophy, concerned that students learn to live their lives "glorifying God and worshiping Him as He should be worshiped."

15

PHYSICAL EDUCATION

Roger G. Soule

As we teach physical education classes, conduct and promote intercollegiate and intramural sports programs, and have recreational fun time sport activities in a Bible-based college, it is essential to keep in mind the overall value of these programs for the young people. Many students who have decided to attend a Christian college believe they have been called of God to do so. In their immaturity, however, they fail to grasp the "whole man" concept of biblical anthropology and therefore may have to be convinced of the fact that organized physical activity is a valuable aspect of their preparation to serve God as pastors, missionaries, doctors, educators, or in some other profession. The Bible college, from its most primitive foundational course to a myriad of physical education activities and sports programs, must have a clear philosophy of how these activities contribute to the overall educational and spiritual objectives of both student and institution.

Introduction

Definition

It seems apparent from the Scriptures that exercise, in its broadest sense, has been part of God's plan for man from the very creation of the world. Exercise in its earliest forms was primarily related to the military, but it now includes sports, games, recreational activities, and physical fitness programs; all of these are aspects of physical education.

Many textbook definitions of physical education are exemplified in the following excerpt from Freeman:

> When we speak of physical education we are referring to a broad field of interests. The basic concern is human movement, primarily in the sense of gross [larger] movements rather than the more minute or finer movements of the body. More specifically, physical education is concerned with the relationship between human movement and other areas of education—that is, with the relationship of the body's physical development to the mind and soul as they are being developed.[1]

Perhaps a more traditional definition of the term "physical education," (and incidentally one that is still in use), is the one put forth by an early leader in the profession, Jesse Feiring Williams: "Physical education is the sum of man's physical activities selected as to kind, and conducted as to outcomes."[2] Such definitions are valuable but I prefer a simple working definition: Physical education as a discipline is the study of how man moves in God's creation. As a discipline, physical education includes the study of the various aspects of movement—games, sports, exercise—and how activity better promotes a general well-being for individuals so they might better perform the duties or professions to which God has called them.

Rationale For Inclusion

The Bible college which is genuinely concerned about the student's *physical well-being* will place a strong emphasis on exercise or physical fitness in its course offerings. The integration of physical activity with the total development of man should be based on sound biblical principles. However, we in the profession must be careful to realize that in God's total plan an overemphasis on the physical is as dangerous as no emphasis at all. We must be concerned, then, for those activities which contribute to the development of the physical attributes of our young people.

In addition, we must be concerned for those activities which have *lifetime recreational values.* Our graduates entering Christian vocations toil long and hard in a variety of ministries. In such stress, relaxation and refreshment are beneficial, but our students often find themselves inadequately prepared to participate in physical activities. Such deficiency is not necessary. Bible college can offer proper instruction in physical care. We sometimes call these lifetime sports or leisure time activities. A long list could be given, and many of them are obvious: swimming, walking, bicycling, golf, tennis, racquetball. Other involvements could easily be included to which a person might devote some minutes of physical relaxation after a long work session.[3]

Another area is *skill development*. Many times these activities take the form of intercollegiate or intramural sports and games, and it is here that the gifted person gets the opportunity to develop skills in such areas as soccer, basketball, or baseball. Such skills and abilities can be used for only a relatively short period of time in a person's life. Obviously if the sport is a lifetime sport, e.g. golf or tennis, there is a more lasting value.

In addition to the universal need for physical well-being, the lifetime need for exercise, and the development of sport skills, there is also a special need for the *professional preparation* of young people for ministries in physical education. Professions in physical education are for those who demonstrate a keen interest and talent and who believe that God has called them to teach and/or coach physical activity in camps, schools, or colleges. Thus some Bible colleges have decided to include a professional curriculum in physical education to prepare the Christian young person to utilize physical education as an avenue of ministry to others.

The study of how a person performs physically is a worthwhile area of concern in the Bible college. The reasons for studying physical education are related to the doctrine of creation and the consequent responsibility of man to maintain physical, spiritual, and mental fitness as he strives to be the person God intended.

Biblical Foundation

Many references in Scripture allude to sport and exercise. In many of these physical exercise is used as a metaphor for spiritual development. One of the most outstanding references in the Old Testament is Isaiah 40:31: "But those who hope in the Lord will renew their strength. They will soar on wings like eagles; they will run and not grow weary, they will walk and not be faint" (NIV). Obviously an untrained person would not normally be expected to run without becoming weary, and that rather quickly. To be able to run or even walk briskly, is to have a pattern of consistently running or walking. The application is obvious. Just as we must work at intellectual development and spiritual growth, so too we must train our physical attributes.

Paul specifically uses running and competition as a metaphor for spiritual preparedness in 1 Corinthians 9:23–27.

> And I do all things for the sake of the gospel, that I may become a fellow partaker of it. Do you not know that those who run in a race all run, but only one receives the prize? Run in such a way that you may win. And everyone who competes in the games exercises self-control in all things. They then do it to receive a perishable wreath, but we an imperishable. Therefore I run in such a way, as not without aim; I box in such a way, as not beating the air; but I buffet my body and make it my slave, lest possibly, after I have preached to others, I myself should be disqualified (1 Cor. 9:23–27, NASB).

Paul is indicating that the body should be subject to its owner and that it should be controlled, controllable, and integrated into the totality of what God wants in a mature person.

In The Amplified Bible the last two verses read this way:

> Therefore, I do not run uncertainly without definite aim, I do not box as one beating the air and striking without an adversary, but like a boxer I buffet my body, handle it roughly, discipline it by hardships, and subdue it for fear that after proclaiming to others the gospel and things pertaining to it I myself should become unfit, not stand the test and be unapproved and rejected as a counterfeit.

One of the concepts that we must share with our students is that as Christians we must teach by model as well as by concept. It would be inappropriate if we ask others to perform physical exercise and could or would not perform it ourselves. We must not be phony— faith and practice must be compatible in our lives. In physical education, Christian teachers use this passage as one of the backbone verses for the value of physical exercise. Paul's metaphor refers to boxing, running, and other physical activities used in those days.

In addition to running and competition, Paul uses the soldier as an example of training. Though we do not engage in military drills or procedures in the physical education curriculum, it does seem appropriate to use the soldier in conjunction with exercise and discipline. The concept of discipline is important for the soldier and athlete. It is also strategic for the Christian. An old volume (1907) contains a short essay on training written by R. A. Waite, Jr., that has truth for us even today:

> What athlete does not realize the necessity of training? Nevertheless to the Christian it is infinitely more necessary. That we may be fit to endure any test which may come to us we must pursue a course of suitable exercise.[4]

In 1 & 2 Timothy Paul makes reference several times to running, fleeing, and being a good soldier, as for example he does in 2 Timothy 2:3: "Thou therefore endure hardness as a good soldier of Jesus Christ." Here he is referring to the discipline and the hardening of our bodies. So often students get taken up in the business of studying that they neglect the hardening of their bodies as good soldiers or athletes. It is important that we—students and instructors alike—have strong, healthy, conditioned bodies in order to better carry on the tasks to which God has called us.

In addition to the above discussion, there are other scriptural references to running and walking. Galatians 5:7 talks about running. Hebrews 12:1 talks about running with endurance, meaning to be able to exercise for an extended period of time. It is scriptural that we should be able to work hard all day. It is important that we be able to perform a task for a work day and, even though this passage is really talking about running with endurance in the race of life, it also has implication for running with endurance in the sense of performing a task. If one can literally run all day, he can surely perform other tasks! In Psalm 18:29, David is talking about running and jumping, we might even term it leaping, which implies that a great deal of energy is expended. There are also many references to walking as a mode of exercise: 1 John 2:6 and 2 Corinthians 5:7 are just two.

It is important that the scriptural concepts of running, walking, exercising, and disciplining our bodies refer to endurance in many aspects of life. God calls us to be disciplined individuals and integration of these principles is needed in the physical activity classes we teach.

Practical Application

Faculty Qualifications

Most Bible college people involved in the teaching of physical education activities should recognize the importance of these activities for all students, and especially for Christian young people. Furthermore, the teacher of physical education activities must feel that God has called him to this profession. It might be noted that instructors of physical education and coaches of the various sports in Bible colleges almost always have diversified backgrounds: professional sports, secular university teaching, public school teaching, among others. They come trusting that God has called them together to teach and coach His people in His school and ultimately for the sharing of His truths.

The relationship of truth to college activities and sports must be of major importance to this faculty. Unfortunately, we have not always invested sufficient time and effort in trying to justify the presence of physical education activities on the campus of Christian colleges. We all realize that God has a hierarchy of importance and most of us involved in physical education and athletics would agree that the development of physical skill ability is probably not number one on God's priority list. Yet we do know physical activity has *some* importance and consequently are content to share that importance with the students that God brings under our direction. A supportive, servant mentality is basic to our ministry.

Interdisciplinary Integration

When discussing the academic or classroom preparation of the physical education major, we must communicate to our students a genuine understanding of how the human body operates structurally (the anatomical) and functionally (the physiological), as well as an understanding of how man operates sociologically and psychologically. Consequently, there is important integration with other academic areas of study including nursing, biology, and medicine.

It should be noted that it is in the study of the physical, social, and psychological disciplines that a further integration of faith and learning takes place. Man as a created being, in all of his fearfully and wonderfully made properties, fits into a created society. Even the nonmajor receives exposure to this concept as we try to encourage all students to understand that good health, good physical endurance, and good eye-hand coordination are important to the total development of a Christian, no matter what his chosen profession.

As our students complete their general education requirements in physical education (usually two to four semesters of classes), they should have gained a better understanding of how their bodies function, a better ability to perform some of the intricate skills that the body is capable of performing, and a greater capacity to do long-term exercise. Further, they should have learned how to keep the body disciplined and under subjection to the mind, the will, and the direction of God's Spirit.

Conclusion

In no other area of the organized college curriculum, except maybe in the arts or medicine, is so much attention given to how the body performs. In no other area is the emphasis so strong on how the body performs while engaging in recreational leisure time, non-occupational types of physical activities. The Bible college curriculum should offer opportunity for both study and relaxation, a balance that can enhance a person's Christian commitment. Though there are many areas of academic pursuit, and although there are many biblical study opportunities, there are often few possibilities of physical recreation activity. Consequently, the contribution made by having physical education integrated into the curriculum of a Bible college education is not only unique, but essential.

As we run the race that is set before us, that of progressing from birth through life to victorious death, it seems apparent that the ability to run that race with a strong body, great endurance, and capability for rest and relaxation is esssential to the accomplishment of the other tasks that God has planned for that race, including leading others to Christ, glorifying God, and worshiping Him as He should be worshiped. Integration may be more obvious in academic disciplines such as Bible study, theology, ethics, philosophy, English, mathematics, and history. Yet it is also essential that the student have the opportunity to pursue physical education activities which are grounded in the doctrine of creation and an awareness of God's ownership of our bodies. As our students tread across the platform on graduation day, it should be apparent that their education has been based on an integration of faith and learning in *all* fields of study, including that most closely related to walking across that stage in good health.

Notes

1. William H. Freeman, *Physical Education in a Changing Society* (Boston: Houghton Mifflin, 1977).
2. Jesse F. Williams, *The Principles of Physical Education* (1927; reprint ed., Philadelphia: Saunders, 1964), p. 13.
3. Handy sport and recreational guides are readily available in bookstores. See David A. Armbruster, F. F. Musker and D. Mood, *Sports and Recreational Activities For Men and Women* (St. Louis: Mosby, 1979).
4. R. A. Waite, Jr. *The Gospel in Athletic Phrases* (New York: Young Men's Christian Association Press, 1907).

BIBLIOGRAPHY

General*

Armerding, Hudson T., ed. *Christianity and the World of Thought.* Chicago: Moody, 1968.

Clark, Gordon H. *A Christian Philosophy of Education.* Grand Rapids: Eerdmans, 1946.

Gaebelein, Frank E. *Christian Education in a Democracy.* New York: Oxford, 1951.

_____. *The Pattern of God's Truth.* New York: Oxford, 1954; Chicago: Moody, 1976.

Holmes, Arthur F. *All Truth is God's Truth.* Grand Rapids: Eerdmans, 1975.

_____. *The Idea of a Christian College.* Grand Rapids: Eerdmans, 1975.

LeBar, Lois E. *Education That Is Christian.* Old Tappan, N.J.: Revell, 1958.

Smith, Robert W., ed. *Christ and the Modern Mind.* Downers Grove, Ill.: Inter-Varsity, 1972.

Zylstra, Henry. *Testament of Vision.* Grand Rapids: Eerdmans, 1958.

English Bible

Gray, James M. *How to Master the English Bible.* Chicago: The Bible Institute Colportage Association, 1904.

Lee, James Michael. *The Flow of Religious Education.* Mishawaka: Religious Education Press, 1973.

Schaeffer, Francis A. *Art and the Bible.* Downers Grove, Ill.: Inter-Varsity, 1973.

Witmer, S. A. *Education With Dimension.* Manhasset, N.Y.: Channel Press, 1962.

Theology

Bredenberg, Richard R. "An Appraisal of Current Procedures Used in Teaching Introductory Bible Courses in Liberal Arts Colleges." Ph.D. dissertation, New York University, 1959.

Carter, John D. and Bruce Narramore. *The Integration of Psychology and Theology.* Grand Rapids: Zondervan, 1979.

Hiebert, Albert A. "Expository and Discovery Teaching of Systematic Theology: An Analysis of Instructional Models Preferred by Teachers

---

*Many of the writers referred to the same books on the broad topic of the integration of faith and learning. These have been cumulated into the general bibliography and deleted from the subject bibliographies which follow.

and Students of Systematic Theology in Accredited Schools of the American Association of Bible Colleges." Ph.D. dissertation, New York University, 1978.

Johnson, Richard A. "A Study of Christian Theology Books used as Texts in
A.T.S. Schools." Master's thesis, Western Evangelical Seminary, 1975.

Rogers, Jack B. and Forrest Baird. *Introduction to Philosophy: A Case
Study Approach*. San Francisco: Harper & Row, 1981.

Pastoral Studies

Adams, Jay E. *Shepherding God's Flock*. Vol. 1. Nutley, N.J.: Presbyterian
and Reformed, 1974.

DeHaan, Richard. *Your Pastor and You*. Grand Rapids: Radio Bible Class,
n.d.

Hendriksen, William. *New Testament Commentary Exposition of the
Pastoral Epistles*. Grand Rapids: Baker, 1965.

Kent, Homer A., Jr. *Ephesians*. Chicago: Moody, 1971.

_____. *The Pastoral Epistles*. Chicago: Moody, 1966.

_____. *The Pastor and His Work*. Chicago: Moody, 1963.

Murphy, Thomas. *Pastoral Theology*. Philadelphia: Presbyterian Board of
Publications, 1877.

Ryrie, Charles C. *Balancing the Christian Life*. Chicago: Moody, 1973.

Sugden, Howard F. and Warren W. Wiersbe. *When Pastors Wonder How*.
Chicago: Moody, 1973.

Thayer, Joseph Henry. *Thayer's Greek-English Lexicon of the New
Testament*. Grand Rapids: Zondervan, 1965.

Towns, Elmer L. *America's Fastest Growing Churches*. Nashville: Impact
Books, 1972.

_____. *The Ten Largest Sunday Schools and What Makes Them Grow*.
Grand Rapids: Baker, 1967.

Turnbull, Ralph G., ed. *Baker's Dictionary of Practical Theology*. Grand
Rapids: Baker, 1967.

Vine, W. E. *Expository Dictionary of New Testament Words*. Westwood,
N.J.: Revell, 1966.

Evangelism

Armstrong, Richard Stoll. *Service Evangelism*. Philadelphia: Westminster,
1979.

Autrey, C. E. *Basic Evangelism*. Grand Rapids: Zondervan, 1959.

Barclay, William. *Turning to God; A Study of Conversion in the Book of
Acts and Today*. Grand Rapids: Baker, 1964.

Boer, Harry R. *Pentecost and Missions*. Grand Rapids: Eerdmans, 1961.

Coleman, Robert E. *The Master Plan of Evangelism*. Old Tappan, N.J.:
Revell, 1963.

Cook, Luther T. *Calling For Christ*. Chicago: Moody, 1974.

Douglas, J. O., ed. *Let the Earth Hear His Voice*. Minneapolis: World Wide,
1975.

Downey, Murray W. *The Art of Soul-Winning*. Grand Rapids: Baker, 1957.

Engel, James and W. Norton. *What's Gone Wrong With the Harvest?* Grand Rapids: Zondervan, 1976.

Fish, Roy J. and J. E. Conant. *Every Member Evangelism*. New York: Harper & Row, 1976.

Green, Michael. *Evangelism—Now and Then*. Leicester: Inter-Varsity, 1979.

————. *Evangelism in the Early Church*. Grand Rapids: Eerdmans, 1970.

Henderson, Robert T. *Joy to the World: An Introduction to Kingdom Evangelism*. Atlanta: John Knox, 1980.

Kennedy, D. James. *Evangelism Explosion*. Rev. ed. Wheaton: Tyndale, 1978.

Kraus, C. Norman. *Missions, Evangelism and Church Growth*. Scottdale: Herald, 1980.

Kuiper, R. B. *God-Centered Evangelism*. Grand Rapids: Baker, 1961.

Little, Paul E. *How to Give Away Your Faith*. Downers Grove: Inter-Varsity, 1966.

McPhee, Arthur G. *Friendship Evangelism*. Grand Rapids: Zondervan, 1978.

Moberg, David O. *The Great Reversal: Evangelism and Social Concern*. Philadelphia: Lippincott, 1977.

Packer, J. I. *Evangelism and the Sovereignty of God*. London: Inter-Varsity, 1961.

Peters, George W. *Saturation Evangelism*. Grand Rapids: Zondervan, 1970.

Prior, Kenneth F. W. *The Gospel in a Pagan Society: the Relevance for Today of Paul's Ministry in Athens*. London: Hodder and Stoughton, 1975.

Sanny, Lorne. *The Art of Personal Witnessing*. Chicago: Moody, 1957.

Scharpf, Paulus. *History of Evangelism*. Grand Rapids: Eerdmans, 1966.

Sweazey, George E. *The Church as Evangelist*. Grand Rapids: Eerdmans, 1978.

Torrey, R. A. *How to Bring Men to Christ*. 1893. Reprint. Minneapolis: Bethany, 1977.

Towns, Elmer L. *Evangelism Thru Christian Education*. Wheaton: Evangelical Teacher Training Association, 1976.

Watson, David. *I Believe in Evangelism*. Grand Rapids: Eerdmans, 1976.

Missions

Bavinck, J. H. *An Introduction to the Science of Missions*. Philadelphia: Presbyterian and Reformed, 1964.

Beyerhaus, Peter. *Shaken Foundations: Theological Foundations for Missions*. Grand Rapids: Zondervan, 1972.

Boer, Harry R. *Pentecost and Missions*. Grand Rapids: Eerdmans, 1961.

Conn, Harvie M. *Theological Perspectives on Church Growth*. Philadelphia: Presbyterian and Reformed, 1976.

DeRidder, Richard R. *Discipling the Nations*. Grand Rapids: Baker, 1971.

Grunlan, Stephen A. and Marvin K. Mayers. *Cultural Anthropology: A Christian Perspective*. Grand Rapids: Zondervan, 1979.

Hesselgrave, David J., ed. *Theology and Mission*. Grand Rapids: Baker, 1978.

Kane, J. Herbert. *Missions in Biblical Perspective*. Grand Rapids: Baker, 1976.

Lindsell, Harold. *An Evangelical Theology of Missions*. Grand Rapids: Zondervan, 1970.

Luzbetak, Louis J. *The Church and Cultures*. Pasadena: William Carey Library, 1970.

McGavran, Donald. *The Clash Between Christianity and Cultures*. Grand Rapids: Baker, 1974.

Nida, Eugene A. *Religion Across Cultures*. Pasadena: William Carey Library, 1968.

Peters, George. *A Biblical Theology of Missions*. Chicago: Moody, 1972.

Smalley, William A. *Readings in Missionary Anthropology II*. Pasadena: William Carey Library, 1978.

Stott, John and Robert T. Cook. *Gospel and Culture*. Pasadena: William Carey Library, 1979.

Tippett, Alan R. *Church Growth and the Word of God*. Grand Rapids: Eerdmans, 1970.

Church Education

American Association of Bible Colleges. *Preparing Bible College Students for Ministries in Christian Education*. Wheaton: AABC, 1973.

LeBar, Lois E. *Focus on People in Church Education*. Old Tappan, N.J.: Revell, 1969.

Neill, A. S. "Can I Come to Summerhill?" in *Readings in Educational Psychology Today*. Del Mar, Cal.: CRM Books, 1970.

Richards, Lawrence O. *Creative Bible Teaching*. Chicago: Moody, 1970.

_____. *A Theology of Christian Education*. Grand Rapids: Zondervan, 1975.

Sacred Music

Best, Harold M. "Church Relatedness, Music, and Higher Education." *Proceedings of the 52nd Annual Meeting, National Association of Schools of Music, Atlanta, Georgia 1976*. Reston, Va.: NASM, 1977.

_____. "Music: Offerings of Creativity." *Christianity Today*, 6 May 1977, pp. 12–15.

Blume, Friedrich. *Protestant Church Music: A History*. New York: W. W. Norton, 1974.

Forkel, Johann Nikolaus. *Johann Sebastian Bach: His Life, Art, and Work*. 1802. Reprint. New York: Vienna House, 1974.

Geiringer, Karl. *Instruments in the History of Western Music*. New York: Oxford, 1978.

_____. *Johann Sebastian Bach: The Culmination of an Era*. New York: Oxford, 1966.

Hofstadter, Albert. *Truth and Art.* New York: Columbia University Press, 1965.

Langer, Susanne K. *Feeling and Form.* New York: Scribner's, 1953.

Lewis, C. S. *Reflections on the Psalms.* New York: Harcourt Brace Jovanovich, 1958.

Lunde, Alfred E. *Christian Education thru Music.* Wheaton: Evangelical Teacher Training Association, 1978.

Luther, Martin. *What Luther Says: An Anthology.* Compiled by Ewald M. Plass. 3 vols. Saint Louis, Mo.: Concordia, 1959.

Macaulay, J. C. "The Ministry of Music." *Accrediting Association of Bible Colleges Newsletter,* 16 (Fall 1972): 6–9.

May, Rollo. *The Courage to Create.* New York: Norton, 1975.

Nettl, Paul. *Luther and Music.* Translated by Frida Best and Ralph Wood. New York: Russell and Russell, 1948.

Ortlund, Anne. *Up with Worship.* Glendale, Cal.: G/L Publications, 1975.

Rookmaaker, H. R. *Art Needs No Justification.* Downers Grove, Ill.: Inter-Varsity, 1978.

Santayana, George. *The Life of Reason.* New York: Scribner's, 1905.

Sayers, Dorothy L. "Toward a Christian Aesthetic" (1947). Reprinted in *The Whimsical Christian* by Dorothy L. Sayers. New York: Macmillan, 1978.

Schaeffer, Francis A. *Art and the Bible.* Downers Grove, Ill.: Inter-Varsity, 1973.

Stravinsky, Igor. *Poetics of Music.* Cambridge: Harvard University Press, 1942.

Stravinsky, Vera and Robert Craft. "Stravinsky's Early Years." *Ovation,* 1 (May 1980): 18–21.

Wilson, John F. *An Introduction to Church Music.* Chicago: Moody, 1965.

Speech/Communications

Brooks, William D. *Speech Communication.* Dubuque, Iowa: Wm. C. Brown, 1974.

Brooks, William D. and Philip Emmert. *Interpersonal Communication.* Dubuque, Iowa: Wm. C. Brown, 1976.

Communication Yearbooks 1, 2, 3. New Brunswick, N.J.: Transaction Books, 1979.

Fisher, B. Aubrey. *Perspectives on Human Communication.* New York: Macmillan, 1978.

Hybels, Saundra and Richard Weaver. *Speech Communication.* New York: D. Van Nostrand, 1974.

Jaarsma, Cornelius. *Human Development, Learning and Teaching.* Grand Rapids: Eerdmans, 1961.

Jourard, Sidney. *Self-Disclosure: An Experimental Analysis of the Transparent Self.* New York: Wiley, 1971.

McKeachie, Wilbert. *Teaching Tips.* Lexington, Mass.: Heath, 1969.

Minirth, Frank. *Christian Psychiatry.* Old Tappan, N.J.: Revell, 1977.

Monroe, Alan and Douglas Ehninger. *Principles of Speech Communication.* Glenview, Ill.: Scott, Foresman, 1975.

Ruben, Brent D. and Richard W. Budd. *Human Communication Handbook.* Rochelle Park, N.J.: Hayden Book Co., 1975.

Toffler, Alvin. *The Third Wave.* New York: Morrow, 1980.

Watzlawick, Paul; Beavin, Janet Helmick; and Jackson, Don D. *Pragmatics of Human Communication.* New York: Norton, 1967.

English and Literature

Batson, Beatrice. *A Reader's Guide to Religious Literature.* Chicago: Moody, 1968.

Evans, Frederick. "Dilemma in the Study of Literature." *The Christian Teacher,* January-March 1968, p. 5.

Frye, Roland M. *Perspective on Man: Literature and the Christian Tradition.* Philadelphia: Westminster, 1961.

Kilby, Clyde. "The Novel." *His Magazine,* February 1963, p. 11.

Moeller, Charles. *Man and Salvation in Literature.* Notre Dame: The University of Notre Dame, 1970.

O'Connor, Flannery. *Mystery and Manners.* Edited by Sally and Robert Fitzgerald. New York: Farrar, Straus and Giroux, 1957.

Ryken, Leland. "Literature and the Arts: A Christian Approach." *The Christian Teacher,* March-April 1970, p. 27. Reprinted from *Christianity Today,* 5 Dec. 1969.

_____. *Triumphs of the Imagination.* Downers Grove, Ill.: InterVarsity, 1979.

Scott, Nathan A., Jr., ed. *The Climate of Faith in Modern Literature.* New York: Seabury, 1964.

_____. *The New Orpheus: Essays Toward a Christian Poetic.* New York: Sheed and Ward, 1964.

Tennyson, G. B. and Edward E. Ericson, Jr., eds. *Religion and Modern Literature: Essays in Theory and Criticism.* Grand Rapids: Eerdmans, 1975.

TeSelle, Sallie McFague. *Literature and the Christian Life.* New Haven: Yale University Press, 1966.

Humanities

Brown, Colin. *Philosophy and the Christian Faith.* Downers Grove, Ill.: Inter-Varsity, 1968.

Buswell, James Oliver, Jr. *A Christian View of Being and Knowing.* Grand Rapids, Mich.: Zondervan, 1960.

Cairns, Earle E. *God and Man in Time: A Christian Approach to Historiography.* Grand Rapids: Baker, 1979.

Clark, Gordon H. *A Christian View of Men and Things.* Grand Rapids: Eerdmans, 1952.

Dillenberger, Jane. *Style and Content in Christian Art.* New York: Abingdon, 1965.

Eversole, Finley, ed. *Christian Faith and Contemporary Arts.* New York: Abingdon, 1957.

Guinness, Os. *The Dust of Death*. Downers Grove, Ill.: Inter-Varsity, 1973.

Henry, Carl F. H. *Aspects of Christian Social Ethics*. Grand Rapids: Eerdmans, 1964.

_____ . *Contemporary Evangelical Thought*. New York: Harper, 1957.

Kilby, Clyde S. *Christianity and Aesthetics*. Chicago: Inter-Varsity, 1961.

Niebuhr, H. Richard. *Christ and Culture*. New York: Harper, 1951.

Rookmaaker, H. R. *Modern Art and the Death of a Culture*. Downers Grove, Ill.: Inter-Varsity, 1970.

Schaeffer, Francis A. *How Should We Then Live?* Old Tappan, N.J.: Revell, 1976.

_____ . *Art and the Bible*. Downers Grove, Ill.: Inter-Varsity, 1973.

_____ . *The Church at the End of the 20th Century*. Downers Grove, Ill.: Inter-Varsity, 1970.

_____ . *Escape From Reason*. Downers Grove, Ill.: Inter-Varsity, 1968.

Stewart, Randall. *American Literature and Christian Doctrine*. Baton Rouge, La.: Louisiana State University, 1958.

Young, Warren, C. *A Christian Approach to Philosophy*. Wheaton: Van Kampen, 1954.

Physical Education

Armbruster, David A., F. F. Musker, and D. Mood. *Sports and Recreational Activities for Men and Women*. St. Louis: Mosby, 1979.

Freeman, William H. *Physical Education in a Changing Society*. Boston: Houghton Mifflin, 1977.

Waite, R. A., Jr. *The Gospel in Athletic Phrases*. New York: Young Men's Christian Association Press, 1907.

Williams, Jesse F. *The Principles of Physical Education*. Philadelphia: Saunders, 1964.